CHANGING CHILDREN'S MINDS

CHANGING CHILDREN'S MINDS

Feuerstein's Revolution in the Teaching of Intelligence

by

HOWARD SHARRON

A CONDOR BOOK
SOUVENIR PRESS (E & A) LTD

For Susan, Kerrie, Hannah and Eliza.

ACKNOWLEDGEMENTS

I would like to thank Professor Reuven Feuerstein for the hospitality he and his family, particularly his wife, Berta, showed me while I was in Israel researching this book. I am also grateful for the patience of the very over-worked staff of the Hadassah Wizo Institute in Jerusalem who, nevertheless, found time to answer my endless inquiries.

I would also like to thank Sara Elkes of the Elchannen Elkes Association for International Understanding, who interrupted her punishing schedule to give me a great deal of practical support in Israel.

To two people in particular I am especially indebted. Andrew Sutton first pointed me towards Professor Feuerstein as being a worthy subject for investigation, and advised me throughout the writing of this book. Issacher Ilan, an officer of the Jewish Agency and an internationally respected social worker, went to enormous trouble to make my first visit to Israel a success, and arranged my first meeting with Professor Feuerstein. I have not been able to thank him enough.

In addition, I would like to thank Alma Craft and Keith Weller for permission to quote extensively from the report *Making up our Minds*, originally published by the Schools Council. They have fought consistently for Instrumental Enrichment and for Cognitive Education generally, in difficult conditions. I would also like to thank the American publishers, Stratton and Grunne, for permission to quote from L. Mann's *On the Trail of Cognitive Process: A Historical Perspective on Cognitive Education* (1979).

I would like to acknowledge the work of researchers into Instrumental Enrichment around the world; those mentioned here and those who could not be included because of pressure of space. Their determination to find a method which will help children, often abandoned in the past by psychologists and educationalists, and which will also stand up to rigorous testing, is worthy, in my view, of great commendation.

Instrumental Enrichment illustrations are the copyright of Professor Reuven Feuerstein and are reprinted with permission. Much of the research by Feuerstein and the Instrumental Enrichment material was originally published by Scott Foresman and Company.

Howard Sharron

CONTENTS

INTRODUCTION

It is no coincidence that the ideas of Reuven Feuerstein are now finally gaining a wider currency, after almost 30 years in the intellectual wilderness. The conditions that led to his ostracism are crumbling away as the doubts grow apace on the nature of intelligence and the causes of educational retardation, not to mention the effectiveness of present remedial techniques and placements for 'children with learning difficulties'.

In the 1950s, when Feuerstein began his controversial work with very backward children in Israel, the West was full of confidence and complacency about its ability to measure children's intelligence and to place them in a school system graded to suit their varying ability levels. In Britain there were Grammar Schools, Secondary Moderns, Technical Schools and Special Schools for the Educationally Subnormal. Placement followed tests based on the 'science' of intelligence measurement—psychometrics.

There was no independent questioning that intelligence was both inherited and immutable and, since this was so, most psychologists thought measurement was able to predict future performance at school and in society at large.

The last thing such psychologists wanted to hear about was the astonishing results of a renegade Israeli clinical psychologist who had practically demonstrated that intelligence was a much more fluid phenomenon than hitherto supposed, and that it could be taught to many children wrongly characterised by IQ tests as 'defectives'. They were not interested in his remedial methods or in the special environments through which children with severe learning, psychological, behavioural and medical problems were being integrated into mainstream education and society. The West had its system of discrimination and segregation and a powerful set of vested professional interests relied upon it.

The West's edifice was built upon the assumption of an individual's intelligence being a once-and-for-all, God-given endowment. But such notions became increasingly vulnerable to attack. Because poor intellectual performance corresponded so closely with low social and economic status and membership of ethnic groups, it became necessary to consider broader determinants of intelligence than heredity.

Crude and supposedly incontrovertible meanings deduced from IQ test scores were also challenged and there is now a belated recognition of what many parents have always intuitively known (and which provided a large part of the gut reaction against the 11-plus), that the one constant feature of childhood is change. Trying to determine a child's whole future with a test at 11 years old is an inhuman nonsense: any snapshot of a child's intellectual performance at one particular time can only be of very limited significance. IQ tests have no way of measuring the effect of past influences or of future potential; they sacrifice everything to the Manifest Level of Functioning—what a child can do, unaided, at the time of testing.

It seems an absurdly obvious point to make, particularly to educational psychologists and teachers who resort to IQ tests, that conventional testing cannot measure the effect of teaching on the child, or a child's ability to learn! Nevertheless, T. E. Vernon, a British critic of intelligence tests, had to say in 1969: 'It is indeed curious that we use intelligence tests mainly to predict capacity for learning and yet none of our tests involves any learning, instead they give us a cross-section of what has been learned'.

Despite the growing objections to the premise that intelligence is a once-and-for-all endowment at birth, the final death-blow to crude IQ testing has been a long time coming. In Britain, such tests are still widely used as a matter of routine on children in many mainstream state schools. And they continue to be used by the majority of educational psychologists in the assessment of mentally and physically handicapped children and those with other learning difficulties.

Part of the reason for the persistence of conventional psychometrics is professional inertia. Psychometrics has played an important rôle in justifying the development of educational psychology as a profession based on the same sort of rigorous methods as the natural sciences. There are vested interests in local educational authorities and universities determinedly defending it. But perhaps the more important reason is that there has been nothing satisfactorily to take the place of IQ testing and the theories of intelligence which underpin it.

Teachers' experiences in the classroom tend to confirm apparently commonsense, but in fact deeply ideological, views that children have either 'got it' or 'haven't got it'. It is a comfortable and myopic view which fails to take account of the fact that children who fail in school and who cannot cope with formal learning situations, can often function well outside school in games or work where complex skills are involved.

But teachers' overly black-and-white view of children's intellectual capacity is also an understandable response to some confusing and frustrating phenomena which every teacher has experienced. This is the way that some children, after painstaking instruction, can apparently master some problem or new skill, but, within a day or even hours, lose that ability so completely that it seems as if it was never taught. Or a child may manage to master a problem, but then simply cannot apply the problem-solving principles to new tasks.

The response of educationalists to these children is to try to measure their lack of ability and—armed with a battery of intelligence test results—categorise them along a 'continuum of need' as having (in the new argot) severe learning difficulties, moderate learning difficulties or just plain learning difficulties.

Whatever the terms, the effects of this type of assessment and placement on children are the same. The teaching they are given is reduced in complexity according to their assigned intellectual status, and the children never progress beyond what is officially expected of them. Whatever potential they may have had becomes well and truly buried beneath the assumptions and the reality of their IQ scores.

This passive approach to children's intellectual performance is based on the conception of intelligence as an ineluctable substance endowed by genetics, or by God. But what if we had a less mystical and more practical notion of intelligence as a set of skills or thinking processes which enable us to make sense of the world and creatively use information to tackle new tasks—the ability, in other words, to learn from experience?

It might not seem like it, but this formulation of what constitutes intelligence has the most profound implications. What we might call endowment still remains important but it loses its primary rôle in development in favour of the way children's minds are fashioned to enable them to see, understand and act upon the world. Rather than being a passive and pessimistic view of the ability to modify children's intellectual performance, it allows for an optimistic and interventionist outlook. It suggests that the thinking skills we need in order to learn effectively, and which are normally absorbed by children as they develop in their family and culture, can, if absent, be instrumentally remedied. With this approach educationalists are encouraged to retain a sense of children's potential to develop and change, and warned away from too readily passing life-sentences of 'sub-normality'.

It has also allowed for the opening up of the whole new field of Cognitive Education—teaching children how to think more effectively—which is gradually being seen as one of the most rewarding innovations in education in the Western and Third Worlds. This achievement is in some large part due to the work of Professor Reuven Feuerstein, the subject of this book.

Feuerstein's main tenet is that children who are unable to learn from experience or to benefit from teaching are usually suffering from cognitive deficiencies—put more simply, they have not learned to think coherently. They therefore have no apparatus with which to organise, store and re-use the mass of information which bombards children every minute of their waking lives. Instead of considering new problems and thinking them through with the benefit of past lessons learned, such children either react impulsively or become inert in the face of tasks or information that they do not have the intellectual means to solve or process.

Such responses will immediately strike chords with parents and a whole range of professionals dealing with both low-achieving and delinquent children. Feuerstein points out that impulsiveness is one of the most striking features characterising these children: they do not have the structured thought needed to learn from their mistakes, to act rationally in new situations or to absorb the values of the culture in which they are brought up.

Here it is possible to glimpse the explanatory power of Feuerstein's theories and the remedial techniques—collectively called Instrumental Enrichment (IE)—which spring from them. One should add that both the theories and the techniques have been successfully tested in a large number of countries: in the USA and Canada where Instrumental Enrichment is used extensively, and in South American countries, like Venezuela, where it is part of the education programme for state-trained teachers. And there is a growing body of research evidence that Instrumental Enrichment is effective with a wide range of client populations.

For example, it is now accepted in the Canadian penal system that Instrumental Enrichment is of great benefit to prisoners of all ages. Third-world countries have found that it helps children to develop the thinking patterns and concepts that they need to live in industrial societies. It has been shown to improve the performance of working-class, immigrant and ethnic-minority children in Israel and other countries where it has been tested in state education systems. In clinical or group situations it has been shown to have a range of beneficial effects for children with mental handicaps or other disruptive conditions, enabling them to achieve levels of performance previously considered absolutely impossible by other established medical and psychological opinion.

A word needs to be said here about Feuerstein's work with children who are mentally handicapped. In many ways it is his most inspiring, but his claims for his methods are slightly different with these children. He categorically maintains that children who are low-functioning and educationally retarded as a result of cognitive deficiencies which are 'social' in origin can be brought to function at average or above-average levels with Instrumental Enrichment. He does not say this for children who have genetic or organic conditions like Down's Syndrome or brain damage. He does claim that he can dramatically improve their intellectual performance and their quality of life even though they will probably never achieve average ability. In some ways, though, the degree of change is far greater, and far more unexpected and exciting, with these children than with those who have only been socially handicapped.

With children who have been severely socially handicapped or disabled by organic or genetic conditions, Feuerstein often combines Instrumental Enrichment with specially designed placements which are usually residential in character. These therapeutic settings, as much as his theoretical work and Instrumental Enrichment techniques, constitute Feuerstein's revolution in special education. Some of the principles behind them will be described in this book. It is astonishing to consider that many of these environments were developed in the years just after the war and yet they are still, in my opinion, years ahead of anything that the British special education or care system has to offer.

The objectives of this book are to introduce the reader to the broad span of Feuerstein's ideas and work, from the theories behind Instrumental Enrichment to his commitment to plastic surgery for children with Down's Syndrome. It will also offer a taste of the way some of the Instrumental Enrichment materials are used by practitioners, and discuss some of the research carried out on their effectiveness. Much of this material has never been collected together before. Little of it has been accessible, physically or intellectually, to those parents and professionals without the academic background or time to hunt out and plough through some very difficult documentation. Educationalists in many far-flung countries are greatly excited by Feuerstein's work and his ideas remain too important not to be disseminated in a more popular form. As well as to parents, I believe this book will be of interest to teachers in ordinary and special schools, social workers and probation officers, prisons officers and psychologists in their various services, and the medical and paramedical professionals involved with the mentally handicapped.

There is another reason for this book, a more political one. Education, like every other social endeavour, is a political arena in which opposing theories, notwithstanding their claims to scientific objectivity, slug it out for supremacy. Until now the advocates of hereditary intelligence, fixed for all time by genetics, have held sway. The opposing, purely sociological argument that rich kids always do better, has never satisfactorily been able to explain why some materially-deprived immigrant groups do better than others. Or why some children from working-class backgrounds, with similar material disadvantages, leave their peers behind and go on to university. The sociological argument is too crude to be able to explain the many exceptions.

Feuerstein offers a more sophisticated and plausible explanation of how the effects of social class and cultural deprivation can work through family relations to affect the psychology of the individuals, producing educationally retarded children, or 'low-functioning' children as he calls them, and how the seeds of delinquency are sown in children from disadvantaged groups.

In Feuerstein's understanding of child development children are placed firmly in the context of their families which interpret the world for them and, in so doing, instil the means for understanding and appreciating their own culture, and for operating as intelligent beings within it. He has analysed how this complex process of acculturation can break down, impoverishing children's intellectual capacities. To Feuerstein, cultural deprivation is alienation from one's own culture, not the dominant culture of the society that one lives in.

By insisting on a psychological and social explanation to educational backwardness, rather than a fatalistic genetic one, Feuerstein has been able to develop an interventionist and optimistic approach. The significance of this, in the contrast it represents to conventional psychological and educational practice in the West, is best summed up by Feuerstein himself in a critical comment on conventional psychology which recalls Marx's famous dictum on the way that academic philosophy sought merely to interpret the world rather than change it. 'What,' he asks, 'is the point of just measuring a child's intelligence and labelling him with a tag of slowness or subnormality? The point, surely, is to change the child.

PART 1
THE HISTORICAL IMPERATIVE

OUT OF TRAGEDY . . .

As the Second World War drew to its close a major operation was launched by Zionists to bring the surviving Jewish children of Europe to Palestine. It was controlled by Youth Aliyah—the wing of the Jewish Agency formed in the 1930s to assist the escape and immigration of young Jews from Europe to the Homeland. With the help of the now semi-clandestine network of Jewish committees, Jewish Agency officers and Jewish troops in allied armies, the children were transported to Mediterranean ports and smuggled into Palestine under the noses of the British Mandate forces.

With the establishment of the Israeli state in 1948, and throughout the 1950s and 1960s, Israel experienced a second great wave of immigration from North Africa and the Middle East. These oriental Jews came from very different lands and cultures, sometimes hundreds if not thousands of years removed from the western technological culture of Israel. In many cases they came from communities that had been atomised by repression and which had lost most of their cultural bonds.

The accounts of these vast movements of people have tended to concentrate, understandably, on the heroic achievements of the rescuers and the rescued. But in fact they presented Israel with a set of social problems equally if not more heroic in scale. Not the least of these was the discovery by educationalists in Youth Aliyah and Jewish society at large that great numbers of children from European and oriental Jewish immigrant communities were failing to thrive in their new country. The former were often too traumatised by the Holocaust to be able to integrate easily into schools, while the latter seemed unable to perform at the appropriate level in school; they rejected or were rejected by the mainstream culture and were beginning to form the basis of a marginal underclass.

It was not ideologically possible, however, for Israel simply to take the conventional Western route and try and contain their youth problem in the ghettos of low-achieving schools or young offender institutions. These children were too important; they were symbols of the tragic past and of the optimistic future of the Jewish people, and of the Israeli state. This exceptional commitment is important to mention because it determined how services were constructed to assist them, and allowed an environment favourable to a much more radical, interventionist and humanitarian approach to child care than is our experience in the West.

A major instrument in this massive rehabilitation programme remained Youth Aliyah. It had the advantage of being a 'voluntary' organisation, outside the official education system, even if the state gave it considerable backing—and was, therefore, more flexible in its theoretical and practical approaches to disturbed and retarded youngsters. And since its whole conception was based on the premise of 'rescuing' Jewish children, its commitment to rehabilitation was more intense than elsewhere. Knowing and understanding, and more importantly, sympathising with their past, Youth Aliyah invested enormous resources of money, expertise and patience in these children.

Rehabilitation was carried out, by and large, in Youth Villages or other residential settlements, usually within Kibbutzim, which acted both as induction centres for new young immigrants to Israel and as therapeutic communities for children too disturbed to exist for the time being in ordinary Jewish society.

Professor Feuerstein, who had fled Nazi-occupied Romania in 1944, became a key figure in the development of Youth Aliyah's services. He had started with Youth Aliyah in 1945 as a special teacher and counsellor for children who had survived the concentration camps and became the director of psychological services, Europe, in 1951, eventually establishing, in 1954, its Jerusalem Child Guidance Clinic. He remained its director until 1983 and is now the director of the Hadassah Wizo Canada Child Research Institute in Jerusalem.

His work has consisted of two concurrent and merging themes: the reintegration of severely emotionally-disturbed children through a programme of general enrichment and socialisation, and helping socially and culturally-deprived, as well as handicapped children, with very poor intellectual functioning, to raise their performances through Instrumental Enrichment. This is the programme of structured exercises which are based on Feuerstein's theoretical analyses of children's thinking failures and which are designed to tutor 'intelligence'.

The Youth Villages

One of the most basic principles of Feuerstein's work has been that disturbed, delinquent and retarded children should never be completely cut off from their normal peers. For Feuerstein special education has only one purpose, to prepare problem children for re-entry into normal schools and ordinary society. And contact with ordinary children is one of the most powerful agents for achieving this. In cold print this might seem merely commonsensical: but it stands in sharp contrast to the desperately confused special-education, child-care and juvenile justice systems in the West.

Our special-education systems, for example, including that part of the state system in Israel influenced by the West, is based on the premise that retarded performers should be segregated for their educational lives in special schools. Now, at least rhetorically, it is guided by the principle of integration. Yet, once inside the system, with its separate and autonomous existence, it has been virtually impossible to get children out. Attempts by the British, Americans and Europeans to integrate educationally retarded or disabled children into ordinary schools, often without any preparation, are failing. In the UK the same proportion of children are still going into special schools as ever. In the juvenile justice system, Community Homes with Education (formerly approved schools) and other penal institutions isolate children and youths because of their delinquency. None of these institutions is run by the education system, and education is often a poorly-executed afterthought to care or control objectives.

The approach of Feuerstein and his colleagues could not have been more different. Instead of total and permanent segregation of disturbed or retarded children on the one hand, or a hapless integration with normal children on the other, they insisted on a planned and structured 're-entry' of problem children into the mainstream, in the context of an educational institution. The Youth Villages and Kibbutz-based residential camps, it must be remembered, were educational institutions in the widest sense, and were ideal for the purpose. They sought to educate and socialise children from widely varying academic and cultural backgrounds in order to forge new Israeli citizens.

'Treatment groups' of 25 very psychologically–and emotionally–disturbed children were established within the Youth Aliyah Villages and these received separate instruction and care, as well as a controlled interaction with their normal peers. This afforded the problem children protection from damaging competition and rejection, while preventing the establishment of a delinquent sub-culture. Feuerstein maintains, as do many others, that this deviant sub-culture always establishes itself in institutions where all the adolescent inmates are considered by the authorities, and by themselves, as social problems of one sort or another.

Writing in 1974 on the type of child placed in the treatment group, Feuerstein explained that the qualifications were rather severe. 'Total or functional illiteracy, low conventionally-measured intelligence, (40 to 75 IQ), primary emotional disturbance and severe behaviour disorders. About 20% of these children were considered to be borderline psychotic. They had either been hospitalised or hospitalisation had been seriously considered. Others had been rejected from special or normal school systems because of the severity of their disturbance.

The treatment groups provided the setting for much of Feuerstein's later and more famous work. They were the basis for other innovative types of placement for children who would normally be segregated. I will return to these later because of their importance to practices of childcare and special education in the West.

The most important development of Feuerstein's work—the elaboration of the theory of the Mediated Learning Experience and Structural Cognitive Modifiability, and the techniques to improve children's thinking skills called Instrumental Enrichment—occurred within the context of the Youth Village treatment groups. The Youth Village which pioneered the 'treatment group' work was the Swiss-sponsored village Kyriat Yearim. Studies of children from Kyriat Yearim, later tested by the army, showed that they had not only recovered normal functioning but performed better than the average for the population as a whole. Only graduates of the highly privileged Kibbutzim fared better.

To gather the significance of this, an analogy is in order. It is comparable to the majority of children in our own schools for the moderately educationally retarded, those in schools for the maladjusted and those in suspension units, children's homes and increasingly those being sent into Detention Centres and Youth Custody, turning out to be responsible and capable citizens with a higher-than-average intellectual performance. In Britain the chance of this happening is unthinkable (*see Part 4, Changing Environments*).

CHILDREN OF THE MELLAH

A fundamental tenet of Israeli nationhood is the Law of Return, which gives all Jews the right to emigrate to Israel. One of the few times this principle was seriously questioned was over the children of the Moroccan Mellah—the Jewish enclaves in Morocco—who were found to be so backward that it was suggested that many of them could never integrate into Israeli society, at least without placing an impossible burden on the State.

Moroccan Jews, like other oriental Jews, did have very different lifestyles and customs from the western, Ashkenazi Jews. Because of their comparative technological backwardness and, some would say, because of the subtle bias of the Ashkenazi-governing establishment of Israel, they were destined to take up the rôle of unskilled, working-class and frontier settlers on poor agricultural land. It was declared at the time that the bias against oriental Jews was clearly apparent in the readiness of professionals to condemn the children of virtually a whole population group as 'sub-normal'.

On the other hand the conventional tests, including those designed as far as possible to be culturally unbiased, revealed exceptionally low functioning in a wide band of Moroccan Jewish children—more so than in any other group of immigrant Jews. The implication was that Moroccan Jewish children were somehow genetically impaired.

Feuerstein, as head of Youth Aliyah's psychological service in France and Morocco, refused to accept either position. A wide variety of tests did indeed show very poor intellectual functioning, even when compared with other pre-industrial oriental Jewish communities like the Yemenites. 'They had a very poor grasp of reality; poor perception; they failed to use all sources of information available to them; some children of

14 years could not even name the days of the week. There was not the slightest doubt that they were functioning at very low levels', explained Feuerstein.

But the genetic explanation of their consistently low IQ scores did not convince him either. Unlike the other professionals who had tested these children, Feuerstein was aware, as a keen student of Jewish history, that Moroccan Jewry had in the past a culture which had created one of the greatest traditions of Talmudic scholasticism in the Diaspora. Something had clearly happened to the Moroccan Jewish community, and to a lesser extent to Jews from other North African countries, which might be responsible for the strange deficiencies in the children. Whatever it was, the conventional psychometric tests were not explaining it, he recalls:

> One of the great confusions of psychometric testing, which became very clear to us in those times in Morocco, is that it could not distinguish between performance and potential. All our tests on the Moroccan children showed us that they were performing unnaturally badly. We felt obliged to see if the children really had more hidden potential than was being manifested in the tests. But there was no test, European or American, that could help us discover if these children really had more capacity to learn than we were giving them credit for.

Testing for Potential

The system that Feuerstein and the famous Swiss psychologist, André Rey, finally constructed was exceptionally simple. They tested the children in order to locate some of the intellectual problems they were experiencing, then carried out some highly focused teaching and psychological treatment, and then retested the children to see how their performance had changed. The results of this test-teach-test routine confounded those of the conventional tests: children previously assessed as having IQs of 55–65 were found to have the potential to obtain at least normal functioning.

At the Hadassah Wizo Canada Research Institute in Jerusalem, Feuerstein still has some of the records of the Moroccan children tested in Israel and Morocco, with their original low IQ scores. He also has records of their academic achievement after his and Youth Aliyah's interventions. Apart from those originally thought to be mentally handicapped, who reached average attainment, there are those that went on to university and academic careers. One of the boys is quoted in Feuerstein's books: at the age of 14 years he was given an IQ of 55 and, like many of the Moroccan Jewish children, would draw human figures with arms sticking out of their heads. The child grew up to be a professor of social sciences.

The 'dynamic' test-teach-test routine was subsequently elaborated into Feuerstein's 'Learning Potential Assessment Device', which will be discussed in more detail in Part 2. Dynamic testing has now become much more commonplace (although it is often done without the radical critique of the theory and procedures of conventional testing which is so important to Feuerstein's Learning Potential Assessment Device). But when it was first used in 1960 the device represented a highly controversial departure from conventional psychometric practice. Because it was devised not only to assess learning potential, but to diagnose deficiencies in performance, it was more than a clinical tool; it functioned as an instrument for suggesting new insights about the way 'intelligence' operated and the main factors influencing it.

For example, the Learning Potential Assessment Device showed that the Moroccan children were not stupid (except in every conventionally tested sense) but had enormous gaps in the cognitive processes or thinking skills which ordinary children pick up through interactions with their families. They found it hard to make comparisons between things and events, so that they could not reach conclusions based on these comparisons; they had very poor logical reasoning; their perception was sweeping—it failed to differentiate items sufficiently to discover the difference between figures, shapes, patterns, letters; they had poor spatial and temporal orientation —asked to draw a body, the head, rather than the torso, would grow limbs. Reality itself was blurred for these children.

Most of us have experienced this blurring. When we are tired our perception can lose focus and our analytical powers seem to go into suspension. For short periods life washes over us. For the children of the Mellah it was a permanent condition of their existence. They were bombarded with information and stimuli which they had no way of organising for use or re-use. Because it was not properly ordered it was impossible to store properly and, as a result, the children, typically, had very inadequate short-term memories. Problem-solving was exceptionally difficult because they had no store of experience to apply to new tasks: they had to approach each problem completely afresh, as would a baby.

Victims of Information

These children were, says Feuerstein, victims of information. They simply had not learned how to master and creatively use information for either their school or daily lives, although in some particular aspects which they had somehow mastered, they often excelled. Typically, however, in the face of a deluge of data they could not begin to utilise, and problems they could not begin to solve such children were passive. Or they were impulsive, either through the hope that a snatch at a possible solution might be lucky, or out of frustration. They had, in a phrase, failed to learn how to think.

Since the Moroccan children dramatically improved with remedial instruction, genetic barriers to learning were ruled out. But there was no question of the retardation of the children being purely a question of inadequate upbringing on the part of pathological individual families: the phenomenon was far too widespread.

Cultural Deprivation

Feuerstein compared the societies of the Moroccan Mellah with other immigrant Jewish communities. His conclusions were quite stark. Some pre-industrial Jewish communities, like the Yemenites and the Ethiopian Jews—the Falashas who have recently received so much publicity—produced children who did not suffer these cognitive deficiencies, who were very adaptable and who had enormous capacities for learning. Yet the North African Jews, which had come into contact with advanced technological cultures through colonialism, did produce low-functioning, unadaptable children with very limited capacities for learning. The impact of colonialism on the culture of Moroccan Jewish society seemed to have produced more than just a disastrous social effect; it left a psychological disaster in its train. Says Feuerstein:

> Moroccan Jewish culture was an exploded culture. The metropolitan French culture did not really reach the Arab-speaking cultures—what came out was what we would call a very inadequate representation of French culture—its marginal fringe aspects. But this was enough to disintegrate the indigenous cultures.
>
> The forces which led Moroccans to become alienated from their own culture were numerous, but among the most important was the internal migration to the urban colonial centres. Traditionally the Jews lived in small, very closely-knit ghettos in which the culture was transmitted to the younger generation through the grandfather and the old people generally. It was a patriarchal mode. The nuclear family could not ensure transmission because the fathers spent most of the week travelling around the markets as artisans and were too tired on return on Friday night to offer their children much. The mothers were also too busy with babies, housework and looking after whatever livestock and land the family had. So the grandparents were the teachers and the preservers of the culture.
>
> The moment the nuclear family migrated to Casablanca and other urban centres, this system broke down. The grandparents were often left behind, and even if they went with them they often couldn't live-in with the family because living space was so overcrowded. So you had a kind of discontinuity of the cultural transmission. It was made worse because the urbanised children rejected the traditions and values of their uprooted, but still basically rural, parents.

These children were culturally deprived—but by this Feuerstein means they had been alienated by sociological and psychological factors from their own culture, or, more exactly, their own historical culture, which had been reduced to a shadow of its former richness and cohesion.

Comparisons with the Yemenites and the Falashas from Ethiopia—the most technologically primitive groups to emigrate to Israel—were instructive. Groups of Yemenites and Falashas had lived in very isolated communities before arriving in Israel and their culture had persisted in a more or less integrated way for thousands of years. The Yemenites were air-lifted en masse to Israel out of their messianic desire to return to Zion, not because they were oppressed and needed refuge in Israel.

Tradition's rôle

They had, according to Feuerstein, a system of cultural transmission which proceeded through a highly elaborate and very strong system of community-wide relationships where the children were respected participants and had special rôles in the customs of the community. The children had the same rights and duties as the adults as regards the prayers: they gathered together around the Torah praying together and were accorded real status. This had a tremendous impact on the children, all of whom were literate between the ages of three and four years.

Moreover, how they read was an interesting metaphor for the way that culture influences learning. Because there was a great scarcity of books in the villages, everyone had to sit round to read the same book. As a result the children learned to read from every angle—upside down, straight on, left to right, right to left. There were no illiterates in the Yemen and their incorporation into Israel was remarkably free of major problems: the community showed a readiness and ability to learn rapidly about their new environment and to negotiate a relationship to a new culture. The Yemenites have continued to do well in their adopted country, but it is a much more sophisticated and differentiated society. Some children of the poorer members of the community in Israel's urban centres are now beginning to manifest hitherto unknown cases of illiteracy. The weakening of their historical culture, Feuerstein believes, is responsible for this.

The culture of the Ethiopian Jews was very different and if anything more technologically primitive. But it was no less rich. Their form of Judaism was based on the strict observance of the five books of Moses—they lived separated off from all rabbinical teachings of the period following the destruction of the First Temple. The customs and rituals were dominated by a Coenate—a priesthood—which was only recently, and even then only partially, transformed into a less powerful Rabbinate by contact with Western Jews at the turn of the century.

The Rabbis remained priestlike in their authority, however, and continued to dominate Ethiopian Jewish society, which remained a pre-literate society especially in the more rural Tigre province. They were the only group which developed literacy skills required to officiate at religious ceremonies and to interpret the Law. Nevertheless, their teachings and the age-old customs of the people were transmitted through the generations very efficiently, even rigidly, by the oral culture. But then oral cultures generally are, says Feuerstein, very effective transmission belts.

> If you give someone a book to read they may read it or not; you may have sustained attention or not, you may not have understood the words used. Literary transmission is much more hit-and-miss than oral transmission where a mother will relate to a child, repeat something if it is not all grasped, use different words and gestures if one means of communicating something has failed, and attract a child's attention if it is wandering off. It is a very, very efficient means of transmitting culture from one generation to another.

Like the Yemenites, the Ethiopian Jews have shown extraordinary adaptability in their new and comparatively very strange society. Their teachers and social workers have universally expressed surprise at the speed with which the children and younger adults learn, and a large number of them are now beginning to progress to further education and universities. Even the elders have shown a pragmatic willingness to change their customs and even their religious rituals to suit their new country. But this could be a very mixed blessing because it might well undermine the very cultural traditions that gave the ability to learn a new culture so rapidly.

Culturally Deprived and Culturally Different

A very important hypothesis of Feuerstein's is that individuals from different but nevertheless rich and still coherent cultures, having learned one culture, usually have the means to learn another. Those children who had been deprived of their own culture do not. This insight convinced Feuerstein that, as a matter of Youth Aliyah and State policy, it was vital to support and reinforce the culture of immigrant groups to enable them to integrate into their new society. It was those children lucky enough to have firm cultural bases who were able to develop the necessary skills to keep a foot in two cultural camps—the old and the new.

Whatever intellectual difficulties they had from moving into a new culture, the difficulties were much more superficial than for those children who were culturally deprived, or who were unfortunately both culturally deprived and different. This insight had immense ramifications for social and educational policy regarding immigrant children in Israel. (It also, of course, opens up large areas for investigation into the problems associated with different immigrant groups like the Asians, and West Indians, and other minority groups, in Britain and the USA.)

But the issues involved far transcend the problems of immigrant children. Feuerstein found not only that there were different abilities within different incoming cultures, but that the Yemenites and the Falashas often had better learning skills, and were therefore more adaptable and better able to acquire a new culture, than the children of the poorer immigrant families from Britain and the USA. Equally as startling was that children from seemingly very primitive societies were able to acquire Israeli culture more readily than deprived Israeli-born children.

TRANSMITTING CULTURES

'You can take a child to a zoo and he might find it very interesting, but it won't teach him logic'. Feuerstein uses this quaint aphorism to challenge some of the most widespread theories of child development. The most important of these, argued by Piaget, is that children's minds respond to the development in their sensory and motor abilities, and then to new stimuli. These constantly widen and alter their view of the world and their intellectual framework, so that they can assimilate new levels of information.

Through ceaseless interactions with the world children are continually modifying their ability to process new information. There is a partial analogy here with computers—the greater the capacity and sophistication of a computer's central processing system, the more complex the information that it can handle.

Piaget presumed a structure in the mind which could organise and process data, in the same way that computers need processing systems. The difference, of course, is that Piaget believed children's processing powers are continually being modified and expanded to the point where they can undertake highly formalised and abstract mental operations. Computers do not have this growth potential—their structures are fixed.

Piaget's philosophy of child development has been so widely disseminated that it now forms part of the 'common sense' of child-rearing and education. One of the interpretations of his work is that children must be exposed to as much stimulation as possible to grow intellectually—the more the better—and children deprived of stimulation will suffer. Failure of parents to stimulate their child adequately is one of the grounds on which our social services attempt to prove parental neglect and to remove children from the home of their parents.

Feuerstein, who was a student of Piaget from 1950 to 1954,

does not discount his former teacher's work. But he says it is an inadequate and still too mechanical explanation of child development, which fails to explain many things. Why, he asks, if the Piagetian progression towards formal mental operations is automatic and universal, does so much of humanity fail to reach this level? Why and how do children from different cultures and socio-economic groups manifest a different receptivity to stimuli—such as going to a zoo or museum—and why do the children of some cultures show an inability or resistance to learning, despite being bombarded by stimuli?

In Feuerstein's view, the Piagetian concept of development cannot explain the very large differences in learning abilities between individuals, and between and within groups, classes and cultures. It could not, for example, explain the poor performance of the Moroccan children compared to the Falasha or Yemenite children, or of working-class children generally.

The basic premise that one's environment, or at least a child's 'free' interaction with that environment, produces a mental framework or structure that allows steady and automatic progression, fails adequately to explain two other phenomena. It cannot elucidate why an achievement in one small area can completely transform the personality of the whole child and its intellectual performance; and it is unable to explain the sometimes radical changes wrought by 'teachers' (used here in the broadest sense). In fact Piagetian theory, Feuerstein maintains, is in some senses an anti-educational ideology, because it presumes that children learn simply through contact with stimuli: teachers are reduced to the providers of these stimuli and of learning opportunities. Yet this is one of the bases of much liberal educational thought in Britain.

Enter Human Intervention

Feuerstein changes Piaget's formula for the 'free' and 'transparent' interactions between children and the world, denoted by the formula Stimuli-Organism-Response (S-O-R) by inserting the rôle of a mediator—a parent, grandparent, sibling or caretaker—who shapes the way the child perceives the world. This insertion of these mediators of stimuli into the equation of child development does no more than theoretically recover for us our daily experience of bringing up children. Parents, particularly mothers in our society, are not simply one source of stimulation amongst others; they control stimuli for their children and, in so doing, construct a universe for the child which is similar to their own. In this way culture, which determines perception and behaviour, is transmitted in normal conditions from one generation to another.

The formula now becomes S-H-O-R, the **H** standing for human intervention. With this seemingly slight theoretical shift, it is possible to leave behind a mechanistic process of child development. Instead it starts to become possible to examine the way in which mediation takes place to create mental structures in children and to look at the interplay between child upbringing, culture, social conditions and history. Great tragedies and great migrations do, after all, disrupt families and cultures; they have been the stuff of our times and were the starting point of Feuerstein's work.

Contrary to what conventional theories tell us, the way in which parents and other mediators construct their children's world is not through bombarding them with stimuli but by selecting, ordering, emphasising and explaining some stimuli at the expense of others. 'Culture,' says Feuerstein, 'is not absorbed by children, it is imposed upon them.'

Common to all human cultures are cognitive or thinking processes which enable people to function at levels well beyond those required to meet biological needs. An anthropological cliché about man's success is our ability to adapt to new and widely varying conditions. But the highly conscious and controlled forms of human adaptability are a very complex feature of our cultural existence, way above and beyond basic responses to our environment. The development of these cognitive processes is the basic pre-condition, or building foundation, upon which the content of particular cultures is established.

Parents, siblings or caretakers of children, in their rôle as mediators, build up these basic human thinking skills by giving children what Feuerstein calls Mediated Learning Experiences (MLE). He uses this term to highlight the difference with learning through direct exposure to stimuli, which would enable people to develop responses to meet their biological and limited social needs, but could never be responsible for the quantum leap into the higher mental abilities like logical thought.

An interesting example is the way that mothers with newly-born children sequence and group objects and events to give the children a sense of order in time and space. They wipe their hands *before* eating, and they give their child one spoonful *after* they have finished the first. These are toys to play with, those are not. If you touch this, such and such happens. The significance of the adult's intervention in mediating stimuli, acting in effect as censor to some while emphasising and repeating others, can be glimpsed by the importance of the word 'No' to young children. Long before they acquire language children have learned by the sound of the word what they must not do or touch, while mother's smiles and clapping of hands, and repetitions in order to explain something, stress the importance of other stimuli.

This mother-baby behaviour is often termed stimulation or conditioning—as in the research on the bestowal of sex rôles. But the first does not describe how and why types of 'stimulation' produce certain effects on the child. It is a global term, a blunt instrument that does not help our understanding of the intricacies of child development.

The concept of conditioning is also too crude to explain how it is that children ever develop the ability to think for themselves rather than to respond to outside control, or acquire their own powers of adaptive behaviour.

What is really happening in this and other mediational relationships, believes Feuerstein, is that the child is being invested with a series of thinking skills—a structure with which he can perceive and make sense of the world. By scheduling and sorting stimuli, the mother is giving the child a sense of time and space through which experience can be organised. This constructed spatial and temporal universe is very much a cultural phenomenon, and, although the precise content might vary from culture to culture, it is a universal human creation which is not a product of meeting basic needs.

PUTTING IN THE SYSTEM

The story of Moshe K is a tragic one, but it is typical of many of the grossly deprived children Feuerstein was presented with in Youth Aliyah. His history shows the shocking effects of inadequate mediated learning and how professionals too often jump to the conclusion of 'mental defective'.

Moshe's father was a merchant in one of the Sephardic communities of the Diaspora and married a young girl very late in life. While Moshe was still a young child his father died and the mother, absconding with a young lover, abandoned him.

Moshe was rejected by the remainder of his father's family and was forced to live the existence of a street urchin, receiving only occasional shelter from one of his father's former colleagues.

As an illiterate adolescent Moshe's extremely disturbed and aggressive behaviour caused his village to contact Youth Aliyah to see if he could be helped in Israel.

When first examined by psychologists Moshe had a very limited number of intellectual functions and was thought to be mentally handicapped. It was thought, says Feuerstein, that his condition of mind had caused his rejection rather than vice versa. When taken to the transit camp in the South of France before being shipped out to Israel, his reaction to lessons was extremely hostile and unruly.

Attempts to assess him showed phenomenally low, almost unmeasurably low, levels of functioning. He could not use language properly and communication was mainly through pointing gestures. He was highly impulsive and unable to use whatever cues for behaviour or thinking were given to him.

Going by test scores and assessments of behaviour, Moshe seemed a poor prospect for any educational system. Yet by trying to assess his potential rather than his present performance

Feuerstein and colleagues uncovered signs that the child could be affected by teaching.

He was recommended for placement in a preparatory residential setting for cognitive as well as emotional remedial training, so that he could eventually be integrated into one of the mainstream residential units of Youth Aliyah. This never materialised. It was discovered he had a contagious scalp disease and the residential institution refused to accept him before medical treatment had successfully removed any risks to other children.

Fortunately, Moshe was obliged to go to Paris for treatment of his condition and was placed in a ward of very young children with the same disease. He was forced to behave as a small child, eating at small tables, reading infantile booklets and submitting to the same type of treatment from the nurses, that was given to the other children.

This hard and violent, angry, young man literally melted down under the regressive impact of the environment. The nurses became surrogate mothers—in rather an intensive way because of the condition—but also the training and visits of the other mothers became a source of mediation to him.

Moshe, who was formerly completely closed to learning, had started to listen, to be attentive to what one was saying to him, to open his eyes to the booklets, to point out with his finger and to name objects and colours as if he had discovered them for the first time in his life. Whenever someone came to visit him he reacted in an unusually positive way. At the end of five months after the medical treatment was over we reexamined Moshe and found he no longer needed preparatory treatment, but could go straight into a mainstream residential placement in Israel. In fact he joined a very good level adolescent group in a Kibbutz.

Moshe K learned to read and write in French and Hebrew, rose to be the military commander of his village and became subsequently a career soldier. He is now an officer teaching social work to military welfare staff.

The most crucial factor in causing the extreme changes in Moshe's level of behavioural and cognitive functioning was the intensive mediated learning experience he received at the hospital. He was given the chance to be unconditionally accepted as a small child and to receive the type of interactions naturally given to children by parents. These gave Moshe the cognitive apparatus which became one of a person who could judge, learn and develop.

Feuerstein points out that Moshe's case illustrates how modifiability, even of very extreme kinds, can occur naturally as a result of environment rather than of a focused, deliberate intervention. But making this phenomenon happen more frequently and systematically required the analysing and conceptualising of such modifying experiences into an intervention programme.

From their experience of the holocaust and immigrant children, and of the vast army of deprived and delinquent children which flooded into Youth Aliyah after the 1970s, and through the study of hours of video-tapes of behaviour between mothers of normal and developmentally delayed children, Feuerstein and his colleagues have theorised the main characteristics which adult/child interactions must have if they are to mediate, or transfer, important intellectual behaviour to children.

Key features of Mediated Learning Experience

Our parents and relatives, acting as the agents of culture, impose meaning on the otherwise neutral stimuli that continually bombard us, and, in this way, ensure the transmission of values from one generation to another. When parents say, for example, that objects or events are 'good', 'bad', 'sad', 'happy', 'important', 'unimportant', 'worthy of respect', 'unworthy of respect', 'right', 'wrong', they are assigning cultural meanings to our daily environment. These meanings can be very sophisticated and can link a child's experiences with a subtle and pervasive emotional, moral and motivational significance.

Our senses alone cannot do this. It must be through the human endowment of meaning onto a non-human physical environment that a child's cultural universe is established, and different cultures continued. Feuerstein calls this very important activity 'The Mediation of Meaning' and it is one of the key features which defines and sets apart mediated learning experiences from other child-adult interactions.

There are nine other of these broad characteristics which tell whether or not interactions with children will provide them with any of the necessary intellectual functions, needs and behaviours. If only all child-adult interactions were also mediated learning experiences, Feuerstein claims that the extraordinary gap between high-achieving and low-achieving children would not be so wide.

A failure to transfer these meanings to the younger generation will produce anti-social and criminal tendencies which will undermine any culture, says Feuerstein. In response to questions from teachers and some very 'liberal' parents who ask what right they have to impose their values on children, Feuerstein replies that they have no right *not* to. Children need to be given meanings because they act as bearings in an otherwise impenetrable world. And they alone give children the starting point and the opportunity to challenge some or all of the offered meanings at a later stage. Unsocialised or criminal behaviour is not radical or revolutionary behaviour, it is inadequate behaviour.

One of the greatest causes of failure in school is the attempt by many teachers to remain neutral toward the material they are conferring on children. Instead of seeing themselves as mediators of values and morality they often seek to act as objective perpetrators of information, after some notion of an academic tradition.

But children have a need to discover meaning in stimuli and are often left unsatisfied. The stimuli, and even learning itself, are then seen to lack vitality or relevance.

Meaning is the emotional and energetic principle that requires mediators to ensure that the stimulus they are presenting to children gets through. It is the needle that carries the thread through the cloth. If the stimulus carries no real significance, why bother too hard to direct the child to it? We are driven by the need to continue our culture and ourselves in our children. The mediation of meaning is very important to humanity: its absence can be seen in people who do not look for meaning in their lives or behaviour, or in the way they handle themselves and others.

There are two other criteria which have the same 'universal' status as the Mediation of Meaning and one of these must be present, in combination or alone, for an adult-child interaction to constitute a Mediated Learning Experience. They are Intentionality and Transcendence.

Intentionality

Intentionality can be seen in mother–baby relationships from the earliest age and describes the conscious intention with which the mother controls access to stimuli. The purpose of the mother in showing or doing something, or getting the baby to do something, is conveyed to the child who, as it were, becomes part of the intention which frames the different stimuli. In Feuerstein's view this completely alters the nature of a stimulus—compare, for example, a toy train which is static and one that is pushed by the mother from A to B.

The intention of the mother to convey something produces an orientation in the child towards the goal sought by the mediator—in our case to get the child to understand that the toy not only has physical properties but also certain functions. This dramatically intensifies the stimulus, making both child and mother more attentive, and so producing what Feuerstein calls a 'state of vigilance' towards the stimulus which can be evidenced by increased sharpness, focus and acuity of perception.

Transcendence

This is closely linked to intentionality and refers partly to the goal and partly to the character of an interaction between, say, a mother and child. A vital characteristic of Mediated Learning Experience is that it produces *more* than just the behaviour required to meet a specific need. In the practice of conveying to the child some explanation, activity skill or prohibition, something of much more general value is smuggled in which transcends the child's immediate needs and understanding.

A parent counting a number of objects in a set can lead to

more general summative behaviour; allowing children to play with typewriters or even word processors can become a vehicle for teaching cause and effect—'Hit that key, son, and up pops a letter!'—and playing with building blocks can orientate the child to the subtleties of space. A family outing, on the other hand, can become an opportunity for conveying planning behaviour and aspects of time relations, before, during, after. In response to simple questions parents often provide much more than they were asked for and, by so doing, transcend the original need that provoked the question or request.

Virtually every situation has the potential for mediated learning experiences, yet this potential is not always exploited. Toys can be left unexplained, children can be dragged along behind adults on outings, and they can be told not to play with grown-up things like typewriters. When children become mere extensions of adults, the potential for mediational interactions is lost. Telling a child to 'Shut that door' cannot be a Mediated Learning Experience. But 'Shut that door because there is a draught and it is cold' can convey cause and effect—open doors create draughts; shut doors stop draughts—as well as conveying notions of before and after.

The character of an interaction may be transcendental without the mediator fully realising it. But it is surprising how much adults consciously provide goals for children over and above an immediate activity. An example is table manners. Through the basic need to eat parents have developed a social ritual which, among other things, conveys that there are rules of socially acceptable behaviour for certain activities.

Transcendence is a very powerful force for shaping children's behaviour and is responsible for the continual expansion of children's needs beyond their basic requirements for sustenance and comfort. And one of the most important transcendental needs that children develop is the need to know and understand—curiosity.

Among the less constant but nevertheless vital features of Mediated Learning Experiences are that they can mediate feelings of competence; the self-regulation and control of behaviour; sharing behaviour and a sense of individuality. They also instil the need for challenges, for novelty and complexity, and the psychological need to set goals for oneself and then achieve them, which, like the other five, occur in specific situations and, by interacting with the first three necessary criteria, turn child-adult interactions into forms of mediated learning.

Within these broad criteria, child-adult interactions construct children's thinking and behaviour. A child's success at solving intellectual problems, for example, is as dependent on his feelings of competence as on his actual competence, for if the first is not present children become so convinced of their likely failure that they do not attempt to solve problems, or do so only half-heartedly and with an expectation of defeat.

A Sense of Competence

Unfortunately this is one of the cognitive deficiencies that is most difficult to reverse. Once children conceive of themselves as incompetent, nothing, not even the most brilliant successes, can shift a poor self-image. Feuerstein quotes one of his own cases to illustrate this—that of a brilliant student whose over-demanding parents destroyed his self-esteem and who, despite achieving 95% in Israeli matriculation exams, refused to believe in his own abilities.

> His inability to get the other five per cent was more convincing to him than his positive achievements and he tried to minimise his success. It was luck. Or it was just that he revised the right questions. This poor child lived in a perpetual nightmare of imminent failure. He never believed he could repeat a success.

Poor motivation is one of the common results of this feeling of incompetence and teachers must often carry the blame for exaggerating it, says Feuerstein. If children get one out of five questions right, the teachers stress the four that remain to be done correctly—reinforcing children's self-confidence is not something that many teachers see as an over-riding goal.

But the inadequate mediation of feelings of competence can have more unusual psychological effects. Among low-functioning children who have been encouraged to see themselves as having very limited concentration or memory, and who have been taught 'down' to in special schools, a common trait is to be over-anxious to start and complete a task before the instructions have been properly grasped.

In their anxiety they forget what the teacher told them or how they executed the task, resulting in their own very erratic, unplanned behaviour. Here, says Feuerstein, the child's feelings of incompetence are often more important than any other cognitive deficiencies.

He goes so far as to say that feelings of inadequacy and poor self-image represent an inevitable tendency in children because, as they become more conscious they also become aware of the number of tasks their parents and other adults can accomplish, which they cannot. Children compensate for their inadequacy by 'fantasising competence' in their play. While this should be encouraged, children should be given realistic assessments of what is and is not possible for people of their age, so that competence is seen as a process rather than an inherent possession or weakness.

Need for Challenge
Framing tasks that are achievable and explaining the reasons for success reinforce the idea that competence is a process of investment, of time and thought and practice. The emotional reinforcement from parents makes the child willing to cope with new and strange experiences. The excitement of success that is conveyed by parents when they are mediating competence to their children, provokes a need in children to seek goals for themselves and to try and reach those goals. 'I want to do it myself' seems like the natural cry of every child: in fact, it is natural only in the sense that it is learned behaviour normally mediated to children by their parents. Children with an inadequate upbringing frequently do not have this internal need for challenge or for setting their own goals.

Control of Behaviour
When parents or siblings mediate the regulation of behaviour they teach the child that different situations require different responses. In most areas of life instinctive or impulsive behaviour has to be inhibited so that children can successfully gather, process and express information which then determines their actions. Crossing the road is one simple example where

parents insist on controlled, unimpulsive behaviour. But in many interactions adults, either explicitly or through acting as models, encourage controlled and considered responses to stimuli.

Encouraging children, for example, to take problems slowly and break them down into parts; or aiding them to take a systematic and logical approach to finding answers instead of guessing wildly, are all common, almost unconscious forms of mediation through which children are taught to regulate themselves and learn to regulate their own behaviour. This interaction in turn encourages children to take responsibility for their own actions—to understand that certain types of behaviour are more likely than others to lead to satisfactory conclusions, and that choices have their own effects.

In mediating to children the ability to self-regulate their behaviour, not only by inhibiting but by initiating actions, parents and teachers are also mediating judgement. Low-functioning children often suffer from impulsiveness. They do not take the time to work out the information required to achieve something, so they cannot judge what they can and cannot do. Because they do not assess the information that they need, they also fail, when they make an error, to come back and look for the missing data. Feuerstein's Instrumental Enrichment exercises are designed to create an orientation in such children towards reflective thought.

Sharing Behaviour

This is one of the foundations of our social existence and is, says Feuerstein, created in the first instance through children's closest emotional bonds with their mother. It is a very basic mediation which starts soon after birth with eye contact, continues with the baby pointing and sharing an object with the mother and, of course, vice versa, and then reaches more sophisticated forms in play, social relationships and intellectual development. Because of its highly-charged emotional quality, sharing behaviour ensures the effectiveness of the mediator in other adult-child interactions.

The absence of this type of mediation in young children results in the phenomenon of the lonely, emotionally-isolated child who cannot make friends and who cannot engage with the teacher or with other mediators, which, in turn, can result in a range of cognitive deficiencies. Teachers can counter this by acting as a rôle model and really emphasising sharing behaviour, perhaps by admitting their own educational difficulties or working through tasks with the child.

Individuality

The mediation of individuality and psychological differentiation seems to contradict sharing behaviour. It does, says Feuerstein, but then life *is* very contradictory. Encouraging the child to see itself as different from the mediator and from the rest of the world, by allowing children some elements of 'control' in the child-adult interactions, giving children their own special possessions, encouraging an active relationship with the environment and an idea that they legitimately think and feel differently from others. In normal human development there is a healthy tension between a child's need to imitate and share, and to develop his or her own personality. Differentiation is most easily accomplished by not allowing children to become too passive in relation to their parents or environment. As Feuerstein says:

> In normal human development there is a healthy tension between the need for children to develop their own personality and to distinguish themselves from their background, and the need to imitate and take comfort from belonging to a family or group.
>
> At adolescence these tensions become extreme; there are both strong rejection drives and belonging drives, and contradictory drives for change and stability. In fact, the changes are so rapid that adolescent children often wonder if they are the same people from one day to the next, and so do their parents. Hence their very disturbed behaviour. Perfect equilibrium in all these drives is rarely achieved even by adults.

A Need for Goal-Setting

With the mediation of goal-setting and goal-reaching there is a critically important inculcation of the need to plan and achieve. The need to look for goals is produced by such interactions as, 'What shall we do now?' or, 'Where shall we go and how should we get there?' It is surprising how quickly children develop a taste for strategic thinking and hypothesising. 'If we walk to the shops and it doesn't rain, we won't need our umbrellas!' Encouraging children to set goals and then making them explicitly state the means for their achievement, is a very enriching form of mediation—the elaboration of the process of some task being as important as its accomplishment.

An Awareness of Change

The final characteristic for Mediated Learning Experience is that it produces a consciousness of change in the child. This is the exact opposite of what many parents and teachers do, when they talk about children's abilities and characteristics as if they were fixed for all time. Some do mediate an awareness of change by pointing out to children that they can achieve things now which they found impossible before.

Such mediation gives children the tools to evaluate themselves —for example, they can now do something alone for which they required help before. Or, they can now complete tasks with greater efficiency, with greater precision. By so doing mediators build within the child an internal need for change and improvement. Unfortunately, teachers often fail to give their pupils any idea of the progress they are making.

The absence of these types of interactions with adults can bestow on children grave cognitive deficiencies which can give the false impression that, to some degree, such children are mentally handicapped. How much potential has been hidden beneath this lack of thinking skills, and in what areas one should concentrate one's remedial efforts, are questions addressed by Feuerstein's Learning Potential Assessment Device. The means for the intellectual recovery and advancement of retarded children is his Instrumental Enrichment programme.

THE MISSING LINKS

Accumulated experience and research have allowed Feuerstein and colleagues to draw up a list (far from exhaustive) of interactions in real life which can offer children Mediated Learning Experience, and which can play a rôle in shaping their ability to interpret and act upon the world.

The list has some fifty or so interactions but it is unnecessary to discuss them all here. Many are, in any case, self-explanatory. Others are less so and still others, because of their great significance for low-functioning children, have played a crucial rôle in the construction of the remedial exercises of Instrumental Enrichment.

Crucial to a child's cognitive development is the transfer of the ability to focus perception and attention. Very young children are now known to be able to see clearly much earlier than we previously thought, but their natural style of seeing is to scan the environment around them. The mother, by exposing herself to her child and, by various means, making the child follow her eyes (this can involve the mother and baby in very strange positions!), mediates focusing. The child needs the mother's intense investment in this activity to learn how to focus on a particular item. Feuerstein calls the parent-child interactions which develop this skill '*mediated focusing*'.

The absence of one particular adult to help the child learn to focus attention and see single objects in great detail can have very profound effects. It leads to an inadequate perception of reality—blurred and sweeping perception—which means the child is automatically excluded from acquiring a whole range of cognitive functions. Perception skills are required for comparisons between objects. Comparison, one of the basic cognitive functions, is required for categorisation, which in turn is necessary for much logical thought.

Children who do not focus by habit often have not had a constant mother figure to mediate this skill to them: such children, Feuerstein explains, cannot invest attention in an object a moment longer than it takes them to perceive its existence. They find it hard to linger on a particular object because they lack the criteria for discrimination and selection. They cannot tell what interests them or not. Instead their perception roams aimlessly and superficially, with all stimuli competing equally for attention. This can be seen in children isolated at an early age from mother or father, living in orphanages where there are many adults but no one special figure. Feuerstein further explains:

> There are secondary developments from this imposed act of the child focusing on the mother. The mother's figure has some characteristics which no other object has. The very long and quite exceptional exposure the child has to the mother's face breeds familiarity in the child which also gives it the power of discrimination—what is and is not the mother's face. From this discrimination flows a differential treatment of the mother compared to others and then a hierarchy of familiarity—mother, less familiar figures, strangers. Once familiarity is established, some claim by the second week, others claim by the third month, the mother feels the child responds to her and strengthens her intentions—her desire to influence the child's behaviour. The child, also, in responding establishes a reciprocal behaviour that is vital for all other learning.
>
> And then what happens? By being totally familiar with the mother's face, perhaps most familiar with the mother's expression during feeding, the baby can notice differences or transformations in expression. An understanding of transformation is only possible when you have grasped how things look normally.
>
> This opens up the way for the child to ask *why* the transformation has taken place, why is she sad or happy or angry? This is a primitive quest for an understanding for causality between events. I must say that blurred and sweeping perception and the inability to appreciate transformations is very common in the deprived child and

its correction is of the greatest significance in raising intellectual performance.

Vital Censorship

Where a mother mediates focusing to her child she selects the things she wants her child to see, and selects out those she does not. All forms of mediation, in fact, act in this way as a filter through which stimuli pass and, in the process, are strengthened, weakened, regulated or edited right out.

In this way parents do not so much construct as frame their child's universe. When children are young parents select out dangerous or disturbing stimuli covertly or overtly.

In asking a child to see or think about an object or an event in a certain way, the mother or other mediator usually insists that other stimuli in the environment are temporarily down-graded or removed. When the parent says, 'Switch off the telly while I read to you'; 'Look at this, not that, so that you can concentrate', or, 'Don't eat before dinner because you won't be hungry', she is transferring to her children an understanding of the *need* for selection of stimuli. If children are to become able to think for themselves it is vital that this need is internalised. Those without this selectivity have very short concentration spans and a range of other cognitive deficiencies.

One of Feuerstein's students, Jay, a 13-year-old Jewish boy from Canada, had this problem in an extreme form. He had no selectivity in either the information he absorbed or the endless verbiage he poured out. His concentration span was clearly stated in reports as being less than five minutes and he was considered by many psychologists to be psychotic and ineducable, with a very low IQ.

After an initial meeting Feuerstein conducted a two-hour session with the child, in which Jay was asked to perform very difficult mental tasks throughout that time. By subsequently removing the boy from home and, in his treatment with Instrumental Enrichment, stressing the exercises which consciously seek to instil the need to select information and to transmit it with precision, Feuerstein broke down a disastrous psychological barrier to learning. It has transpired that Jay is exceptionally bright, has learnt Hebrew and is now attending a residential school before he re-enters the ordinary school system.

Organising Living

Parents unconsciously and consciously instil into their children the *need for scheduling* and planning events from the time that they are very small babies. Having a bath before going to bed or having a nappy changed before finishing a feed—all routine creates a notion of scheduling in children, which is explicitly reinforced as they grow older. 'Do this before you do that'. 'Unless you do this first you won't be able to succeed in your efforts'.

As a young baby the child sees itself at the centre of a schedule of events—assuming the mother has at least some routine—and is therefore able to associate events and give them some sort of order and direction. The process of living through a day or experiencing a meal-time is broken down into its component parts which the child learns to link into some kind of relationship, leading to a particular denouement.

The transfer by the parent of the ability to recognise a schedule and to plan ahead—termed *'mediated scheduling'*—gives the child the skill to represent the future abstractly. In fact planning, attempting to schedule events, and keeping in mind a goal to which one is working, are extremely sophisticated abstract activities. Parents can assist their children by asking them to help plan holidays, days out or even small expeditions to the shops.

Visualising the future is a most important cognitive function since it is one of the basic abstractions for children. Without it, socialised existence is impossible and the lack of any need for planning or thinking behaviour, based on anticipation, means that the need for logical thought does not even present itself.

Encouraging children to look into the future, positively reinforcing their anticipation of future events, is therefore a crucial mediation which parents often achieve by saying: 'It will be your birthday soon (in a few days, tomorrow'),' or, 'If you're good you can go to the park this afternoon,' or, 'Grandma is coming next week.' Many parents feel slightly guilty at continually bribing their children to be good with promises of jam tomorrow. In fact it is a very positive aspect of child-parent relationships, particularly as it links a happy representation of the future with the need for control in the present. These interactions are called '*mediation of positive anticipation*'.

The Question of Control

Parents need to teach children self-control. If they did not, children would tend to respond impulsively to every stimulus—they would grab food off the table; they would never be able to control their behaviour in a potential conflict; they would be reluctant to think about solutions to problems because the most obvious, but often partial facets would immediately dominate, as would the most attractive course of action.

Teaching children to defer gratification, to control their impulsiveness, to think before they act, is vital in every activity in life, from thinking to any social behaviour. Simple examples which show how parents, to use Feuerstein's description, '*mediate inhibition and control*' include making children eat what is in their mouth before they take another spoonful; eating their main meal before they eat something sweet; ensuring they do not snatch toys off siblings or friends (usually as soon as they have been picked up) and that they wait until other children have finished with them, and so on.

In many ways the second part of the deferment of gratification is the positive representation of the future. It is more specific than mediating a habit of anticipation because it refers to the way in which parents help their children represent a future, based on an incident or experience in the present or past. Seeing a squashed rabbit in the road could prompt a parent to say: 'This could happen to you if you don't cross the road carefully.' A great many children's stories in fact relate the dire consequences of a naughty rabbit carrying out a silly act!

It need not always be such a negative future that is represented. The work-ethic is based on the dictum that if you work hard you will succeed in the future and get . . . whatever your culture deems worthwhile. The future represented certainly need not be a future with a moralistic message attached. The ability to construe imaginatively a future scenario based on facts, experiences and advice can come, for example, from a mother telling a pre-school child what her first schoolday will be like. The mother will, consciously or instinctively, base the presentation on past experiences to make it live in her child's mind. Feuerstein calls this *'mediated representation of the future'*.

A failure to instil in children the ability to represent the future has grave moral implications. It means that children and adults have no cognitive control over their acts and react irrationally to stimuli. It is, says Feuerstein, a pronounced and well observed feature of delinquent youths that they have an impaired ability to conceive of the future in relation to any of their acts. Most juvenile crimes are 'situational' in that the stimuli and the opportunity combine to coerce into stupid crimes a child who has limited control or who lacks the ability to consider the future.

Cognitive Control and Crime

Youth workers, probation officers, magistrates and solicitors speak in amazement of the way in which children out on bail go and commit the same offence again. It seems a sort of imbecilic madness, but in fact the children lack the cognitive apparatus fully to control their behaviour. Their inability to visualise the future means they cannot learn from past experience. Their lifestyles, too, tend to reflect this impulsive day-to-day reaction to events—the future is never conceived in a way that will influence present actions.

The impulsive 'situational' character of juvenile and much adult crime has now been recognised by criminologists on both sides of the Atlantic. In the Canadian penal system Feuerstein's Instrumental Enrichment programme has been implemented for adult prisoners with enthusiastic reviews from the prison administrators involved. It is precisely the emphasis of the programme on reducing impulsiveness, and in developing higher critical abilities for prisoners in their dealings with their environment, that has attracted them. In California an experimental project has just started on the effects of Instrumental Enrichment on delinquents, although it is as yet too early for any results to be available.

One of the most pervasive interactions, performed consciously and unconsciously by parents, is the verbal stimulation of the children. Parents tirelessly insist upon children describing or saying exactly what they want, rather than just grunting or pointing. Such 'mediation of verbal stimulation' goes on so relentlessly in early childhood that children develop a need for precision about what things are called and this is then thrown back at their verbally-lazy or inaccurate parents. Verbal stimulation, where it involves the use of language for pleasure, can also occur at a level above that of accurate functional language. Songs and nursery rhymes, for example, clearly inculcate a pleasure in words and rhymes that goes beyond the need to be understood; and recent research has suggested that these play a very important rôle in the development of language and literacy skills.

The need to instil in children precision in the way in which they take in information and apply and communicate it, is a more general need, affecting all the senses and cognitive functions. 'Look or listen carefully' are, of course, two simple ways in which adults insist on precision in the way that children learn.

But seeing and hearing do not take place independently of past experience or thinking processes. And as a result of inadequate mediation in these areas it becomes impossible for children to be precise in the way they absorb reality: in comparing two objects, for instance, they might not collect all the data about similar or dissimilar attributes. If this is the case, then this amounts to a serious dysfunction: such children would be unable to differentiate or compare accurately enough to carry out many simple intellectual operations. As we have mentioned before, it is impossible to discern how something changes—an object, a situation, or a problem—if its original attributes have not been picked up correctly.

A very common problem concerning lack of precision among children at the level of input is that they often cannot use more than a single source of information at any one time. If you set them a problem which requires them to spot and utilise three different clues or attributes, they invariably fail. They might 'see' the different elements but not appropriate them intellectually in a clear enough way to assist them in working out the solution to the problem. They might be too impulsive to be able to go beyond the first information source.

Parents 'mediate precision' simply by encouraging care in all activities, language, drawing, carrying things, any motor or verbal response. The absence of this mediation can have a devastating effect and produce educationally-retarded children. Problem-solving is very difficult with a child who lacks the precision necessary to collect the data to reach a correct solution, or who lacks the need to reach exact solutions.

If children's speech is unclear, or, as often happens, their conceptual grip of an issue becomes garbled in the communication of it, then this problem of output becomes a cause of school failure and is frequently seen as a problem of simple handicap or of some irremediable brain damage.

Cognitive Deficiencies

Even minor impairments could, however, have a very significant impact on children's thinking processes because of the knock-on effect onto other parts of the cognitive structure. A child who cannot be precise cannot compare effectively and this affects the ability to classify, categorise, to draw analogies and to make conclusions.

A child with poor spatial and temporal orientation would find it hard to order his work or analyse cause and effect, understand logical progression or construct abstract representations of situations. In fact his ability to develop abstract thought at all would be greatly impeded.

Cognitive deficiencies can interact with each other, and with emotional and motivational factors, to make children school failures. But the precise nature of a child's deficiencies, resulting from inadequate Mediated Learning, are likely to be confused by teachers' and psychologists' preference for gross descriptions of poor functioning.

Feuerstein has attempted to map out, albeit fairly schematically, the act of thinking and the location of typical deficiencies within this act. Called the Cognitive Map, it is used with the Learning Potential Assessment Device to diagnose the root causes of a child's intellectual problems with unprecedented sophistication.

Mapping the Causes of Failure

In order to pinpoint a child's thinking difficulties the Cognitive Map (Figure 1) advises the break-up of the act of thinking into three theoretical parts or stages: the input of information, the

Input phase: Impairments concerning the quantity and quality of data gathered by the individual.	*Elaborational phase*: Impairments concerning the efficient use of data available to the individual.	*Output phase*: Impairments concerning the communication of the outcome of elaborative processes.
Blurred and sweeping perception.	Inadequacy in experiencing the existence of and subsequently defining an actual problem.	Egocentric communicational modalities.
Unplanned, impulsive, and unsystematic exploratory behaviour.	Inability to select relevant, as opposed to irrelevant, cues in defining a problem.	Blocking. Trial and error responses.
Impaired receptive verbal tools and concepts which affect discrimination.	Lack of spontaneous comparative behaviour or limitation of its appearance to a restricted field of needs.	Lack of, or impaired verbal tools for communicating adequately elaborated responses.
Impaired spatial organisation, including the lack of stable systems of reference which impair the establishment of topological and Euclidian organisation of space.	Narrowness of the psychological field.	Deficiency of visual transport. Lack of, or impaired need for precision and accuracy in communicating one's responses.
Impaired temporal orientation.	Lack of, or impaired need for summative behaviour.	Impulsive acting-out behaviour, affecting the nature of the communication process.
Lack of, or impaired conservation of constancies.	Difficulties in projecting virtual relationships.	
Lack of, or deficient need for precision and accuracy in data gathering.	Lack of orientation towards the need for logical evidence as an interactional modality with one's objectal and social environment.	
Lack of, or impaired capacity for considering two sources of information at once, reflected in dealing with data in a piecemeal fashion rather than as a unit of organised facts.	Lack of, or limited interiorisation of one's behaviour.	
	Lack of, or restricted inferential-hypothetical thinking.	
	Lack of, or impaired strategies for hypothesis testing.	
	Lack of, or imparied planning behaviour.	
	Non-elaboration of certain cognitive categories because the necessary labels are either not part of the individual's verbal inventory on the receptive level, or they are not available at the expressive level.	
	Episodic grasp of reality.	

Fig 1   The cognitive map. Deficient cognitive functions classified according to the input, elaborational, and output phases of the mental act (from Feuerstein, 1979).

elaborational phase where the data is processed and the output phase where it is applied and expressed. It is an attempt to systematise the insights gained from Feuerstein's clinical work on the effects of cultural deprivation on children, so that the manner in which deficiencies disable children's 'practical' thinking skills can be effectively located and analysed.

This 'input', 'elaborational' and 'output' topography of an intellectual act has an obvious analogy with computer systems, and Feuerstein admits that, despite its comparative sophistication, it is still an over-mechanical analysis of the way children think. Likewise, the thinking deficiencies are separated, for theoretical purposes, in these three stages but rarely, if ever, occur separately in real life. However, it has allowed Feuerstein to progress from a general analysis and description of the causes of inadequate intellectual functioning in children to a system of diagnosis which can be picked up and used by teachers, parents and other professionals with a limited amount of training.

Input Phase
Normally, when we address a problem, we accumulate the information that we need to solve a task and, if this is perceived as inadequate, we return to the problem to find the data we need to reach a solution. But this is very difficult for low–functioning children and adults. Perception, although it is based on sensory input, is also reliant on past experience, usefully retained, to make sense of what we perceive. Children who have had inadequate mediated learning experiences do not have this fund of useful history to interpret new information and to find the relationships between the stimuli they perceive. Consequently they have an episodic grasp of reality and very poor analytical perception. The two are mutually reinforcing. Such children might see something, but they do not know what it means. They cannot relate parts of information to a whole structure and so often cannot appreciate that parts of a structure are missing or require changing. Problem-recognition and initiative exist at very low levels.

Typically, too, they will find it difficult to consider more than one source of information at a time, even though there might be several clues obviously presenting themselves for use in the solution of a problem. This is because they do not have the ability, or the need, to try and impose order on information. They perceive it in a piecemeal way.

Children with an episodic grasp of reality often suffer from a blurred and sweeping type of perception: they have not learnt to focus their perception long enough to mine an object or problem for all its significant attributes. Their perception is therefore partial. This can easily be seen in young children or in those with concentration difficulties. Ask them to describe something they have just seen and they will miss out the most salient features. They will have very poor short-term memories and an impaired ability to conserve in their mind constancies of an object—shape, colour, orientation—in order to compare it with another. Their visual transport—the capacity to see an object and hold it mentally long enough to spot a similar one in a different place—will be very undeveloped.

These children will also have poor powers of analytical perception, which is often marked by something called field dependence. Here a child has not developed a set of internal rules or frame of reference through which to impose organisation on space. The field dominates the child rather than the other way round.

The most common example and simple (but very effective) diagnostic 'trick' is to ask a child to stick out his right hand and then point to yours; and then for you to turn round and, with your back to him, ask him to repeat the action. Children who lack these cognitive controls over space will be unable to complete the task while face to face. Their immediate, impulsive act is to point to the arm directly opposite their own outstretched one. Such children have poor conception of perspective and dimension, and an inability to project anything other than very superficial relationships onto what they see. They might know about concepts like 'up', 'down', 'back', 'front', 'left and right', but they are not used as operational tools for categorising objects and events. They will also find it very hard to respond or to give clear and accurate geographical direction, although anyone who has lost his way in a strange town knows this is not limited to children.

Children deprived of mediation often have an inability to conceptualise, structure and organise space. Yet, ironically, intelligence tests designed to be 'culture free' and 'culture fair', so as not to penalise culturally-deprived children, often require the children to analyse and discriminate in space. 'The weaknesses of culturally-deprived children in this area make failure automatic in the tests designed by clever psychologists specifically in order not to penalise culturally-deprived children,' says Feuerstein.

In clinical work, Feuerstein and his colleagues have found that simply by inhibiting gestures like pointing or touching, which children with bad spatial orientation prefer because it is easier than thinking more abstractly about space, great improvements can occur. The children are forced to represent spatial relationships mentally. It is an interesting example, says Feuerstein, of the way in which crude means for organising stimuli, like pointing, touching or moving objects around, can interfere with higher ways of abstractly thinking about space.

Along with an impaired orientation in space, the absence of an internal reference system, caused by a fragmented conception of reality, can reduce children's abilities to orientate themselves in time: they do not fully comprehend sequences of events or the concept of succession, or the organisational significance of time in many day-to-day activities. Information collected on this basis is often either distorted or inadequate. A sense of order is often a sense of order in time, and children with impaired temporal orientation often have both a poor conception of before and after, and cause and effect. Consequently they might find comparisons and logical thought very difficult, even alien.

Such children do not use past experience or anticipations of the future to control themselves; in fact without a clear internal reference system of time and an understanding of intervals and sequences, it is impossible for them to organise their time effectively. They live or drift from moment to moment and from impulse to impulse.

One of the ways in which weak orientation manifests itself is when qualitative or subjective time is allowed completely to dominate standard measures of time. Subjectively, time during periods of excitement, danger, depression or great anticipation can burst far beyond its 'real' barriers and inappropriately affect our behaviour, if it is not cognitively controlled. With children this frequently happens during exams. The excitement, and the danger of failing, means that many children feel unable to spend those few vital but seemingly interminable minutes assessing the whole exam paper properly and then making sure they have read the questions correctly, before they start writing.

Teachers will repeatedly try to reinforce examinees' cognitive control over their subjectivity by setting real time limits before they pick up their pens. An equally disastrous failure of temporal orientation during exams is to spend far too long on just one question.

Feuerstein gives the interesting example of prisoners whose escape attempts increase as the time of their release from prison draws near. Subjectively, the days become unbearably long as freedom approaches and the prisoners lack the cognitive controls to analyse and gain insight into their emotions and so adopt strategies for coping with their distortion of time. For those prisoners who give way to their subjectivity, freedom can recede more quickly than it approaches.

Time is a relationship—an artificial, man-made relationship between events or between other relationships: the time it takes to travel between A and B is a relationship of speed to distance. Speed, which children often confuse with time, is a relationship of time and distance. Time has no material existence; it is an abstract phenomenon and children who are well orientated towards time are also well orientated to some elements of abstract thought.

On the other hand, children with poor orientation in space and time find systematic exploration of the facets of a problem more or less impossible. They do not care where they start or move to next; they do not have a need to do things sequentially; they cannot impose any order on their behaviour in collecting relevant data to solve a problem. If they have misplaced their glasses or a toy, for example, they start to search randomly rather than carrying out a mental search first to try to think of the last place they possessed the lost object. They also fail to give priority to the most likely places in their order of searching. The lack of systematic exploratory behaviour, which makes the collection of data totally haphazard, is a very common cognitive deficiency in children whose parents have not shown them how to 'do one thing, and then another, and then another' in space and time.

The lack of, or impaired, receptive verbal tools causes some deprived children to have a very limited conceptual repertoire. They might have the label for a concept such as 'identity', 'detail', 'characteristic', 'symbol', or 'similarity', but do not really know what it means. They cannot use this label as a tool to receive information accurately because they do not have the conceptual/verbal tools to discriminate between stimuli in the desired way. It is important here not to confuse culturally-deprived with culturally-different children. The latter might have the concept, but not the label specific to the language.

Some children do not have a sufficiently highly developed need for precision or accuracy in their gathering of information. It is a common failing, but it can have very serious repercussions on thinking ability and other people's estimation of such children's intelligence. If children are not encouraged to be precise in their requests and information they will tend to see accuracy in what they do as a waste of time and energy. Wrongly or partially collected data inevitably lead to a failure to solve tasks. But the deficiency can be present in the next 'phases' of elaboration and communication. Children may have great potential abilities, but this deficiency in input, elaboration or output could render them retarded. Trying to evaluate a child without looking for this weakness is, says Feuerstein, like evaluating a dumb child with verbal tests.

Poor 'input' of information results in a very severe difficulty of elaboration, an inability to recognise the existence of a problem, which is the most crucial and fundamental of all. Problems simply do not present themselves in the same obvious way for such children as for ordinary children. Teaching them to recognise the existence of problems is one of the main enterprises in the Learning Potential Assessment Device and Instrumental Enrichment.

Elaborational Phase
Confusion, perplexity and doubt are the signals that make us stop and think. Something is wrong that needs attention, a problem is perceived. Our cognitive skills are brought into play

to try and re-create a comfortable equilibrium which satisfies our ingrained expectations.

For the culturally-deprived child this process, which seems to us almost automatic, does not operate very efficiently, if at all. Without attention and skill in the collection of data it becomes impossible fully to comprehend the existence of a problem. The cues which normally trigger our highly sophisticated awareness of problems are not picked up and incongruous, incompatible or missing elements in a situation, which define the problem more closely, are not grasped.

To stimulate our confusion and perplexity, a situation or problem must somehow fail to conform to our experience—but it is the inadequacy of usefully retained experience that defines culturally-deprived children. Because they lack experience or cannot learn from it, they have fewer ingrained expectations to act as alarms when they come up against new situations which, to us, do not make sense.

Selection of relevant data. Poverty of usefully retained experience, which normally instils in children principles of analysis and organisation, prevents low-performing children from selecting relevant rather than irrelevant cues from a problem. Ask deprived children to tell you the bare bones of a story and they will get side-tracked in minutiae. Go beyond a request for a summary of the narrative and ask for the lessons from the story, and they will have even more trouble. Relevance is defined by goals that you have been set in the problem; if you do not fully understand the nature of the problem—perhaps because you have simply not understood words used to express it, or more seriously, because you lack the cognitive skills to appreciate it fully—then you will not be able to select the important, relevant cues for its solution.

One of the most important of those skills by which normal children organise reality is spontaneous comparative behaviour. It is through comparisons that children move from the act of simple recognition of an object or event to establish relationships between them. This leads to judgemental and 'iffy' or inferential thinking, and also to abstract logical thinking, to the possibility of children saying of a story that certain characters were like or unlike each other, that they were goodies and baddies; that unhappy events followed from one course of action and happy events from others and that, therefore, the moral of the story was . . .

Deprived children, says Feuerstein, are often unable to make comparisons between objects and events which limits tremendously the way they understand what they see. If they are shown two geometrical shapes and asked to compare them, they will invariably only describe one or one at a time, without referring at all to the other, and without any mention whatsoever of their relationship. Comparative adjectives such as 'similar', 'like' or 'unlike' are largely absent in the speech of children with this deficiency.

This does not, of course, mean that the children are unable spontaneously to compare things because of some inborn biological/psychological incapacity, as many psychologists might immediately suggest when confronted with failures of this magnitude. These children can compare when it suits their immediate needs, such as deciding which piece of cake is the biggest. And when provoked by direct instruction they can function as well as their nondeprived peers in their perceptual discrimination. They do not, however, compare spontaneously, because their environment and upbringing have not demanded it of them.

Linked to this is a series of deficiencies associated with children's episodic grasp of reality. Their inability to construct relationships between pieces of information means that they find it difficult to retain data for any length of time; they can gather information in quantity, but they do not know how to use it and only a little is retained. This is termed narrowness of mental field and refers to the inability of some children to process much information at any one time. Poor short-term memory is characteristic of these children because it is so difficult to store and retrieve disorganised information.

The lack of a need to impose a structure on reality, by projecting relationships on to objects or events, or organising things in time and space, means that stimuli act on children rather than being mastered intellectually by them. Such children often have no desire to sum up or make conclusions about their experiences, to assess the significance of the data they have collected, or to measure their progress towards a goal. Alongside this lack of summative behaviour and inability to project virtual relationships (from the French word *virtuelle*, meaning 'almost real'), there is no strong need to pursue logical evidence when confronting a problem or to give logical reasons for their opinions. Nor do they request this vital information of others.

Without an orientation to at least the pursuit of logical evidence, the construction of strategies for advancing on problems is impossible. And the ability to construct hypotheses of possibly correct solutions is often impaired because they cannot use past information or a system of relationships to infer or 'represent' something outside the immediate data. They cannot generate information from other, given information. And, if they have some facility for hypothetical thinking, they do not have the means to check their hypotheses before becoming committed to them. This is reflected in a form of impulsive behaviour.

Output Phase
Some deficiencies already mentioned can crop up in this phase of mental activity, with disastrous results. Lack of precision and accuracy, although a highly remediable deficiency, can drastically cut IQ test scores, even though, unbeknown to the tester, the child has successfully collected and processed the information necessary for the successful completion of a task. This is due much more to the way attitudes, lifestyle, and cultural milieu have failed to inculcate an internal need for precision, than to a paucity of inherent intelligence.

Another major failing is egocentric communication, when children do not bother to express themselves clearly because they assume everyone else automatically understands what they are thinking. There is a very interesting instrument in the more advanced lessons of Instrumental Enrichment, where one child is asked to give another a set of clear, unambiguous directions which, if followed correctly, would result in the drawing of a completed geometric pattern. In 1984, at a conference in Oxford University on Feuerstein's work, held by the then Schools Council, psychologists and educational administrators were asked to do this task. Not one communicated to a partner, with complete success, the way to draw the pattern, and the majority found that the instructions, when they were comprehensible at all, resulted in anything but the required figure. Egocentricity of communication is a very relative phenomenon.

'Blocking' is the term used by Feuerstein to describe the phenomenon which impedes the expression of ideas. It has several causes, some of which are cognitive—poor short-term memory, for example. Others are emotional and may involve a reluctance to remember difficult processes. It is also, perhaps, a form of intellectual rigidity which prevents the use of alternative strategies to pull something out of one's memory—one set of cues has failed to evoke the right word or information.

A very common and unfortunately often teacher-exaggerated problem for culturally-deprived children is the continual resort to trial-and error procedures for solving problems. As a tactic it is undertaken in the absence of more sophisticated processes in the elaborational phase. But whereas, in non-handicapped children, trial and error is a perfectly acceptable strategy, with low-functioning children it is not. This runs contrary to what many teachers in special education practice believe, because they believe trial and error is a simpler strategy than more abstract approaches.

Nonetheless, it is an impossible strategy for children with an episodic grasp of reality, who have not learned to look for relationships, or to draw conclusions, or to infer patterns, or to learn from mistakes. They cannot absorb direct experience in a useful way because they have no system for interpreting it. Their errors will be followed by more errors unless they accidentally hit upon the solution, and even then they will not be able to learn the route to a successful answer again. Moreover, the extra emphasis in special education on physical manipulation of objects to aid learning is an extra obstacle—motoric acts frequently get in the way of children's attempts to formulate strategies abstractly. Feuerstein and his colleagues take great pains to avoid and discourage trial-and-error procedures in children.

Impulsive acting-out behaviour is a common deficit in the output phase which can be seen in children suffering from impulsiveness and lack of planning behaviour, or in those who, eager to please their teacher's harmful demands for quick and snappy answers, say the first thing that comes into their heads. Even if they get it wrong they might get a pat on the head. This type of behaviour often has an emotional cause, stemming from children's insecurity about whether they can attack a problem successfully. But it can occur in children who have well-developed elaborational skills.

A lack of vocabulary can also inhibit the ability to communicate problems that a child has solved mentally. It is impossible to classify objects without being able to assign a label to the type of classification, and the lack of verbal tools can give conventional testers very false impressions of a child's intelligence.

Normally, such cognitive deficiencies are compensated for by the use of others, but in low-functioning children just one or two deficiencies can spell failure in school, in IQ tests and in life. They can interact with each other, and with emotional and motivational factors, to form very complicated obstacles to learning. The different deficiencies we have discussed, crude and artificially distinct though they are, reveal, with the other elements of the Cognitive Map, why children are failing in their responses to the Learning Potential Assessment Device tasks. This enables remedial work to be targeted to the dominant causes, and potential to be assessed on the effectiveness of that educational investment.

The other criteria of the Cognitive Map, used to analyse children's responses, are generally straightforward, although they show how selfconscious and cautious a Learning Potential Assessment Device tester must be, and how naïve and reckless conventional testers are (not, one should add, by virtue of their personal characteristics, but because of the inadequate theories and instruments they are using).

A factor which can be vital in determining whether children from a culturally-deprived or different background can function well in a test, is whether or not they are familiar with the content of the test. If, for instance, their educational and cultural experiences have not equipped them to deal with geometric shapes, this alone will require so much investment that little capacity will remain to perform the cognitive operations involved in the test. 'Culture-free' tests often include content which, like geometric shapes, might be very strange. In the Learning Potential Assessment Device there is a test where children's short-term memory is assessed by asking them to recall one object which is associated with another linked object. If the child is not familiar with these objects, which include garden implements and other tools, successful recall becomes very difficult. But failure might have nothing to do with any incapacity.

We have already touched upon the different languages found in different tasks. The inclusion of this factor in the Cognitive Map is a reminder that both children and adults have preferred modalities, and that this can affect thinking performance. The efficiency in the use of some 'languages'—verbal, pictorial, symbolical or numerical—and not others, may, of course, go beyond individuals and affect cultures or socio-economic groups. Simply because children cannot perform an operation in one modality does not mean they cannot perform it at all.

Feuerstein uses the term 'operation' to refer to the strategies or sets of rules which allow individuals to organise, transform and generate information to construct a mental act which produces a solution to a problem—an intellectual pathway, as it were, requiring one or more cognitive skills as prerequisites. Operations are the most sophisticated part of the interpretive system which analyses reality for us. A requirement for the development of these sets of rules is, however, the cognitive functions that are often absent in culturally-deprived and, to a lesser extent, culturally-different children. The classification of objects, for example, is a complex operation which, depending on the sort of task, might require analytical perception, spontaneous comparative behaviour, the pursuit of logical evidence, systematic exploration, the conservation of constancies, and so on.

Other operations which Feuerstein and his colleagues have commonly found to be inadequately mastered by deprived children are serialisation (understanding and organising things and events into series), logical multiplication, analogical thinking, syllogistic thinking, inferential thinking, comparison and recognition. The latter two are obviously much less complex than the others.

The inability of testers and teachers to distinguish between children's efficiency in carrying out intellectual tasks and intelligence itself, is a tragic source of error in the judgement of children's abilities. Says Feuerstein: 'The lack of efficiency shown by slowness and imprecision, may be totally irrelevant to an individual's ability to grasp and elaborate a particular problem.'

These phenomena can all be produced by the problems exposed in the other elements of the Cognitive Map. A high level of complexity, due to the unfamiliarity of the subject-matter, can result in a *relatively* inefficient handling of a task, whereas the modality or manner of a problem's expression can result in extra hurdles being placed before the child.

Inefficiency can also be caused by outside factors such as fatigue, stess, lack of motivation. The more recent children have acquired thinking behaviours, the more subject they are to disruptive emotional factors, for instance, carrying out tests in very unnatural and stressful conditions.

The root of cognitive deficiencies lies in the quality of children's relationships within their families. Parents who completely lack routine, drag their children around behind them, and impose restrictions that are not explained, or parents who fail to instil the habit of picturing the future or of precision in gathering and expressing information, could impair the development of thinking skills in their children. But one should be wary before jumping to conclusions. Mediated interactions between parents and children can be very subtle, and may be accomplished in non-linguistic codes that convey immense information but are very difficult to spot. It is rare to find a complete absence of routine, or an absence of any reciprocal communication between parents or caretakers and children. The success or failure of parents to mediate effectively to children is a question of degree.

Moreover, parents often compensate in other areas for certain weaknesses, with the result that all adults tend to have some cognitive deficiencies. Many professors, pyschologists and teachers have had to face this uncomfortable fact when confronted with Instrumental Enrichment exercises which they cannot complete, while their supposedly retarded children have no difficulty.

If black, working-class or immigrant children are functioning poorly, Feuerstein does not hesitate to say so. The first priority is not to look for social excuses or causes, it is to remedy the situation. Feuerstein further runs against the grain of liberal educational values by locating the origins of individual children's problems in their family background. That is not to say, however, that his views conform to the moralistic conservatism of blaming parents for the sins of their children. Rather, he sees the failure of parents to mediate effectively to children as a process of cultural breakdown, as a hiatus in the transmission of a culture from one generation to another.

THE GENERATION GAP

Contained within the break in the transmission of culture from one generation to another is the failure to transfer values and habits of thought and perception which can enable a child to interpret reality. In Feuerstein's theories reality might have an independent existence, but for human beings it can only be 'appropriated' or grasped through culture. Hence, a culturally deprived child, a child who has often not sufficiently absorbed his own culture, suffers from what Feuerstein calls an 'intermittent grasp of reality.'

Much depends on the degree of deprivation and the particular characteristics of an individual. But severely deprived children typically do not have the intellectual apparatus to make use of new experiences. They cannot rely upon any past stream of experience to help them understand new problems or situations; they are downtrodden by new information. As Feuerstein says:

> Children who do not have adequate mediated experience do not just have low intellectual functioning, they also tend to have narrow, rigid personalities. They are in the grip of a constant fear that some new situation will arise or they will be presented with some demanding new task, which they will not be able to handle. They reject new experiences; they cannot accommodate them or adapt to new circumstances. A very typical feature of the culturally deprived immigrant children we dealt with early on in Youth Aliyah was their distance from their old and new cultures and their lack of adaptive behaviour.
>
> Their rigidity was not just a deeply ingrained personality trait. The lack of mediated learning experience meant they were not inclined to want to modify themselves, or even to see the need for it.

Origins of Cultural Deprivation

Although 'deprivation' is often associated with poverty, what Feuerstein understands by cultural deprivation has its origins in many different social circumstances. It is associated, along with poor educational achievement, with the lower socio-economic classes. But while material constraints may be a very significant factor in ensuring that the parents do not have the time and the energy to mediate a wide range of cultural needs to their children, they do not *necessarily* lead to cultural deprivation. Things are much more complex: history, politics and economics as well as cultural traditions all take a rôle.

For example, the strength of Jewish culture in the appalling ghettos of East London at the beginning of this century meant that many children emerged from impoverished East End families to make significant contributions to all aspects of British society.

But for some of Feuerstein's first charges, children from the great intellectual Jewish tradition of central Europe, their culture and their families were physically expunged during the Holocaust. They were orphans in many senses and their deprivation of many basic human needs was more extreme than virtually anything in history. The work of Youth Aliyah with these children required a painstaking emotional and cognitive reconstruction.

The Children of the Mellah had different causes for their cultural deprivation. Their Jewish culture had been 'exploded' by internal migration to urban centres and contact with some of the more obvious aspects of French lifestyles and consumerism. In the move Jewish families not only lost the key agents of cultural transmission—the grandparents—but the values of the patriarchal father no longer carried the same weight or seemed as relevant in the city. The fathers were often unemployed or forced to do menial work and could no longer call upon the same respect and obedience from their children as they had in their villages. Their sons and daughters were attracted to the ephemera of their new society and, while not being able to integrate into it fully, nevertheless, or perhaps as a result, felt a strong need to reject their old culture.

The Impact of Transition

Nor, in many cases, did the parents want to impose their values. Feuerstein points out that one of the most devastating effects of the transition from a rural peasant-based culture to a technologically advanced society is the loss of confidence in parents of the relevance of their knowledge and values to their children. The more rapid the technological progress and social change the more extreme the break in cultural transmission and the bigger the generation gap.

None of this applies solely to immigrants, of course. Working-class culture in advanced Western societies is continually being broken up by the changes in work patterns and internal migration and the subordination of working-class culture to the values of the affluent middle-class. Much of the culture of East London and the shipyards of the North East is already either gone or speedily disappearing with the decline of the docks and the shipyards. Indeed the culture of the working-class in the regions is undergoing profound changes as traditional industries go to the wall, leaving mass unemployment in its place. One of the few distinct working-class cultures to have survived the ceaseless re-composition and re-location of industry and workforces has been that of the miners—precisely because their industries have been fixed and their communities totally dependent on the pit. With the pit closures even this is being threatened and the defence of a 'way of life' was a prominent element in the recent abortive miners' strike against the decline of the industry in traditional areas.

For many families it has proved impossible to survive the trauma of this type of change: there is no greater distance between a culture based on work and one based on unemployment. The responses of parents have varied between the extremes of not being able to accept unemployment for their children and believing that it is their own fault, and acceptance that the values by which they lived are irrelevant to the modern age; they have surrendered their rôle as the guardians of any traditions and values.

According to Feuerstein's theory, a strong culture can enable an immigrant group, and the individuals within it, to negotiate its relationship to the new culture more successfully than a group whose culture has already been fragmented. The

Yemenites and the Falashas arrived in Israel with their culture intact: and, within a few years of the start of their arrival in Israel, the latter have been able to protest as an organised people about the racialism of Israeli society and what they claim is religious and employment discrimination. Few immigrant groups, let alone refugees, could boast their social cohesion or organisation.

The same can be said of Asian families that settled in Britain. They have maintained their cultural identity and, although there are some real tensions between individuals who wish to negotiate a relationship to Western culture which their parents do not approach, there has not been a general fragmentation along generational lines.

For the West Indian community this is not the case. Their culture, arguably already an exploded African culture fragmented by slavery and colonialism, has had great difficulty reproducing itself in Britain. Confronted with racialism and unemployment, young West Indians have rejected the view of Britain and their adoption of the Protestant ethic and rebelled, reconstructing a culture of protest loosely based around Rastafarianism, music and patois. The need to create a protest culture as a defence mechanism against an oppressive and racialist culture suggests that they are insecure in their own historical culture. White working-class youth have also clearly felt the need for some sort of protest culture but no such need has manifested itself among Asian youth.

In many cases the situation of young blacks in Britain is complicated by class issues. Like the Children of the Mellah, many of their parents have made the move from rural and technologically primitive communities; in many cases both parents have had to work, and often the rôle of the grandparents, crucial in the West Indies, has also been lost. There are a great number of similarities with the Children of the Mellah, down to their poor educational achievement and their intense alienation from mainstream culture.

All this has great bearing on the current, rather fruitless, discussion about whether the roots of the poor academic achievement of blacks lies in the home or in the racial bias of the education system. Feuerstein's immediate concern would be to make sure that their intellectual functioning was improved. His theories suggest that he would formulate the problem in terms of the way in which fragmented West Indian culture and the family as the agents of that culture have been unable to fortify its children against a hostile environment.

There are also more prosaic ways that children can be culturally deprived within an otherwise ordinary family which is not directly affected by social upheaval or cultural fragmentation. The last child in a large batch might be overlooked by harassed parents and receive inadequate mediated experience. Or the child might have an organic or genetic problem which makes the parents despair of ever reaching him. Indeed, some children might be quite receptive, but their parents are so demoralised by what they take to be an implacable genetic disorder that they do not invest enough in their child's potential. Many parents with Down's Syndrome or brain-damaged children, discouraged by the negative views of the medical and teaching professions, often give up.

With these children the barriers to learning are real but not insurmountable. A greater intensity of mediation and different types of remediation can overcome or by-pass barriers to the acquisition of new thinking skills. For the culturally deprived children poor functioning can be systematically attacked and normal levels of performance achieved.

How much potential and in what areas one should concentrate remedial efforts are questions that are addressed by Feuerstein's Learning Potential Assessment Device. It was through this highly unorthodox test that Feuerstein discovered the real potential of Moroccan children who, because of their low scores on conventional psychometric tests, had been written off as defectives. From this test Feuerstein theorised a detailed list of cognitive deficiencies caused by inadequate Mediated Learning Experiences and a programme of remediation, Instrumental Enrichment. It is to the Learning Potential Assessment Device that we now turn.

PART 2
THE PRACTICE

LEARNING POTENTIAL ASSESSMENT DEVICE—A TEST LIKE NO OTHER

At the third International Workshop on Feuerstein's methods in Jerusalem, in May 1984, Feuerstein demonstrated the Learning Potential Assessment Device in front of 150 teachers, psychologists and academics from 14 different countries. A small frail girl, greatly undersized for her 14 years, was introduced to the audience. 'Sarah has just been referred to the Institute because her special school wants to reclassify her from being educationally retarded to being mentally handicapped and ineducable. She is now considered only suitable for training and not education,' explained Feuerstein.

Sarah, who also had a genetic condition, worked steadily for Feuerstein on the initial tests of the Learning Potential Assessment Device for three hours, clearly carrying out, with some initial tuition, varying tasks of considerable complexity and abstraction.

At the end of the session Feuerstein was able to say, with the clear agreement of the audience, that the child was a very long way from being ineducable. She had many of the concepts needed to execute the tests, but was not orientated to use them to solve problems. She also suffered from a profound lack of self-confidence which, like her lack of problem-solving skills, had been exaggerated, if not created, by special education. The Institute, said Feuerstein, would place her in a setting which would be able to address her specific deficiencies. He expected her to reach near normal levels of intellectual functioning, and certainly to reach the point where normal life and marriage were considered a matter of course.

Sarah had a genetic condition which required very intensive mediation to overcome. Because of this condition and her age, Feuerstein doubted whether she would ever be completely 'normal'. But his use of the Learning Potential Assessment Device has been frequently observed to reveal potential for *at least* normal functioning in culturally-deprived children whom psychologists had written off as profoundly handicapped. Professor Emeritus J. McVicar Hunt of Illinois University visited Feuerstein in 1969.

> I observed him use his Learning Potential Assessment Device version of the Raven's Progressive Matrices with a 12-year-old boy who had a conventional IQ of 60 and the Learning Potential Assessment Device version of Grace Arthur's Stencil Design Test with a girl of 16, conventional IQ in the sixties. It was abundantly evident, even though the interchanges in Hebrew had to be communicated to me through simultaneous translation, that these adolescents could, with Feuerstein's encouragement and questioning, appreciate and use conceptual schemata of which their conventional IQ indicated they were devoid. I was impressed. Later Feuerstein showed me the test record at age 13 (conventional IQ of 70) of a young man whom I had met. When I had met him he had earned a Ph.D., in psychology from the Sorbonne in Paris.

The Learning Potential Assessment Device was developed for precisely this purpose: to rescue children, brought up through the Holocaust and from the fragmented cultures of North Africa, from the further tyranny of the IQ test and the reduced life opportunities that inevitably flowed from a poor test score. The problem was to ascertain the potential of these children to advance beyond their present functioning and, if potential was found, to discover the obstacles to its realisation. By testing a child, then teaching him the skills requisite for a type of problem, and then re-testing, it was possible to see how far the child could be raised intellectually with a given amount of teacher investment.

In the highly unconventional interactions between the child and the tester-cum-teacher, it was possible to uncover the children's intellectual deficits that were preventing them solving problems. The Learning Potential Assessment Device was both a diagnosis and a broad measure of hidden potential. In some ways, of course, using teaching to indicate potential for learning seems plain common sense. But in terms of the prevailing rules of the game in post-war psychology it has been anything but. It has required a jump, unprecedented in the West, from the values and strident professional orthodoxy of one system into an ideologically and professionally-suspect alternative: from a system of measuring and 'correctly' assigning children their 'natural' place in the educational and social system, to one of changing their performance and confounding 'scientific' measurements of ability and disability.

Breaking the Rules

In making the leap, Feuerstein constructed principles for the Learning Potential Assessment Device which broke every rule in the psychometric rule-book and ensured his isolation from the professional mainstream of psychology for decades. In contrast to the rigorously reserved attitude of the examiner towards the child, the creation of cold clinical and 'standard' test conditions, and the complete non-involvement of the examiner in the task, Feuerstein's testing system required the tester to reassure, encourage and teach the child how to do the test! In other words it was a way of offering the child very intense mediation.

So that psychologists could maintain that conventional IQ tests were scientific and standardised they had to create completely inhuman conditions. The testers would not talk to the child or respond in any way. For a child lacking in self-confidence this was a disaster. Also, of course, the child had a social and emotional history and different access to education which the tests could not account for in the results. These tests assumed non-subjective children in order to give their results objectivity. Absolute madness! Psychologists were more concerned to justify their methods in similar ways to the natural sciences, to ensure their professional prestige, then they were concerned to help children.

The whole point with our tests was that we did not give a damn now well the children scored. We were interested in the process of the child doing the test not its outcome, which was only important in the way it changed over time. The Learning Potential Assessment Device is not, in fact, a test in any conventional sense, it is an assessment of modifiability.

The Learning Potential Assessment Device is organised to make this assessment, and investigates children in several particular areas: the ability to grasp the principle underlying a problem; the amount and nature of teaching investment required for the child to acquire the principle; how well that principle is transferred to different tasks of varying complexity; whether a child responds differently to problems expressed in different modalities, such as language, figures, numbers, pictures, etc., and how different training strategies affect the child's performance. The series of tasks comprising the Learning Potential Assessment Device therefore gradually become more complex, with the principle remaining constant and elements of a problem, such as its expression in different forms, changing.

The emphasis on a human and creative relationship between examiner and examinee in the process of doing the test, rather than on result and on structuring the test so it can be used for both diagnosis and remediation, are all stark departures from conventional testing. But there is another departure which sums up the difference in the systems—the interpretation of results.

In conventional testing a single, isolated, excellent response is seen as an aberration and averaged out of significance in the overall test scores. But since the purpose of the Learning Potential Assessment Device is not to assign a numerical value to a child, but is instead designed to uncover weaknesses and strengths, isolated peaks of performance assume immense importance. They are signs, often seized upon and treasured by the parents of retarded children, too, that the child has potential to operate at a much higher level than the overall current performance would suggest.

For those who believe in conventional psychometrics, current performance is all there is to be measured, and in a very gross way at that. Those who believe in dynamic assessment believe in the possibility of changing a child's manifest performance.

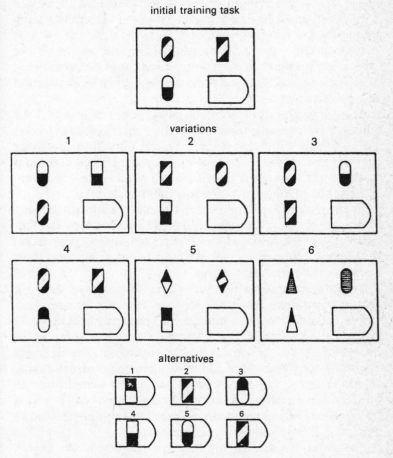

Fig 2   Learning Potential Assessment Device variations I.
Initial training task and six variations.

The Tests Themselves

It was partly an act of impudence for Feuerstein to choose as one of his main tests in the Learning Potential Assessment Device, the *Raven's Progressive Matrices*. (See Figure 2 below). They are a system of designs within a rectangle with one design missing. The missing one is presented at the bottom of a page among several inappropriate ones.

They become gradually more difficult and require of the examinee the ability to carry out several cognitive operations, such as analogical thinking, serialisation, logical multiplication and permutation.

According to A. R. Jensen, the psychologist who has led the school of fixed genetic intelligence, these matrices are inaccessible to people with what he called Level I intelligence—those with IQs of between 60 and 70 on conventional tests—no matter what training is given! People on this level can rote-learn series of objects or numbers and undertake trial-and-error learning if given a behavioural reward on correct responses, but they can never move to Level II which involves much greater self-initiated, complex, conceptual activity. Level II thinkers represent a genetically distinct group and their abilities cannot be 'trained up'.

Feuerstein disproves this thesis every day during his work at the Jerusalem Institute. His studies have shown that individuals and groups of individuals previously in hospital or in specialised residential settings can, through training, solve 20 out of 30 of the problems. At the recent international workshop the 'ineducable' Sarah was able to acquire the skills to master the early Raven's problems, which was all she had time for. On an earlier occasion a Canadian girl of 17, with a tested IQ of 60, completed a section of the matrices more quickly and efficiently than the author.

Very intensive and highly targeted training is the key to these successful performances, made possible by the sophisticated diagnostic tools of the Learning Potential Assessment Device itself and the Cognitive Map.

Figure 2 is a pre-test sample for the Raven's Matrices. Typically, a retarded child would be unable to define the problem, would not understand the relationship between the top and bottom of the page, be unable to describe exactly what

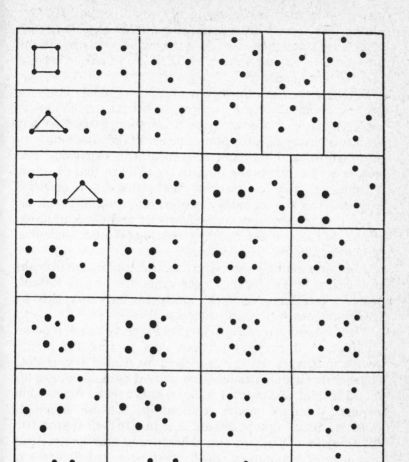

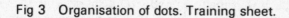
Fig 3   Organisation of dots. Training sheet.

was missing from the main figure (would perhaps indicate merely that some black was missing instead of a shape with black areas); and then, once he or she had appreciated the link between the top and bottom of the page, would proceed to give the wrong answers.

In taking the child through the test the examiner notes the possible deficiencies such as impulsive behaviour; inability to see and define problems; poor orientation toward solving problems; sweeping perception; the use of only one source of information; and the lack of comparative behaviour, and step-by-step mediates the skills to the child so that he or she becomes capable of reaching the solution. A practised examiner can very speedily uncover, after several problems, what are the most resistant deficiencies and concentrate on them, in the process building the logical and analogical reasoning required for the tasks.

Just how strikingly successful it can be, can be seen from the complexity of Feuerstein's own variations on the Raven's Matrices (see Figure 2) which are successfully completed by large numbers of 'Level I' students.

The *Organisation of Dots Test* (See Figures 3 and 4) requires children to draw lines between dots to find the hidden geometric shapes. It was developed by André Rey, a close collaborator with Feuerstein, and is loved by children. For the retarded child, and even for adults, it can be very difficult, for it requires them to impose relationships between seemingly random, chaotic dots and to use clues to plan their approach to the problems—in other words children must draw up strategies and mental hypotheses which must be tested before any solution can be found.

Children who are impulsive, who cannot plan their actions, or who cannot conserve constancies in their minds, will fail, as will those with poor perceptual analysis and an undeveloped need to explore and to be precise. The interactions between the child and the tester must be driven by the need to instil in the child the appropriate attitude to the task; to remedy cognitive deficiencies, such as the lack of comparative behaviour, needed to establish that the form and size of shapes embedded in the dots are the same as in the models, and to counter any lack of summative behaviour, because it is necessary to add up the

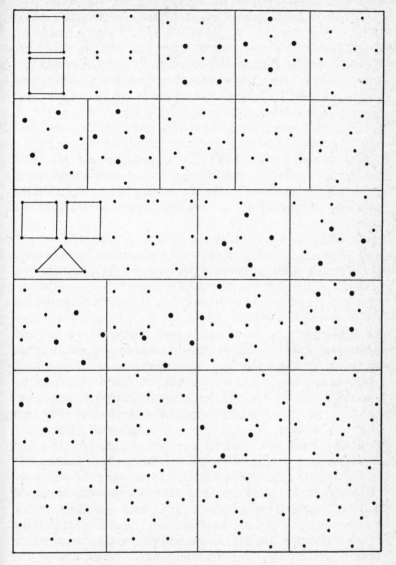

Fig 4   Organisation of dots. Test.

dots belonging to certain groups. It is also important to orientate the child to the message being given out by his own work, so that his own efforts can offer him feedback on his progress for teachers.

The *Representational Stencil Design Test* is the most difficult in the Learning Potential Assessment Device battery. It was developed on the back of a sub-test used by Grace Arthur in his Point Scale of Performance Test, but underwent a typical Feuerstein alteration.

In the original test, children were asked to build up different stencil patterns, one on top of another, until they produced a required configuration. In Feuerstein's test, however, there are no actual stencils and therefore the child cannot manually and overtly use trial-and-error procedures; he has to represent the outcome of placing different stencils together purely in his mind.

Needless to say, this is a very difficult test, even for adults, and watching it being carried out by supposedly backward children is a rather peculiar experience. The children are first trained on the stencil poster which has four rows of designs that are, in fact, components of the integrated designs that the children must compile. The bottom rows are the 'base' figures—solid squares of blue, green, black, yellow, red and white. It is upon these bases that the child must place the other designs to produce the final design required by the tester.

Great care is taken to ensure that the child understands the content of the test and that he is familiar with the shapes and colours, and that he can expressively label everything that needs to be mentally manipulated. The examiner also ensures that the child understands the stencil concept and can anticipate the results of simple moves, such as placing one stencil on top of a solid square and describing the outcome.

The examiner then trains and guides the child into making 20 different designs which each have two or three stencil components placed onto the solid base. The child is taught how to 'look down through the imaginary pile' to discover what the base is, and what succeeding components are on top.

The final test has designs which vary in the number of components, but go up to seven. The progression in complexity through the test is uneven, so that the rigidity typical in many

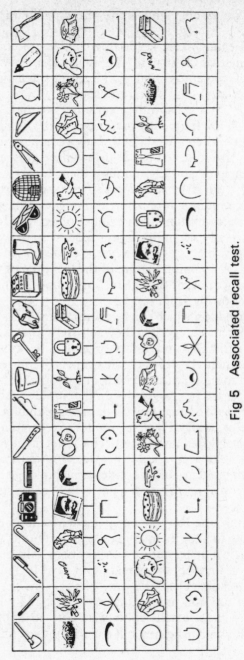

Fig 5 Associated recall test.

children, who assume what went before will always recur, is challenged.

The intellectual skills needed by children to complete the tests include the ability to represent abstractly: changes, anticipation, perceptual analysis, including sophisticated comparisons, seriation and visual transport.

There are other tests in the Learning Potential Assessment Device which are frequently used, such as the *Complex Figure Test*, where children are taught to draw a complex figure. After tuition they are re-tested to see if they have grasped organisational principles and can employ them to draw the figure competently; the *Associated Recall Test* (see Figure 5), where children are required, after some training, to remember items through the recognition of other linked objects, and the human figure test, really no more than a request to draw a man or woman but which can, however, reveal grave perceptual deficiencies. A common feature of the Children of the Mellah was that they drew, at the age of 7 and above, human figures with arms growing from heads.

The information which can be gained from the tests falls into several different categories: they can show the extent of the child's modifiability and ability to generalise skills from one task to another; the level of 'investment' required to bring children up to standard and where, in the cognitive process, the effort needs to be targeted—in the input, elaborational, output or effective and motivational areas of thinking. And the test also helps to identify which modes of communication and learning the children find easiest. This is not merely to alert the teachers to weak areas; it also provides routes through which children can build up their confidence in thinking and can then attack their weaknesses from a position of some strength and self-assurance.

With Sarah, the Raven's Progressive Matrices showed that she was able to spot the missing design in the early tests with very little help, but her output was very poor. Although she had a concept of numbers she would never say, 'It is number six,' for the right design but, 'This one.' She also had the word 'size' but did not use it as an organising concept and refused to go beyond 'big and small'. She was able to spot different characteristics in the figures, but did not see these differences as constituting a relationship between the figures—in other words she had weak comparative skills. And when she was asked why she had picked the right or the wrong figure to go into the rectangle she could not give reasons—she confused reasons with outcome and had no internal need for logical evidence.

Many basic concepts like vertical and horizontal were missing. 'This is years of special education for you,' said Feuerstein. But when they were introduced to Sarah she showed an ability to understand and deploy them. Her input of information was weak when it came to using more than one source, but with training she improved and her elaborative, working-out processes were surprisingly strong for a girl who had been classified as ineducable.

When it came to the *Plateau Test* of the Learning Potential Assessment Device (Figure 6) where physical manipulation was required, it become obvious that Sarah had a very profound difficulty; any motor act seemed completely to short-circuit her thinking abilities. This test comprises four separate but stacked plates, each of which has nine buttons, one of which is not movable in a different position on all the different plates. The examinees are asked to do three different tasks: to remember the position of the non-movable buttons on all four plates without prompting; to draw a diagrammatic represen-tation of the buttons on all four plates as if they were on just one plate; to find the positions of the buttons after the plates have been put through a series of 90-degree turns. The first task is a basic memory test, the second an intermediate and more abstract problem, and the third involves creatively transforming the positions of the buttons in the mind and is a highly complex act.

While many supposedly low-grade thinkers succeed at this supposedly impossible task, Sarah could only make haphazard guesses at which of the buttons were fixed and was very resistant to mediation. Part of her problem, suggested Feuerstein, was due to her particular genetic condition, but it had probably been greatly exaggerated by special education which believes that backward children can only learn through physical manipulation of objects.

Feuerstein tells of the case of Tamara, a Russian child, who was considered defective and had some organic conditions. She

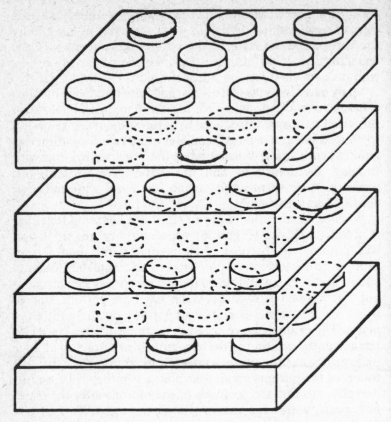

Fig 6   Plateau test by André Rey (reprinted by permission).

had weaknesses on the gathering of data—uncovered in trial-and-error work on the organisation of Dots and the Plateau Test, and in output, because she had such poor motor-coordination. But in work on tests where there was little motor manipulation required, such as the Stencil Design Test and the Raven's Progressive Matrices, she scored maximum points. Her elaborational capacities were greatly underestimated.

As a result of the Learning Potential Assessment Device, Feuerstein and his colleagues decided on a prolonged period of academic study which would use her strengths as the route to re-integration. She was a slow but highly motivated learner at high school, eventually joined the army as a secretary and is now a career civil servant in charge of a secretarial pool. 'Since this child was very slow and unco-ordinated her achievement is not a little amazing,' admits Feuerstein. 'But it shows we were right.'

Many children with motor co-ordination problems, which falsely identify them as mentally handicapped, are advised by professionals involved in their case to go into manual work! The strange logic of this is based on the assumption that children with learning difficulties are incapable of intellectual prowess; it derives from an undifferentiated and unanalysed concept of retardation which has not taken account of the causes. Feuerstein strongly refutes such thinking.

> Children with minimal motor skills are neither suited for manual work, nor do they find it at all rewarding. Instead of searching for whatever cognitive skills the child has, the professionals assume the child is unmodifiable and automatically indicate that training in manual work is their best life option.

A very interesting case of a boy thought to have a form of mental deterioration, caused by a 'schizophrenic psychotic process', is related in Feuerstein's book on the Learning Potential Assessment Device (see Bibliography).

Harry, the eldest son of two parents who had survived the Holocaust, had no problems in school until the third grade when he began to fall behind and show signs of retarded performance. Psychological examinations followed, a low IQ score was awarded and a special school placement made. Harry did not like the school, became very withdrawn and aggressive and eventually was hospitalised. Psychiatrists found that he had a reduced capacity for abstract thought and felt that this indicated a deterioration due to the above mentioned causes.

When tested with the Learning Potential Assessment Device Feuerstein's colleagues found something very different. He was above ordinary intelligence once he was provided with the tools he needed to succeed. The Learning Potential Assessment Device revealed that Harry had no ability to understand stimuli as a series—he saw them all discretely—and was therefore completely devoid of any comparative and summative behaviour. Instead of counting he would use such concepts as 'a lot' or 'a little' and had very poor orientation in space.

These deficiences showed that Harry was culturally deprived, rather than mentally ill, and had not been given the mediation by his very disturbed and limited parents to enable him to think. Hence his growing inability to make sense of school. Once he was provided with the tools, he used them with great precision and his finest achievement was in abstract mental thinking. After a little while he achieved 100% and 90% and became so highly motivated that he would continue to work on the more advanced adult tests of the Raven's Progressive Matrices with great success.

As so often happens, what had been diagnosed as a retardation caused by mental illness or mental handicap, in fact turned out to be the result of highly remediable cognitive deficiencies due to cultural deprivation. How many other children have not been so lucky? It does not bear thinking about.

INTRODUCING INSTRUMENTAL ENRICHMENT

'It's brilliant for your brains.' 'It helps you not to be impulsive—before I used to rush into things.' 'It helped me not to be frightened of new things.' 'It helped me think.' 'It helped me do my other lessons.'

These are children's reactions to Instrumental Enrichment on experimental British programmes, reported by the Schools Council in their document, *'Making up our Minds: an exploratory study of Instrumental Enrichment,' December 1983.*

'If children are low-functioning and cannot think at formal abstract levels, why do we give them very abstract and complex exercises to carry out? Isn't this a form of cruelty completely alien to special education?' asks Feuerstein.

It certainly is alien to much special education. But far from being cruel, the intellectual skills required to complete the Instrumental Enrichment tasks are precisely the cognitive functions and processes which low-performing children frequently do not possess. It is the absence of these that prevents the children's fuller development.

By teaching the means to complete the instrument or set of exercises successfully, says Feuerstein, the teacher provides children with a very intense and structured form of mediated learning experiences. And this can remedy the thinking deficits caused by an inadequate upbringing or other obstructive conditions.

Feuerstein goes out of his way to suggest that Instrumental Enrichment is not the only form of mediation that can be given by professionals to backward children. But it does have the advantage of being systematic, intensive and targeted on the most common thinking deficiences found in children.

The second reason is that the exercises, by virtue of their abstract quality, are relatively content free—they assume very little prior knowledge. Teachers are trained to check, before they start, that children do understand the names and characteristics of whatever figures or shapes occur. This abstract quality enables the most backward children, in terms of acquired knowledge, to attempt the tasks—they do not require the ability to absorb significant amounts of information before they can learn the principles needed to undertake the increasingly complex tasks.

Children suffering from cognitive deficiencies do not have the mental apparatus to sort, store or re-use masses of information. So any attempt at remediation must involve, as far as possible, abstract content-free tasks. Feuerstein maintains that it is one of the great untheorised errors of conventional special education to rely on 'concrete' educational techniques and devices with a heavy emphasis on simple facts, and trial and error procedures for solving problems. This type of approach has failure written in because the child is never given the thinking behaviours that can allow him to organise material and generalise.

The third reason is that children love to do them. It is fascinating to watch children who have been diagnosed as having minimal attention spans work for extended periods on the organisation of dots instrument, for example. The reason why all children, normal or otherwise, like most of the Instrumental Enrichment exercises is, Feuerstein maintains, precisely because they are intellectual games requiring little background knowledge.

The overall aim of the Instrumental Enrichment exercises is to turn children with a reduced ability to be modified—to learn and adapt—into much more flexible and reflective operators in the world. By changing and enriching a child's or adult's structure of thinking Instrumental Enrichment makes them more receptive to stimuli and experience, and increasingly able to cope with new conditions and situations confronting them in life and, of course, in school.

Apart from correcting the deficient functions produced by a lack of mediated learning experience there are a series of other objectives for Instrumental Enrichment. As already mentioned, an important corollary is the teaching of the concepts, verbal tools and relationships which need to be mastered to undertake the Instrumental Enrichment tasks and for other types of sophisticated thought. It is impossible, for example, to teach a sophisticated approach to comparisons without words like 'similar', 'attribute', 'characteristic'.

One of the most essential and unique aims of the Instrumental Enrichment programme is to instil in the learner an intrinsic need for intellectual activity at the right level. This is necessary because many of the children are thought to come from environments that do not impose upon them, from the outside as it were, the need to use their intellectual equipment at any abstract level. Often children from very authoritarian or over-protective families and institutions, as well as those from materially restricted environments, are required to make little use of their minds. They therefore have a limited intellectual repertoire of operations and functions. To use the vernacular, they suffer from 'brain rot'.

Feuerstein and his colleagues claim that one of the reasons why Instrumental Enrichment has been shown to have lasting effects is because of the programme's aim of instilling such an intrinsic need for intellectual activity, which can then give the children some degree of independence from their environment. It can act as a motor, driving forward their development long after formal professional intervention has ceased. Such outcomes are notoriously absent in other learning and social rehabilitation programmes, notably the behaviouristic approaches. They are able to teach some insights and behaviour at a superficial level in specific situations; but they do not change the individual's intellectual structure, or stimulate him to think more incisively about situations and problems, and to seek creative solutions systematically.

To consolidate new thought processes into the general intellectual repertoire of a child, so that their use becomes an intrinsic need, requires a degree of over-learning which can be tiresome and which can encourage an undesirable attitude to work. The instruments have therefore been constructed to try to consolidate thinking habits through varied repetition. Particular functions and skills are represented in different ways, altering the content or using different modalities—representational, verbal, symbolic, diagrammatic. Changing the levels of complexity and abstraction are added ploys. It is the principles and the rules of problem solving, rather than a boring task, which are hammered in.

Efficiency is an important consideration for children who might have adequate cognitive repertoires, but who do not mobilise them if they can possibly help it because the amount of intellectual investment necessary is so high. This is often thought to be mental 'laziness', but Feuerstein points out that the tremendous mental effort required to employ such thought-skills could be 'too costly' when set against their limited needs and the demands placed upon them by their environment. Here, the instilling of a habitual need to think at more sophisticated levels can dramatically enhance the deployment of more elaborate thinking processes by a child.

Instrumental Enrichment, by making intellectual operations less contingent on the environment and its limited or limiting demands, and by reducing the effort required to mobilise the more sophisticated repertoires of thought, has been shown over a period to have an increasing effect. This is of the utmost importance, since the vast majority of programmes are shown to have a decreasing effect the greater the distance from direct instruction.

Insight

The encouragement of insight, too, is a crucial objective of Instrumental Enrichment, and it is here that the teacher plays a major rôle in his or her interactions with pupils. The orientation of a child to examine and understand himself, his activity and how it produces, or fails to produce, particular results can supply a reflectiveness that was hitherto absent in an 'impulsive' child. Teachers need to mediate self-searching questions: 'How did I succeed?' and 'Why did I fail?' are more important for learning than the actual act of succeeding or failing. 'What was the nature of my perceptual and intellectual activity that allowed me to solve that problem?' and 'Why did I become more efficient in handling tasks that I found inaccessible before?' are the next set of questions teachers must encourage pupils to ask of themselves. To these can be added: 'What makes me feel motivated about an activity?' 'What operations did I carry out to produce a given result?', 'Where else can I apply them?', 'What is the relationship between two apparently different tasks?'.

Insight can thus become one of the most powerful means for

transferring and generalising learning processes. However, in an education system geared to the inculcation of useless information rather than critical intellectual abilities, systematic attempts to develop this type of insight in the classroom have not been considered necessary before. This does not mean that the system does not relish the appearance of insight when it appears 'spontaneously' in bright or gifted children. Insight, like intelligence, is supposedly either there or not.

Because the presentation of tasks in Instrumental Enrichment, even when they are very similar to tasks already learned, still requires new adjustments, discoveries and adaptations, it produces a motivation that is intrinsic within the task. The desire of children to go on with the exercises on their own is some evidence to support the success of this objective—children often speak of their pleasure in and commitment to doing the exercises, often in a tone betraying some surprise at themselves.

It is an objective of Instrumental Enrichment socially to reinforce this task-intrinsic motivation. Such is the complexity and difficulty of many of the tasks that it is impossible for teachers, even after considerable familiarity with Instrumental Enrichment, to complete them without a significant and clearly visible amount of investment of time and energy. Feuerstein claims this brings about very meaningful changes in the relationship between child and teacher because the latter appreciates, from his own difficulties, the child's achievement, while the former gains in confidence and motivation from the feeling of equity which the teacher's difficulties bring.

The sixth objective of Instrumental Enrichment is to change children's images of themselves as passive receivers, almost victims, of information, to active, creative masters and generators of information. This is the central goal of the whole programme and has shaped all the instruments. It challenges the way retarded performers are unable to go beyond a limited registration and reproducing of what is learned and experienced—even this often dissipates over a short space of time.

The typical response of such children when asked a question which obliges them to use some intellectual operations they have been taught, where their memory can only be of limited use, is, 'I can't remember.' While psychologists following Arthur

Jensen say this simple response is typical of individuals with Level I intelligence with poor and immutable endowment, Feuerstein says it is the product in ordinary children of a lack of mediated learning experiences. Therefore they are open to change. He sums up the benefits of Instrumental Enrichment as follows:

> It is geared to confront the learner with many opportunities to develop the capacity to change reality, to interpret reality, to produce new relationships and thereby generate new information.
>
> It is the task of the teacher to produce the awareness in the learner of his or her contribution in the solution of a given problem, above and beyond the components which make up that problem. This awareness can become a source of knowledge about one's own capacity to affect the world and may increase the individual's internal locus of control and may lead to a greater readiness to accept responsibilities.

The Rôle of Skilled Teachers
The exercises are so designed to contain elements which can, on their own, mediate certain limited experiences to children. But Feuerstein insists that only by trained teachers using Instrumental Enrichment to transcend the tasks involved and mediate the underlying learning processes—applying them to ever wider areas of life and study—can the full potential of the programme be realised.

Although Feuerstein says Instrumental Enrichment is best used in the classroom where interaction with pupils can amplify the different processes which can be used to interpret and solve problems, it can also be used in clinical settings and different environments for a wide range of populations, including socially–disadvantaged adolescents, school drop-outs, educationally mentally retarded children, organically damaged children, emotionally-disturbed and delinquent children, immigrant children and those from oppressed minority groups. Illiterate adults have also been shown to benefit from Instrumental Enrichment, as have normal and gifted children, and those who are low-achievers because they are gifted.

Researchers around the world are trying it with new populations all the time, and the Institute in Jerusalem has become the centre of referral for a vast network of academics, teachers and students and other professionals working with children.

THE ORGANISATION OF DOTS

'Dots! In real life we have no need to join up dots. So why is the the first instrument in Instrumental Enrichment all about joining up dots to find hidden geometric shapes? Who needs this skill?'

Feuerstein's answer to his own humorous rhetorical question is that culturally-deprived children do. For the skills involved in uncovering the shapes hidden in a seemingly random confusion of dots depend on cognitive functions that are either absent or impaired in the low-performing child.

Take Figure 7 (below). It seems simple and immediately accessible: the model shapes are provided as obvious guides for the student seeking to reproduce them from the dots. To make it yet more simple, the dots comprising the geometric shapes are bigger and blacker—and almost ask to be joined up.

In fact the first basic exercise—they become much more difficult—involves many intellectual functions that, if absent, would lead to a culturally-deprived child being unable to complete the task.

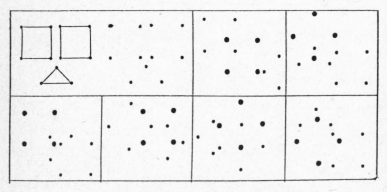

Fig 7   Organisation of dots. Exercise I.

If, for example, a child does not have clear perception, his view of the model shapes, particularly their size, will be distorted, and he might not recognise the cues of the big dots, or perceive all of them, or project them into the right patterns. The child might become confused by the fact that the shapes change their position but still remain the same—in other words he cannot identify the main characteristics of an object and recognise them when they reappear in a slightly altered guise. He might impulsively rush in and draw the shapes haphazardly, using trial-and-error procedures and very little cognitive effort at all.

The instrument is designed to correct these failings, to train the child to have clear perception, a sufficiently adequate spatial awareness to recognise similar patterns and to appreciate and conserve in his mind the stable characteristics of an object. It trains the child to search systematically and to formulate hypotheses about the whereabouts of the patterns rather than to rush in impulsively.

Precision and accuracy are stressed in the instrument because, without careful analysis of the size of dots, their distance, angles and orientation, it is impossible to find the shapes. As with the other functions, the instrument both teaches the need and trains the skill.

Summative behaviour—for instance, counting up the dots in a triangle as opposed to a square—is an important part of planning an approach to a problem and building up hypotheses for testing—something that children with an impulsive and episodic relationship to the world rarely do.

The instrument also remedies any failings a child might have in visual transport. It is necessary in the exercise to carry the models mentally to the unjoined dots, to try and find their equivalents within the disorganisation. Therefore the models must be internalised accurately and comprehensively. In fact many children 'lose' the model more or less immediately after seeing it and cannot transport it anywhere. Although this function is called visual transport, failures in this area require cognitive redevelopment to remedy them, showing just how much our visual apparatus is cognitively structured.

The whole instrument requires a child to project relationships onto a disordered situation and make sense out of it. Dissatisfaction with a disconnected reality is one of the mental behaviours that Instrumental Enrichment tries to instil in children suffering from an episodic grasp of reality. Mastery over disorder is very hard-won in the instrument and needs planning, controlled searching, the use of external cues and rules of geometric figures, flexibility in order to shift from one strategy to another, the creation of hypotheses and their critical examination, and the use of comparisons against a model.

The first frames will have been easy for the average reader to complete. But there are surprises in store as one travels deeper into the instrument.

Hold the Front Page

Before children are allowed to start on the exercises proper, some considerable time is spent discussing the cover page (*See Figure 8*). It contains three different types of emblems in different modalities. The children are asked what they see—invariably the boy is mentioned first—and what the boy is doing and what cues suggest the boy is thinking (the half closed eyes and the pencil in the mouth and the words at the bottom).

The way different pieces of information are put together to reach a solution is discussed. The actual process of thinking, with its different stages—input of data, elaboration and output—are examined consciously, at great length. This terminology is not in the least frightening to children once it has been explained to them. They are told that such terms are like tools to help them express themselves and to aid thinking. One of the most striking reactions from teachers is surprise at the way children of supposedly backward educational levels begin to mobilise sophisticated terms and concepts appropriately.

By reaching the conclusion that the boy on the cover is thinking, the student, or the whole class, has been engaged in successful reflection. Some children might be able to reach the right conclusion at this level almost immediately. But the means might be one of almost subconscious recognition of the image. When asked how they reached that answer the children will say: 'I don't know.' It is important for teachers to reconstruct routes to a solution consciously, so that children develop a systematic approach to problem-solving.

JUST A MINUTE ...

LET ME THINK !

Fig 8   Organisation of dots. Instrument cover.

What is a Problem?

This question, when put to children, produces blank looks. But it is easily explained as a situation in which things or elements do not add up, where there is confusion (even disequilibrium!). A solution is required to make things balanced and clear; it is a form of thinking. But is problem-solving the only type of thinking? What other types are there? All the time the teacher is asking the children to think about thinking and why it is such an important part of our lives. From a single image and a slogan the discussion has moved very far, very rapidly.

The slogan of the whole Instrumental Enrichment programme: 'Just a minute . . . Let me think' provides an opportunity for more training in careful sign recognition, by asking children what the dots after the word 'minute . . .' mean. It is the programme's slogan because it stresses the need to take time to think before acting, cognitively to control one's actions, as well as reinforcing the message that Instrumental Enrichment is about thinking skills.

Similarly, the box containing the Big Dipper constellation offers the chance for discussing one of the central themes of the Instrumental Enrichment programme. Through careful questioning, the teacher can lead the class to the conclusion that the difference between the stars in the constellation and those outside is that the former are organised while the latter are not. 'What does it mean, to organise?' 'Why is it important?' 'Who can give examples of good and poor organisation?'

By the end of the discussion the children should have moved through the idea that organisation is putting things together in some sort of system, to the overall view that it is creating order out of chaos. It helps us in classifying things and in projecting virtual relationships onto objects which allow us to understand the world. But the relationships do not occur naturally. The lines that link the stars do not actually exist in the sky!

The box with the stars is, children are told, like a shop window which tells you what is inside. It is the symbol for the specific instrument, while the words and the image of the boy are the slogan and emblem of the whole programme. They are different ways of representing other things—a form of immediately recognisable shorthand. Pictures that remind you of something else, that represent something else, are known as symbols, children are told. The concept of symbols is a very important one to grasp—they make up an important part of our daily lives, and in much of the language of abstract thought there is inevitably a strong symbolic element.

The cover is a very good example of what Instrumental Enrichment is about; it insists that the children think about thinking—what it is and the way to do it—and is, therefore, a course in meta-cognition. This meta-cognitive level facilitates a conscious learning of basic skills, such as spatial orientation (where on the page is the picture of the boy?) comparison, perceptual analysis, deductive and inferential reasoning, precision and accuracy, as well as the vocabulary necessary to mobilise these skills. By the end of the cover discussion children should have been given the following words at least: emblem, symbol, logo, motto, slogan, cover page, cognitive functions, indefinite, indeterminate cue, input, data, elaboration, output, infer, identify, label, principle, classify, border, constellation, imaginary, association and order.

It usually takes two lessons to get past the cover and, of course, not everything sinks in. But the principles and the vocabulary are constantly reinforced and, according to the observations of sceptical and very hard-bitten teachers, become automatic surprisingly quickly.

Strategies

Very quickly the instrument moves on to problems where there are no obvious cues. It then becomes necessary for the teacher to invest in the children the type of intellectual strategies they need to continue effectively. From the cues it can be seen that the squares have equal sides and sets of dots that are equidistant. But if a child tries to find four dots at once, the same distance apart, without the cues, his search is likely to fail. To spot them immediately within the confusion needs very highly developed skills of perceptual analysis which he is most unlikely to have. The complexity of the task and the unconnected confusion in the frame will instead immobilise his mind.

So children are asked to look for sets of two dots and then to search and see if there are any corresponding dots elsewhere. All directions are checked, vertically, diagonally, above, below.

Once they have found some contenders, the children are told to stop before they rush in to join up the dots. First they must check their hypothesis by seeking proof. Are the dots the same distance apart? Do they form a square that meets the requirements of the model?

A similar approach with triangles is used (*in Figure 9*); their attributes are discussed, two dots are found and then a third is sought which will make two equal sides. But why should one look for the square first and the triangle later? Children and adults with normal abilities would do this automatically, probably without knowing why. But through a process of class discussion and deduction the teacher can overtly explain that because a triangle is smaller and has only three dots, it could fit into a square and therefore lead to a mistake. A square, however, is the bigger of the two figures and has more dots. It cannot, therefore, be included in toto within a triangle. The discovery of a square is relatively more certain, and leaves less ambiguous clues to the remaining figure than the other way round.

Another way of putting this is that the square, because of its greater size and number of attributes, dominates the frame; it helps when organising things to start with the biggest, most dominant object and to work around it. It is a principle of organisation that is normally transferred to children in countless activities and games.

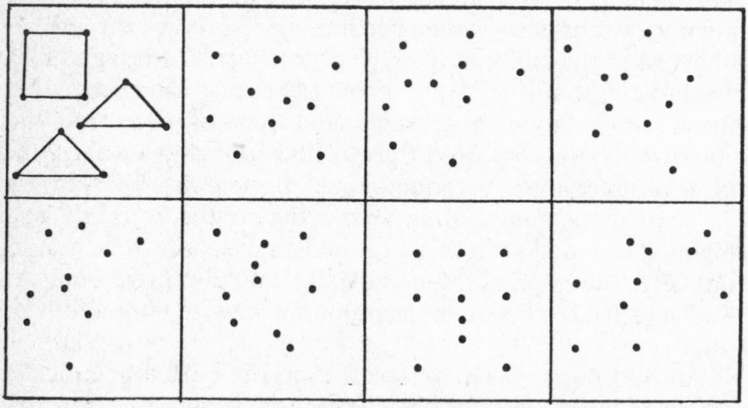

Fig 9   Organisation of dots. Exercise II.

The Costs of Impulsiveness
The tasks become complex very quickly. Figure 9 shows sets of dots that hint immediately at squares and triangles, but which are designed to show that first impressions and impulsive actions can cause serious mistakes. In some of the frames the seemingly obvious but incorrect square is slightly out of shape. If, in the third frame on the second line, a small horizontal square is formed, it becomes impossible to find the triangles. These difficulties reinforce hypothesis testing, precision, comparison with the models and fine discrimination, as well as the conservation of characteristics of shapes (even when they change direction); also reinforced are the use of different sources of information, systematic search and planning behaviour, and internalising and representing the shapes onto the inchoate dots.

The setting of priorities, in this case finding the square first, is a useful tip for the early exercises but becomes essential to solving the later problems. At the end of each page, following considerable discussion and then attempts on their own to find solutions, children are asked to evaluate their own work as a way of fostering independence. This can be done in several ways, all legitimate: they can look at their classmates' work, they can ask the teacher, or they can compare their figures with the models. The last is stressed as being the most independent.

At the beginning of each new page children are asked to compare the exercises with those on the previous page. At the end of each page they discuss the principles of problem-solving that they have acquired. Seemingly difficult concepts like internalisation (knowing what something looks like when you cannot see it) and all the other cognitive functions practised, are debated openly.

Bridging
The final part of any Instrumental Enrichment lesson is to generalise from what has been learnt to other areas of the school curriculum and to life as a whole. In the early pages of the Organisation of Dots, for example, the discussion could centre on the importance of withstanding temptation, on the benefits of systematic search should you lose one of your

belongings, or the advantages of planning and choosing priorities, in games or at home. A typical response to a teacher's request for an example of jumping to conclusions or using the first thing to hand, is ticking the first answer in a multiple-choice test simply because it is first, or wiping up a large spillage with a dish-cloth instead of a floor-cloth.

Systematic generalisation from the principles used in the task to other areas is called bridging. It acts as a way of reinforcing the principle, of expanding the children's intellectual horizons, and of fostering their intellectual independence, by getting them to apply principles and concepts learnt in one context, to another.

However, one of the reasons why Feuerstein insists on quite intensive training for teachers is that it is not enough simply to work through the exercises and discuss bridging at the end. This would be a travesty of Instrumental Enrichment and would overstress the importance of the tasks set in the programme at the expense of the mediation provided by the teacher. The problems really are no more than cleverly designed and carefully structured spring-boards to allow very intensive mediation between the teacher and class, and bridging is a crucial and continuous part of this mediation. It is the *process of learning* rather than the product that is all important.

For a good teacher of Instrumental Enrichment, the above account of the teaching of the cover and first two pages of Instrumental Enrichment would be a dramatic over-simplification of what should happen. Numerous opportunities for instilling in children certain intellectual needs, or reinforcing principles, have not been detailed.

Trained teachers in Israel will spend a very long time discussing the concept of imaginary lines, following on from the constellation of stars on the cover page. Other examples will be requested—national or county borders, for instance—and their uses will be explored. The underlying philosophical principle—of artificially imposing human order onto disorder —will be pressed home.

The construction of constellations will be quoted as a form of organisation in space and will lead on to more ordinary forms of organisation, such as the way food is laid out in a supermarket. A discussion about the absence of organisation and its calamitous effects can result in the class rolling about in hysterical laughter, yet a few minutes before the children may never have thought deliberately about organisation and its uses. A similar discussion can be initiated about the use of labels—such as names—and the confusion that can arise when we do not use them properly.

Planning by Rules

The rules of the construction of a triangle and square will lead to a general discussion of the usefulness of such rules and how, in the search among the dots for shapes, they must guide all efforts. The need for a plan of action during the search will provoke a discussion of the nature of plans and the way they usually contain objectives, a sequence of worked-out moves based on rules—those of a square perhaps—and usually some given information that provides a starting point and a way of checking whether the objectives have been reached successfully.

Below this conceptual level, the trained teacher will use every opportunity to develop basic cognitive functions as habits, like spotting and defining a problem; precision in description comparision and labelling; getting the children to use more than one source of information and to use inferential and deductive thought, requiring them to sum up what they know and to synthesise information to reach solutions.

Wherever possible children are provided with an overview— an insight—into the rôle these skills play in ordinary life, by discussions of what happens when they are absent. A teacher following a child's instructions to locate a figure within a larger frame can deftly show what results from imprecise directions, and the rôle of precision and directional words and spatial orientation can all follow.

This may all seem unnecessarily complicated to the conventional teacher. Many teachers, however, try instinctively to bring out certain cognitive functions and skills in their children, and the growing interest in scientifically researched teaching programmes, particularly in primary schools, has informed teachers more about the processes of learning.

But the theoretical and practical training given to teachers remains very poor. Teaching generally lacks any scientific basis, and the diagnosis and remediation of children's thinking problems is beyond most teachers, not to mention most conventional psychologists. In Feuerstein's work teachers must acquire a theoretical understanding of Mediated Learning Experience and the nature of cognitive deficiencies to enable them to understand their pupils' difficulties. With this knowledge and an understanding of the children in a class it is possible to master the teaching of Instrumental Enrichment and then adapt it both to the needs of the children and to the dynamics of a lesson. A good Instrumental Enrichment teacher has the improvisation skills of a jazz player, moving from the structured tasks to respond to various questions and discussions and to use children's experiences as they surface in class. As the Americans might say, a good teacher must know how to 'go with the flow', while keeping one eye on the cognitive objectives.

Training Flexibility

The exercises continue for some time to reinforce the need for systematic search and the use of logical evidence. They are also confidence-builders because some of the frames are easier than the first two pages. But in the subsequent set of exercises (see Figure 10), the shapes change and become more complex and asymmetrical. Because they are not geometrical shapes, the children are likely to find them strange and difficult.

The children must devise their own labels for the shapes, the most common one being used as the standard (a cue for a discussion on labels). Here, a very important deficiency in the output phase of the mental process can be addressed. Many culturally-deprived children have egocentric styles of communication; they speak in ways not designed for public consumption because they assume that everyone understands what they are thinking about. By telling a child he can have his own special term for one of the shapes, no matter how ridiculous it is, but must use a common label so that others in the class can understand what he is talking about, it is possible to give him an insight into unsatisfactory forms of expression. This is reinforced throughout Instrumental Enrichment by demands for the children to be precise, to use the right

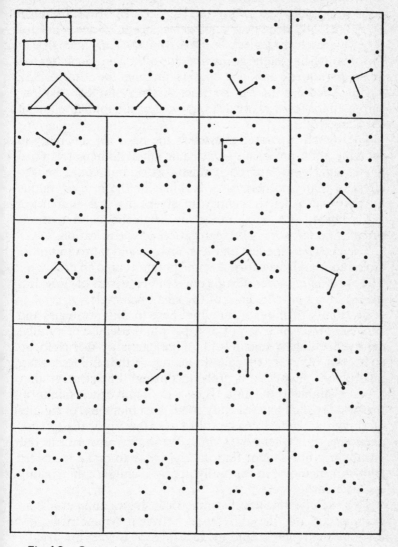

Fig 10   Organisation of dots. Asymmetrical shapes (from Feuerstein, 1978).

terms properly, to use the right vocabulary, to give accurate descriptions and directions.

As usual, they are told to use the cues. But these diminish and eventually disappear and then it becomes necessary for them to switch strategies and move from the tent-like figure to the building-like shape as the first line of attack. The latter has most attributes, and one that is unique: four horizontal, equally-spaced dots. All the other distance/number relationships cannot be so easily distinguished or attributed to one of the shapes.

The switch in strategies stresses the need for flexibility in thinking about problems—one route might no longer work so try another; one approach might work but could be less effective than another. Also, looking for the rare or unique attribute, in order to identify an object that has similarities with others, is a very important principle of all sorts of organisational work, like segregation or classification.

The cues become less and less obvious and more and more ambiguous and, arguably, at some point become obstructions. They proffer a poorer starting point than the pairs of close dots placed along parallel lines of the small rectangle.

Flexibility of thought, required here to shift strategies and avoid obvious cues, is put at a premium because culturally-deprived children manifest the characteristic, discussed on p. 66, which Feuerstein calls 'blocking'. If they fail to reach a satisfactory answer to a problem through one strategy they become unable to function. They cannot move their minds off the strategy they have already tried. This blocking, or rigidity of thought, manifests itself in all of us as the 'tip-of-the-tongue' phenomenon, where we know we have a word in our vocabulary but cannot find the right way to make it surface from our memory. In culturally-deprived children this rigidity is particularly severe.

This exercise also uses asymmetrical shapes and permits an examination of the difference between symmetrical and asymmetrical figures, and the fact that the former are usually easier to identify because of the regularity of their attributes.

The last unit of the Organisation of Dots' instrument, taught in the first year of a two-year programme, is four pages which

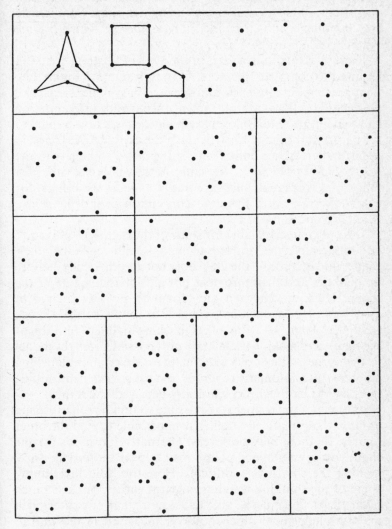

Fig 11   Organisation of dots. Complex shapes (from
Feuerstein, 1973).

carry on from the earlier exercises but add to the variety and complexity of the figures to be identified, and the mental operations to be used. Among the hidden shapes are simple and complex geometric and non-geometric figures, some symmetrical and others not.

There is a qualitative leap in the type of abstract thinking required to complete the exercises in this unit (see Figure 11). There are no obvious cues, and previous easy dimensions, like the length of lines, are no longer effective in differentiating between figures. Much closer examination must now be paid to the nature of the models, particularly the asymmetrical ones, in order that reference points can be identified to help with the search. These need not be the same for the whole class; the idea that some personal cues are just as good as others for conducting a search fosters a conception of independence, flexibility and confidence.

The only universal label for some of the figures is 'polygon', but this really does nothing to help a child remember their shapes and qualities—the label does not automatically conjure up qualities and therefore does not aid internalisation of the shape. Here the children are taught to provide their own associative labels, such as pyramid, or tower for the strange triangular shape, as a way of establishing an internalisation of the figure and making visual transport possible from the model to the frames. The 'looks like' tactic for description, labelling and recall are automatic reponses to most children and adults, but have to be taught to culturally-deprived children.

In many of the frames it is possible to find one figure using dots that automatically makes it impossible to find the other figures, or there may be several alternative positions for the shape, or key reference points may appear more than once, making the choice very difficult. Here the child must apply some of the thinking techniques learnt earlier, but at a much higher level. She must be able to use more than one criterion in making a judgement which, however, must be deferred until all the figures in the frame have been worked out. This, in turn, requires a sequence of work—a strategy, a hypothesis and checking procedures; only then should the lines be drawn in. Because some of the figures are new and asymmetrical, the ability to represent the shapes onto the dots, even when the shapes are facing different ways, is a skill involving a very difficult abstract operation.

During the course of the unit children are taught how to break down complicated tasks into small parts to make them easier, and that dealing with the unfamiliar is more difficult than dealing with the familiar. This is important, because children often feel their confidence ebbing away when confronted with a new problem that requires more time and energy to solve than familiar ones. This loss of confidence can impede their ability and basic motivation to make headway, so they must be prepared for a temporary loss of efficiency and competence when tackling something new. They must also be reassured that different things can be hard or easy for the same person at different times.

The key to cracking the frames in Figure 12 is to find the rectangle in the middle of the G and then locate the three dots that mark the overhead bar and the beginning of the belly. If you try the third frame on the second line you will find

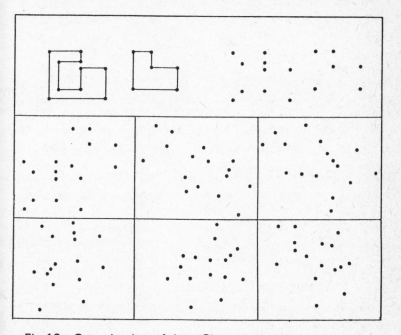

Fig 12   Organisation of dots. Shapes requiring a strategy.

however, that the exercise remains extremely difficult. In Figure 13 children are taught fine perceptual discrimination between a rectangle and a parallelogram, and the rules that distinguish them from each other and from squares. They are also introduced to optical illusions and errors. The first of these occurs in the second line of frames where the rectangle is vertical and seems much bigger. The use of context and the size of other represented shapes around the figure, to check if the size is right, is offered here.

The children cannot use length of lines here because the bottom lines on the 'trousers', on the side of the rectangle and the side of the parallelogram are all the same. It provides a useful lesson about not using dimensions in searches if they cannot help discriminate. Three dots in a triangle do not help either since they, too, can occur in more than one shape. The main cue, arrived at by the very important process of logical elimination, must be tested against several other references before it is safe to proceed. In this case four equidistant dots in

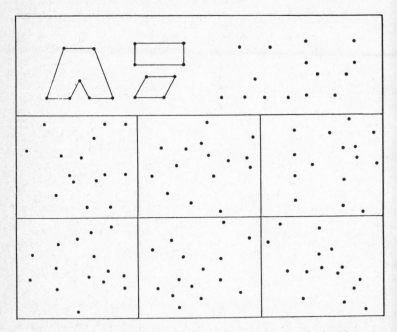

Fig 13 Organisation of dots. Perceptual discrimination.

a line (on the bottom of the tent or trousers' shape) must also have a dot midway above them for the apex of the triangle—marking the crutch of the trousers or the flap of the tent—which must be halfway between two other dots higher up that are the top of the trousers.

The use of context, process of elimination, perceiving the parts of the whole, in relation to the different elements of the trousers, and hypothesis formulation and testing, are all reinforced in these frames. But the introduction of the notion of optical illusions and the fact that the frames show how easy optical errors can be made, provides the opportunity for a very interesting bridging discussion. By using examples of different illusions or perceptual errors, a teacher is able to show that reasoning can often provide us with a better understanding of reality than our first sensory perceptions.

ORIENTATION IN SPACE

Teachers tend to assume that children understand and can follow such terms as left, right, above, below, bottom, top, behind, in front. If they do not, then they are automatically considered stupid. It is, however, one of the common failings of culturally-deprived children that they have not properly internalised a reference system for space, so that even if they do understand what the words mean they have great difficulty in applying them. The crisis often comes when the teacher puts several of these terms together: 'Find the second highest dot in the top left of frame one', will simply lose many children.

Poor orientation in space is part and parcel of that episodic grasp of reality which characterises children who have had inadequate mediated learning. It manifests itself in numerous ways. Children (and indeed adults) might find it very hard to follow or give directions because they cannot clearly abstract and express a route of any complexity. It prevents them forming relationships in space, so that they cannot locate objects and events in their context, and this means that their analysis of situations and problems never gets past first base.

Such children are unable to picture or represent themselves or objects in alternative locations and positions. They tend to conceive of their immediate environment in a crude and egocentric way as mere extensions of themselves: if asked to describe the position of an object in relation to a friend in class they would find it quite impossible. An extension of this primitive relationship to their environment is an inability to picture themselves in other people's shoes, to get their perspective.

From this it is possible to see how a basic cognitive deficiency, like poor spatial awareness, can impede a child's general development. For example, the ability to imagine a change in location of an object or stimulus of some sort, or in one's own position (usually acquired through numerous interactions with parents, often via games and puzzles), is the basis of 'What if?' types of hypothetical thinking which, in turn, form an important part of many logical problem-solving operations.

Playing draughts well, or chess at all, is beyond many children and adults for reasons which, to some considerable degree, are connected with the inability to construct relationships in space. Pieces must be moved geographically across boards, bearing in mind the way that proximity or distance from other pieces sets up relationships which form the context of the games. They also require the ability to anticipate and plan for the effects of one's opponent's decisions to move his pieces through space.

There are a great many cognitive skills involved in the games, but children who have poor spatial orientation will not be able to use enough sources of spatial information even to begin to construct the context of the game indicated by the pieces and their positions. They will be quite unable to assess their situation in the game, any more than in real life. Interestingly, the piece in chess that always causes the most difficulty, and is often an absolute barrier to the progress of many children, is the knight. The reason is that the knight does not move in straight lines, or even along the surface of the board; it jumps, according to complex rules, through space.

Orientation in space is a basic skill even for the 'games' of the Organisation of Dots' instrument. It is a prerequisite for the type of hypothetical thinking used to develop and test strategies for constructing shapes that will solve the problems. Hence the two instruments are always taught together. Orientation in Space seeks to give children an internal system of reference with which they can control space. Its more specific objectives are to attack poor ability in discerning, organising, articulating and abstractly representing spatial arrangements. Under fire is the conceptual and linguistic poverty of children who, when asked where an object is, will always say 'there'.

As with the Organisation of Dots, Orientation in Space has a meta-cognitive goal of bringing children to an understanding of how important it is for humanity to organise and control space. Paradoxically, such discussions—often of a very philosophical nature—form a bridge to the real world, which gives purpose and motivation to the learning of some very basic intellectual skills.

The Nature of Space

A teacher might begin this instrument by asking 'What is space?' 'What are the different notions of space?'. It can extend in all directions horizontally; if it had a vertical dimension, too, it would become three-dimensional space. It could include everything or it could be confined to a classroom, a town or a city; it could be outer space or the psychological feeling of space. The teacher could go on to look at how we parcel up space into manageable relationships, as *on, near, under, behind* and in many other ways. A relationship, children can be reminded, is a connection between two or more things. Space can also refer to both distance and location—something can be so long, or so far, from something else.

Without a reference system for controlling space, social existence would be impossible. Even the most primitive tribes had some sort of directional system for finding their way back to their camps using landmarks, the sun or the stars. Building the simplest house requires the use of a spatial system to ensure that the space inside is useful, and that the house is constructed according to tried-and-tested methods. It is through spatial reference systems that experience, say about house building or navigation, can be transmitted from one person to another, and one generation to another. If such reference systems had never been developed, each person wanting to build a house would be obliged to learn by tedious trial and error.

How we organise space into relationships is an area which should be mined very thoroughly. Children need to be led on from the idea of a book and a table and their spatial connection, to the more general concepts of proximity, separation, enclosure, sequences in space, continuity and discontinuity—for example, a row of books has a continuity within it and a discontinuity in that it begins and ends.

Perspective in space is another relationship we impose and is very much a human cultural construction—peoples who do not live in a sophisticated architectural environment often lack a developed sense of perspective. This, and the ability to understand three-dimensional space, are learnt at various ages up to adolescence. They are complex intellectual/cultural skills often missing in culturally-deprived children and, to some degree, in 'normal' adults.

Even if these concepts are not fully grasped at the early stages of the instrument, they can be mentioned or illustrated with simple drawings on the blackboard to illustrate perspective and three-dimensionality—a cube, for example. In this way, the seeds at least can be sown for later reaping and a questioning attitude to orientation in space initiated. Orientation can be loosely described as direction—the crucial 'where?' question that we consistently ask ourselves with differing degrees of sophistication to help us organise and move about in the world. Disorientation means we do not know where we are because we have no clear reference points to guide us. The discussion can be extended to our adaptation to our environment and how we feel disorientated in unfamiliar surroundings.

The diagram on the cover of the instrument (Figure 14) offers a series of directions noted by the arrow-head. The use of arrow-heads as a symbol of direction is established and the opportunity is opened up for discussions about the use of directions, the planning of quick as opposed to slow routes, whether short-cuts are always shorter (they could be more hazardous) and how different directions need to be given to reach the same point if you start in a different place.

This is a good opportunity for teachers to make directions into a game by choosing a point on the diagram and asking two halves of the class, with different starting points, what directions they would give to reach the teacher's chosen point. The directions, if correct, will be different for each half, but following them, if wrong, can cause hilarity and, at the same time, bring home the importance of accuracy and clarity.

By eliciting the notion of a crossroads from children for the cover page diagram, they can be introduced to some of the ways we use spatial and geographical concepts for other aspects of our lives, making a bridge from abstract ideas about directionality to real experience. Crossroads can also mean a turning point in life in which one of several decisions must be made and then cannot easily be reversed. The reversibility or

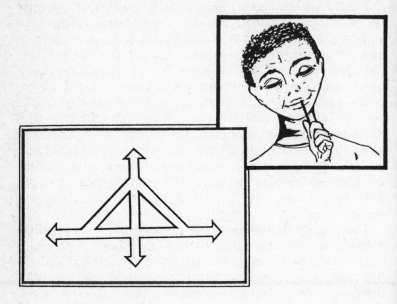

JUST A MINUTE ...

LET ME THINK !

Fig 14   Orientation in space. Instrument cover (from
Feuerstein, 1976).

irreversibility of decisions, with examples, can then lead to the need for thinking carefully and reviewing all the alternatives before making a decision, and *not being impulsive*.

The early discussions serve two purposes for the teacher: they establish an understanding about the need to organise space and provide insights into the particular weaknesses of the children. To instil an internal reference system, the instrument explains and then tests children on the basic system of left, right, front, back. However the content of the system is not the only thing that is elaborated: the properties of systems are stressed so that their rules can be stored and creatively used. Another feature of the instrument, common to them all, is that the system forms the basis of all the tasks, in order to instil it as something that is habitually used by children. But so as not to bore them, it is presented in many different guises, in various modalities and with ever-increasing abstraction and difficulty.

Direction and Side
The spinning pin-wheel or merry-go-round (Figure 15) on the inside cover pages of this instrument introduces the new concepts that are covered throughout the remaining exercises. The four arms may be called sides and, because they are stable and fixed in relation to one another, they form a closed system. Examples of such systems are the days of the week, the months of the year, the circulatory system of the blood, and so on. Its main characteristic is that, from the discovery of one element, it is possible to locate the position, and usually the names of the others. The four arms are in relation to each other, they are connected. This is a chance to reinforce the understanding of a relationship being a connection between two or more things.

It is vital that low-achieving children are taught to go beyond a purely personal reference system, where they locate everything in relation to their own body, as quickly as possible. It is simply too concrete and crude to provide a sophisticated understanding of spatial relations. The arms of the merry-go-round in Figure 15 might be called sides, in the same way that we refer to sides of the body, but not all objects, it should be pointed out, have obvious sides. Houses do, but trees do not. Girls and boys do, but pencils and flowers do not. Those objects that do not, mountains, tables and bottles also come to mind, can be

Fig 15   Orientation in space. Introducing the concepts (from
Feuerstein, 1978).

arbitrarily given sides by their viewer, be it a person, a
newspaper or a photograph, but they are not part of a closed
system.

The spinning pin-wheel or merry-go-round has sides, but it
also has directions, denoted by arrow-heads pointing to the
directions of 'front', 'back', 'left' and 'right'. Direction and side
are not synonymous and can confuse children. It is simply
explained by showing that a child can be facing the front, but
can be moving in a backwards direction. This confusion clears
up when compass points are used for directions and front and
back are superseded.

A chance to consolidate the understanding of a closed

system and the terms of 'left', 'right', 'front' and 'back' is given on a following page. Here the children are asked to infer the terms that are missing from the terms that are given. In the first exercise they are only given one to find, with three given, but in the last they must find the missing three terms from the one provided.

> Fill in the missing word.
> Front, left, right, ...
> ...., ..., ..., Front.

This might seem a straightforward, simple exercise but to the trained Instrumental Enrichment teacher it opens up opportunities for introducing new concepts and vocabulary, as well as establishing what has been taught through real application. It can be seen in the various lines to be completed that, although the number and names of the terms of the system are fixed, they appear in a random way. Random versus fixed order is an immensely fertile ground for discussion, as is the fact that, once a child has chosen which terms he will supply to the blanks, his room for decision-making progressively decreases. One of the properties of a closed system is that it allows the logical deduction of the remaining terms, once one has been given. Logical deduction should be explicitly discussed as a problem-solving strategy.

Children can practise formulating changes in orientation by being asked to describe the location of other students and objects in the classroom in relation to themselves, then between each other, excluding themselves, and then between objects outside the classroom. Some children, however, might have great difficulty in separating their personal frame of reference from their own bodies, and then it would be necessary to ask them to describe the locations of people and objects as they physically turn themselves around, before progressing to the more abstract representational problems. One of the major conclusions to be drawn from the page is that the sides of one's body do not change; what does is direction, orientation and relationships, as a result of changes in position.

Transformations

At this point children may have learnt the four points on the basic spatial system and their relationships to each other. But it is a characteristic of deprived children that they tend to be passive in the face of new situations and problems. Their thinking structures are too crude to allow a self-confident and creative application of knowledge. The frames in Figure 16 deliberately lack instructions, so forcing the children to make several creative leaps of logic. They must infer that the frames carry some problems because there are empty boxes suggesting unsupplied information, and they must assume that these concern the four-point spatial reference system, and that they are required to insert those four points in the boxes as the boy changes orientation in the garden.

Teachers often fail to see the small changes that take place in children as they learn. If children who previously 'froze' when confronted with a new problem are able to make these inferences, then the teacher should be in no doubt as to what has happened. By giving children some basic structures of spatial orientation they have enabled them successfully to carry out a feat of analytical perception.

Children can be told quite straightforwardly that a change in the boy's position results in a transformation—in what he sees and the orientation of the objects to him. Long words do not frighten children if they are explained. However, even though what he sees is different, he still knows where the other objects are because they are in a fixed system and are relative to each other.

There is a natural bridging point here, from the need to put ourselves into the boy's shoes to see what he sees, to the need to carry out a similar intellectual leap to understand someone else's point of view. The inability to see things clearly on the edge of one's field of vision can be raised to explain that different people can see the same thing, but describe it quite differently. The relative nature of perception can be brought home by anecdotes about the inability of different witnesses to recount the same accident in the same way, and that, as well as a visual perspective, there is an emotional one.

The four boys are taken out of their frames and placed at the top of the page in Figure 17, which requires yet more abstract

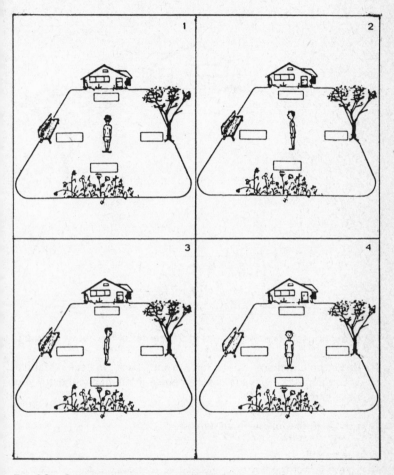

Fig 16   Orientation in space. Points of view (from Feuerstein, 1978).

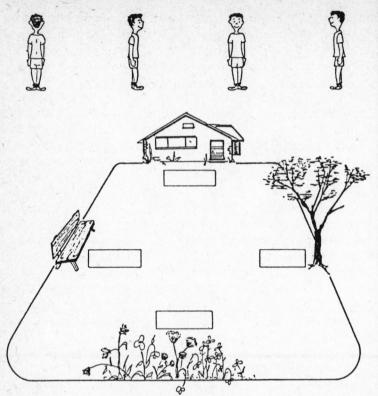

1. Draw or paste one of the boys in the centre of the above drawing.

2. Write the directions 'right', 'left', 'front', 'back', in each rectangle according to the way the objects appear in relation to the boy you have chosen.

3. Complete the following sentences:

The bench is _____

To the left of the boy _____

The house is _____

The flowers _____

Behind the boy _____

Fig 17   Orientation in space. Hypothetical thinking (from
Feuerstein, 1978).

thought and yet more flexibility. Children are asked to paste or draw one of the boys—they always choose the first because it represents their own orientation to the diagram—into the garden and then to fill in the blanks.

In fact, teachers prefer them to draw in the figure because it offers opportunities for them to discuss the uses of modes of representation and symbols. Before this is done, however, the different boys need to be labelled with numbers—and why this use of numerical labels is convenient can be discussed at some length.

When drawing the boy into the garden, the teacher can suggest that the children do not try to reproduce the representative figure but summarise its main attribute—its direction. All that is required is a face and a nose, pointing like an arrow to denote the direction. In this way it is possible to save time 'by sorting the essential from the peripheral attributes, and by deciding priorities in our criteria for drawing the boy. This is a great help to children with problems of visual transport because they have often not been taught to spot key characteristics in objects which can conserve an image over any distance or time.

According to the picture they have drawn, the children are asked to supply answers to certain questions, one of which is 'If the boy turns to the right he will be facing . . . ?' This requires hypothetical thinking based on an abstract representation of the position of the boy once turned round. In other words, the child must carry out a transformation in his head. From a very easy exercise the child must travel a considerable intellectual distance. One of the lessons to emerge from this section is that it is necessary to think hypothetically and to represent routes and directions in your mind in order to give clear directions; and that it is always necessary to define one's starting position, because different positions produce different orientations and directions.

The instrument then insists on a further leap in abstraction and complexity as it turns to challenge children's often limited mental field and their difficulties in holding and using more than one source of information at any one time. They are asked mentally to transport a picture of the boy, in four different numbered positions, into the middle of the garden, and

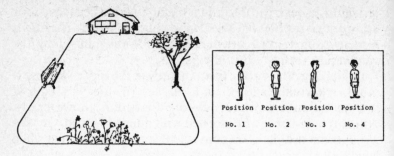

What is the object?

Position	Direction in Relation to the Boy	Object
1	right	
2	front	
3	left	
4	back	
4	front	
3	back	
2	left	
1	back	
4	right	
3	right	
1	front	
2	back	
4	left	
2	right	
3	front	
1	left	

Fig 18   Orientation in space. Working systematically (from Feuerstein, 1978).

supply an answer in the third column of a table from two given parameters (see Figure 18). The task insists on mental flexibility in that it requires the child to use several different languages or modalities: tabular, for the table form of storing information (the convenience of using tables should be spelt out); figurative within the frame (where the direction of the boy in relation to an object is discovered through the position of the figure) which is based on a written command of right and left etc. The symbolic language also appears in the numbers of each of the boy's positions.

Great stress must be laid on systematic work in this section of the instrument because the child is now being asked to hold in his mind several sources of information simultaneously: the two columns in the table, the position of the boy in the garden and the relation of the objects in the garden to the boy. This exercise often provides stunning evidence of how far low-performing children have moved. They must have adequate visual transport to move and hold the boy in the field; they must understand symbolic labelling; they must have the ability mentally to represent changing figures in their context; and they must have a basic understanding of spatial orientation.

The procedure for carrying out the task should be carefully explained: a failure to use systematic exploration is usually an underlying weakness in culturally-deprived children, but no matter how good their grasp of the above-mentioned skills, without a systematic approach they will flounder. Children should be told to move from the column to the frame of four boys, to the garden and back to the second column, then back to the garden, and then to place the answer in the third column. What is being requested is very elaborate hypothetical thinking using three components of information to generate a fourth. By Figure 19, the children are being asked to change the components on every line—making a review of the problem necessary each time. To deduce the position of the boy from other factors is, of course, much harder than anything else because, of all the components, it is the boy who has obvious directionality. At one line there is nothing given—the child has created his own configuration and generated his own information.

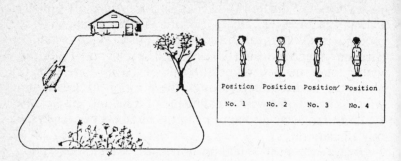

Fill in what is missing:

Position	Object	Direction in Relation to the Boy
1	The tree	
4		right
2		back
	The house	front
3	The bench	
2	The house	
	The tree	left
4		back
	The bench	
		left
3		
4	The tree	
		right

Fig 19   Orientation in space. Changing components (from Feuerstein, 1978).

COMPARISONS

The failure of children to learn to read has many causes, but one of them is often a basic inability to compare shapes of letters. A child with this disability will be unable to distinguish words no matter how many times he is shown them. The recent trend towards 'see and say' sight-recognition methods of teaching leaves many children floundering.

For ordinary children comparisons are easy and spontaneous, enabling them to organise new incoming information by relating it to knowledge they have already stored. Its assimilation is achieved by generating comparisons between the old and the new. Feuerstein describes the act of comparison as the mental superimposition of one object on another in order to distinguish the similarities and the differences. The very act of comparison changes the nature of perception because an individual will find qualities in objects or people that previously were not 'visible'. Relative characteristics such as 'big' or 'small' only have meaning by virtue of comparison. In fact, comparison is one of the basic building blocks of cognition and of abstract systematic thought.

This spontaneous comparative behaviour is, however, learned behaviour. Frequently it remains inadequately grasped and, when this is the case, serious disabilities are produced in children. Since there is no basis on which new information can be assimilated and stored, such children's short-term memory tends to be very poor, and, for similar reasons, their visual transport skills are also very weak. They can generally only use one source of information at a time and, since comparison is the basis of all decision-making, they tend to be very confused and passive or to make completely irrational and impulsive decisions. Inadequate comparative behaviour means that victims can only see reality in a very episodic fashion.

Feuerstein points out that the most low-functioning children can tell the difference between a big piece of cake and a smaller one, or between a smile and a scowl. But this level of comparative behaviour is too primitive to function successfully in the many different arenas of a complex society, one of which is school.

Several cognitive skills are implicit in spontaneous comparative behaviour and it is necessary to target them for remediation as a way of developing the process of making comparisons. The tasks in this instrument, therefore, try to instil and reinforce well-focused perception and adequate visual transport to give stable perception during a child's act of comparison; the conservation of constancies and invariants (so that a child knows which attributes of objects remain the same while others change); systematic and thorough exploration that allows adequate gathering of the information required for comparison; the use of labels, concepts which allow successful discrimination, and summative behaviour where the differences and similarities are assessed to make a comparison judgement. By consistent attention to detail, and through learning to look for those attributes that allow for successful comparison, the children can acquire, remarkably rapidly, some quite sophisticated skills.

The goal of the instrument is to make comparative behaviour automatic. It is only a small step from the comparing of two seen objects to the comparison of a seen and a represented object—in other words, it is an important bridge to abstract thinking. As such it is a vital preparation for other functions, such as categorisation and syllogistic, analogical and transitive styles of thought.

The tasks within the instrument are deceptively easy so that the emphasis is not so much on success or failure, but on the process of comparison, relying more on the creativity and skill of the teacher in unravelling the repertoires of comparative behaviour than on the design of the tasks. Feuerstein warns teachers that many of the tasks in the instrument have numerous answers and these should be elicited and positively encouraged to provoke individual confidence and flexibility in pupils. Different answers to the same question provide heaven-sent opportunities for exploring the different routes and reasons behind particular suggestions, and for raising the wide variety of perceptual and conceptual criteria that constitute exhaustive comparison.

Nevertheless, the teacher must point out that the goals of comparison will determine its parameters, and will usually produce enough constraint to require a 'best' answer. If the object is to find which tool is the best for a particular job, several might be right but only one will be totally appropriate. If one has to compare tools for use by a man with one arm in a wheelchair, the parameters, or criteria of comparison must change according to the new purpose.

Similarities and Differences

By asking children to talk about the two symbols on the cover page (Figure 20), it will become immediately apparent whether or not they compare spontaneously. In the latter case a child will simply itemise the attributes of the symbols without relating them to each other.

As with the other instruments, the cover pages are used to familiarise the students systematically with some of the basic concepts of comparison. The two circles have similarities and differences, both of which are the essence of comparison. Had the two circles been identical, all their attributes would have been the same. Although, it can be pointed out, drawings and plans, as well as manufactured products, are often identical, and that exact identity is important in science and industry, in nature it is very rare. For example, fingerprints are all different, and no two snowflakes have the same patterns. There is a natural bridge here to the rôle of comparisons in identification and social organisation. As with the other instruments, the first pages require children to carry out some basic analytical perception and engage in quite philosophical discussions about the importance of comparisons.

Attempting to go beyond crude comparisons, however, immediately raises serious difficulties for children who have been deprived of mediated learning. Because they have little or no intellectual organisation, all stimuli, and therefore all parameters of comparison, carry equal weight. Ask a child to compare a blue car and a red boat and he will immediately say that the colour is different. In fact, even this is unlikely to be true since it would mean that he had actively compared the two

JUST A MINUTE ...

LET ME THINK !

Fig 20   Comparisons. Instrument cover.

and then found the superordinate concept colour. He would be more likely to say: 'One is red, the other is blue'.

Impulsiveness and the inability to decide priorities among the attributes for comparison produce a totally inappropriate response that would immediately earn the child a label of 'thick as bricks' in most schools. This impression would be confirmed if a teacher then asked the child to find what a boat and a car have in common and received only a silence in return.

If the structures have not been put in, however, it is impossible to expect more from such children. So the instrument sets about establishing a hierarchical intellectual system with which to make successful and intelligent comparisons. This hierarchy entails an understanding of critical attributes, superordinate concepts and levels of generalisation.

Critical Attributes

These occur on the inside cover pages (Figure 21) and denote that both animals are kangaroos. The fact that each kangaroo has a different colour and direction, and position on the page, does not alter the basic similarity of key characteristics which make the animals kangaroos.

If we were comparing for differences, the non-critical attributes of colour, direction and position on the page would assume more importance. The last two are, by the way, parameters added to those on the front page, and throughout the instrument new parameters for comparison are carefully and systematically built in to the tasks, so expanding the repertoire of the child.

When introducing this page the teacher can discuss at some length the strategy for making a successful detailed comparison. The child must scan the page and then move from one element in one figure to its counterpart in the other figure. It requires systematic effort to produce all the similarities and differences.

The object of the comparison determines the relevance of the criteria to be compared (direction of cars in a showroom would not be very relevant), and their criticality. In comparing cars, colour would generally matter less then price, unless one had so much money that price was not a crucial factor. You need different parameters for comparing different objects according to the purpose of the comparison. The nature of the object and

Fig 21   Comparisons. Critical attributes (from Feuerstein, 1978).

the goal in making a comparison therefore place some limits on the almost boundless number of attributes which can be used, say, in comparing cars—or people, for that matter.

Superordinate Concepts and Levels of Generalisation

Returning to the circles on the front cover, the differences are white in black and black in white, so the superordinate term is location of colour; alternatively, within the box the circles are to left and right, which is a question of position.

Comparing two objects with different attributes, such as the faces of two boys (see Figure 22), or a car and a bike, to find what they have in common, is a task of both generalisation and discrimination. The concept, or general idea, used to express this commonality includes the objects in question, or perhaps just their attributes, while excluding other objects and characteristics.

Over-generalisations, such as males, humans, vertebrates, are not good enough because they are not sufficiently specific: it is true that a boy is a sub-set of the above terms, but not all humans, vertebrates or even males are boys. The right superordinate concept is 'boy', but not 'smiling boys' because that term could represent two specific boys, rather than the class of object termed 'boy'. Moreover, 'smiling boys' suggest that both the boys in the pictures are exactly the same—just two smiling boys. In fact they are different in other respects and this can be allowed for in the more general term of 'boy'.

The answer to the second task in Figure 22 is apples, not fruit or food which would be over-generalisations. The difference between the two apples needs to be expressed in two words, one of which qualifies the noun 'apple' e.g. 'small apple', 'big apple'. A principle is thus established that adjectives help to discriminate between objects in the same class (intraclass) while interclass differences are denoted by different nouns.

The commonality between the objects of the first two tasks in Figure 22 can be seen easily because the objects belong to the same class. But for objects which belong to different classes the commonality is not visible; it is conceptual in character. So information must be gathered about both objects. This will focus initially on the differences until a level of generality is reached where a common concept discovers their relationship.

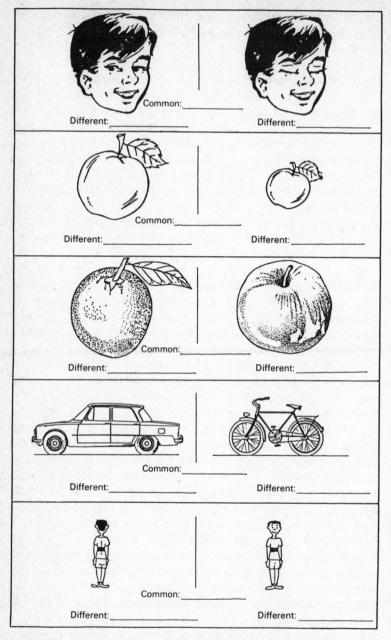

Fig 22 Comparisons. Generalisation and discrimination
(from Feuerstein, 1978).

For an apple and an orange it is 'fruit', for a bicycle and a car it is 'vehicle'. This is more precise than transport which includes ships, planes or railroads that carry goods as well as people as part of their main function, and are, therefore, less personalised means of conveyance. By summing up the differences, eventually to find the common factor, we achieve the ability to say: 'They are both . . .'

When looking at the two boys to find the differences, it is important not to infer more than is reasonable from the given information. A typical response is that one boy is sleeping but the other is not. This is assuming too much, since not everyone who shuts his eyes is asleep. Learning what you cannot say about two objects or events is a critical lesson in realistic comparisons. In life, successful comparison often makes use of logical inferences, but such inferences can easily go too far and allow fantastical assumptions to invade perceptions of reality.

When comparing the differences between objects in the same class, greater discrimination needs relative adjectives of gradation—vocabulary that can allow children to go beyond 'big' and 'small'. Instead, a variety of terms, ranging from 'tiny' to 'medium' to 'gigantic', can be applied to give much greater precision.

Suddenly shifting the modality or language in the instruments, to present the same tasks in different ways, is a feature of all the instruments. It not only relieves boredom but forces children to apply rules more creatively and flexibly. The modality becomes verbal and the children are asked to find the elements in common, and the differences, between church and factory, love and hate, movie and television, baby and old man, amongst others. In this type of exercise the teacher is all-important in bringing out into the open the cognitive lessons that can be learnt.

Words, it can be pointed out, are less concrete than pictures or real things. Using words to compare objects requires us to employ representations of those words that we have stored in our memory. Because they are less concrete than pictures or real objects, words can more easily be made to represent universal sets. 'Ring' symbolises a whole class of objects called rings, which would be much more difficult to draw, and even more difficult to show as real objects.

In order to encourage children to suppress their tendencies for egocentric communication, the instrument stresses the use of 'universal' concepts—relating to the unchanging attributes of objects, events and relationships—rather than idiosyncratic perceptions. Some of the answers children will offer to explain the difference between a church and factory may be: 'My father goes every day to the factory and once a year to church'—too idiosyncratic—or, 'The nearest church has five doors and the nearest factory only has two', which is too dependent on specific objects. The correct answer should be connected with the general or universal difference in function. Churches are for worship, factories for manufacture.

Ways of Seeing

By introducing time and space into the process of comparison the instrument extends the number of parameters through which children can make sophisticated assessments. But it also teaches them that there are divergent ways of seeing the same thing, thus combating the tendency of deprived children to be very rigid in their response to stimuli.

For example, it would be quite possible to say of Figure 23, which appears five pages into the instrument, that the second frame on the first line of tasks contained a square with a hole in it, had we not first seen the frame before it. The circle has an independent existence in that frame and therefore it is logical to assume that, in the next frame, the circle was placed in the square rather than cut out of it. The comparison is based on a transformation. The relationships involved—inside: outside and before: after—are implicit in the sequence of frames.

In lines two and four, the before and after frames reveal an 'in front: behind' transformation. If the second frame was viewed independently it would be natural to assume that a partial square was stuck on to a triangle and a semi-circle was stuck on to a square.

What we are doing in this set of tasks is seeking the relationship between relationships. Put another way, it is the difference in the relationship between the geometric figures in both of the frames that is the basis of the comparison.

Another lesson from the pictures of the jug is that some

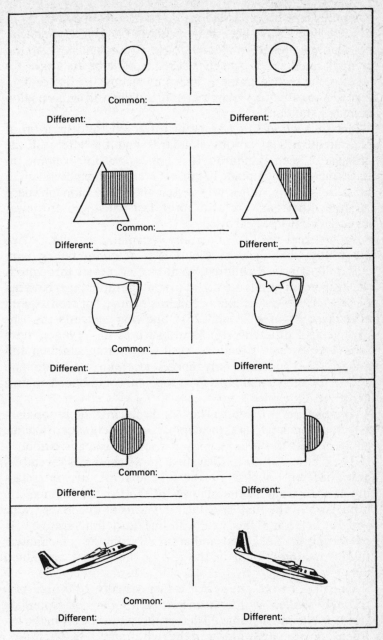

Fig 23   Comparisons. Ways of seeing (from Feuerstein, 1978).

attributes only become obvious in the process of comparison. The jug might have been made with that jagged edge had we not seen it complete in the first frame. The conclusion and the comparison that it is broken is dependent on the first frame. In a sense, the second frame is measured against the first and, in fact, all measurement is comparison, usually with a universally-accepted standard.

This is a good bridging point for a general discussion of measurement via various standards and the effect of the absence of such standards. It is impossible, for example, to sense the speed of a plane because there is nothing by which to measure it. The motorways lessen the impression of speed because other cars are also going fast and there are fewer stationary objects nearby.

An internal need to undertake systematic searching when confronted with new problems is a common failing with culturally-deprived children, so at various points throughout the instrument pupils are asked to spot the differences between pictures. It is a very common children's game, but used to great effect (see Figures 24 and 25). 'Spotting' suggests that the discovery of differences in games such as this is much more spontaneous than it really is, even with normal children and adults. The spotting only comes after an elaborate and systematic search and represents the final comprehension on a perceived difference.

The pictures provide a means of discussing highly sophisticated approaches to making comparisons and this can take the children near to the principles of scientific categorisation.

The pictures of the garden shed, implements and vegetables have different objects in them. There are five interclass differences, while in the pictures of the fish the pictures are intraclass. In the first case, the strategy is to divide the frame with a horizontal and vertical line into four sectors. By narrowing the field, easy and accurate scanning is facilitated; the distracting stimuli in the rest of the picture are edited out.

One object from one sector is then visually, or if necessary through spoken words, transported to the corresponding sector in the other frame. 'There is a round window in the left frame and a square window in the right frame', etc. There is no

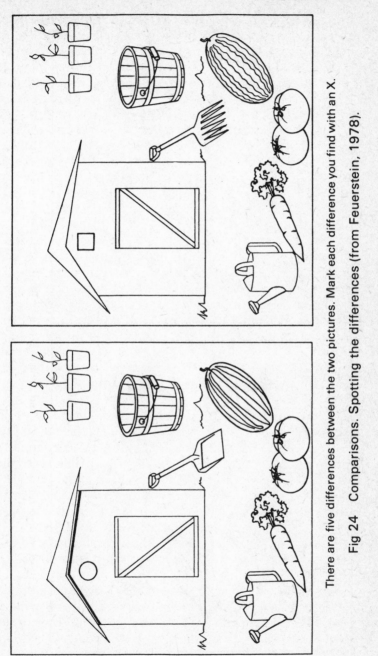

There are five differences between the two pictures. Mark each difference you find with an X.

Fig 24   Comparisons. Spotting the differences (from Feuerstein, 1978).

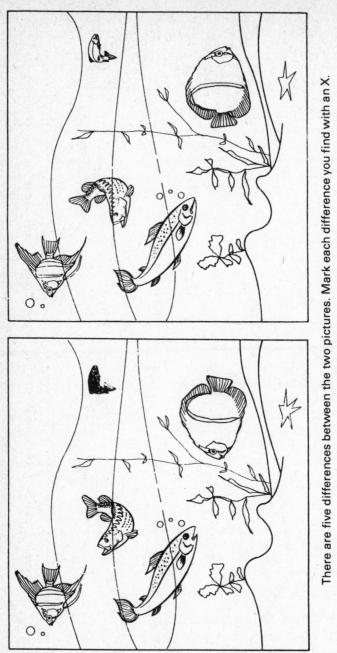

There are five differences between the two pictures. Mark each difference you find with an X.

Fig 25   Comparisons. Spotting the differences (from Feuerstein, 1978).

model, merely two pictures with differences, so it is worth explaining to children that the variations in the second picture are not 'wrong'.

By setting up a primitive table it is possible to get the children to classify the differences according to the parameters of comparison!

The differences in the garden shed picture are those of number, orientation, shape, type of tool and appearance. They are gross differences.

In the fish picture the wavy lines are designed to be used as slightly more difficult sector divides. The intraclass differences are fine and require discrimination between parts of the whole. (See Figure 26.)

Complex Comparisons

Complex comparisons require children to consider several attributes of objects simultaneously. The pairs of words pupils are asked to compare for similarities and differences become much more difficult than previous tasks, partly because they are either very diverse objects or concepts, where the differences far outweigh the similarities, or because they are so similar, or familiar, or because they are abstract. The commonalities between milk and salt, for example, include colour, nourishment, and the fact that both are cooking ingredients. Differences include texture, taste, origin, and so on. Another pair is ugly and wicked, and yet another, newspaper and magazines or, again, lake and river.

The lines drawn in the picture have a double function: to help in a systematic search by dividing the field, and so serve as a reference for positioning of the fish. The task involves scanning and focus.

		Picture on left	Picture on right	Concepts
1	Orientation of fish	Mouth above line 2	Mouth below line 2	Orientation
2	Colour of fish	Black	White	Colour
3	Mouth of fish in 4	Open	Closed	Position
4	Direction of fish	To our left	To our right	Direction
5	Number of arms of starfish	Six	Four	Number

Summary: Differences are fine and require discrimination between parts of whole.

Fig 26   Intraclass differences.

Place an X beneath the two pictures which are identical in each row.

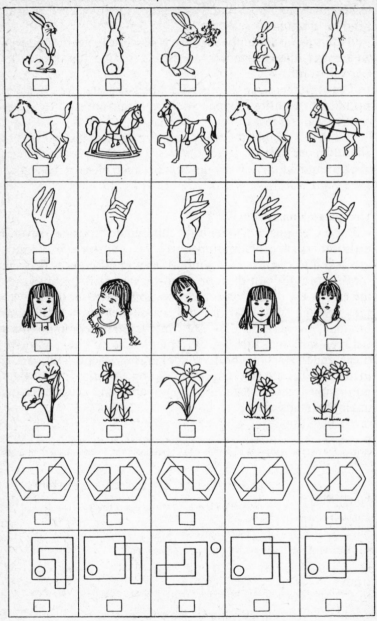

Fig 27 Comparisons. Finding similarities (from Feuerstein, 1978).

The answers will differ from child to child and provide the teacher with an opportunity to explain how some words can connote different meanings to different people and cultures. For effective communication words must denote agreed meanings. Food might be the answer proffered by some children, but others will distinguish between milk, as a drink and as food.

Despite the fact that milk and salt are very familiar, their comparing is quite difficult; familiarity does not necessarily make for easy comparisons, nor do abstract concepts such as 'wicked' and 'ugly'. The highly abstract parameters for comparison within the tasks can be usefully summarised; they are power, function, rôle, and physical attributes.

Using and Creating Models

One way of teaching children how to control the mass of inchoate stimuli that attract them, and how to absorb systematically new information by comparison, is by teaching them how to use comparisons. In the tasks shown in Figure 27 they have moved beyond simple comparisons and are now required to find similarities and differences along several parameters at once.

Choosing two identical objects from a series of similar objects is likely to produce an initial confusion in a child with inadequate mediated learning experience, especially as there is no obvious place to begin. A crucial lesson for comparing is taught through these exercises: when we are not given a model or standard against which to compare, our starting point must be arbitrarily chosen. We must select, for purely personal reasons, a model of our own on which to proceed.

The first rabbit on the right (Figure 27) is chosen to make things simple and to provide a clue to the right strategy for the task. By starting with this rabbit and then hitting upon a cue—its ears to compare with those of the other rabbits, one by one—a process of systematic exploration is established. Once a rabbit with corresponding ears is found, its other attributes need to be checked to see if it is identical. If any cues in the first frame of the other lines fail to find an exact correspondent, then that frame must be abandoned as a model and the next one should be tried, as in line 2 (Figure 27). The final line of this

Look at the sample. In each of the two frames, make a drawing that is the same as the sample *only* in those aspects indicated by the encircled words.

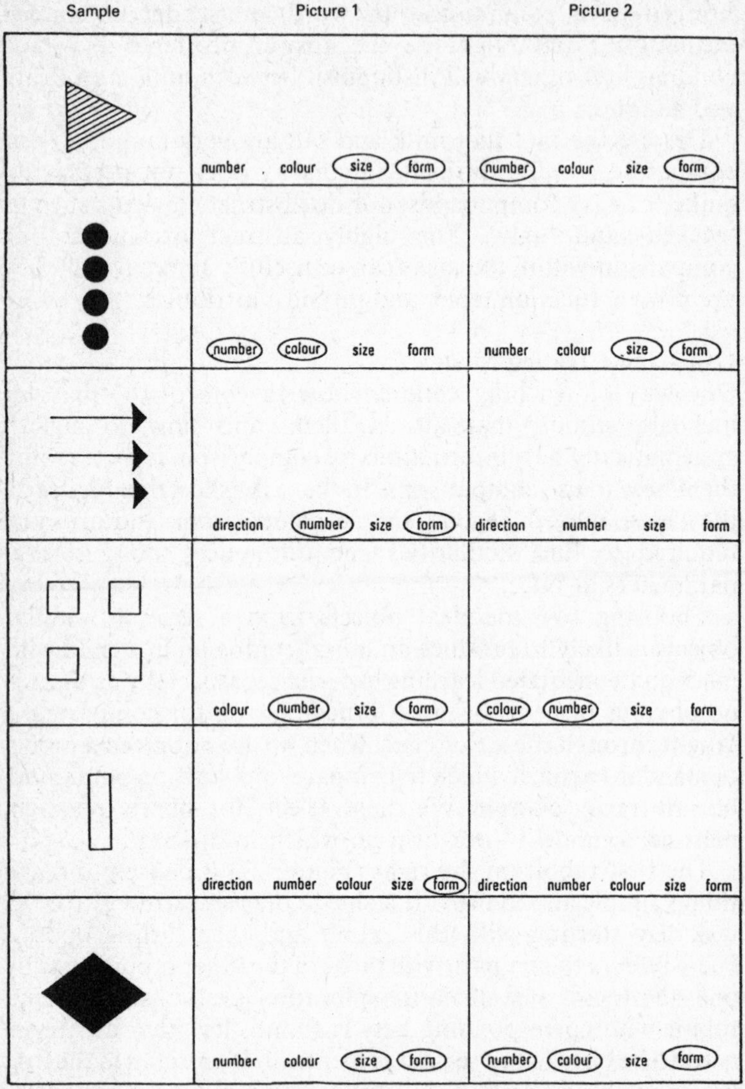

Fig 28   Comparisons. Mobilising parameters I (from Feuerstein, 1978).

exercise is really quite difficult, and, even for adults, there is a need for deliberate systematic search.

Children are then asked to compare to a model, marking the parameters that correspond in the variations to those in the model. These tasks ensure the child is clear about the difference in the parameters and can use them easily. They are asked to mobilise these parameters in the most difficult exercises of the whole instrument (see Figures 28 and 29), where they are provided with a model and asked to draw a figure which is similar on some parameters and different on others.

Every stage of the problem-solving process must be discussed openly with the children before they start because they are likely to both misdefine the problems and flounder in their execution. In effect, the children are being asked to represent in their minds a figure which they have constructed by following directions along five different 'co-ordinates'; these are the four parameters of comparison and the model itself, which must be synchronously applied to build the right figure.

Decoding the instruction (See Figure 28), is likely to lead to misinterpretation of what needs to be done because the word 'only' is quite a difficult concept to grasp and, for want of a better word, to operationalise. A discussion of its meaning can reveal 'only' qualities as being restrictive, and implying that everything else will be different.

This is implied because really it is nothing more than an assumption or a hypothesis. If *only* the parameters that are ringed are the same as the models, those not ringed or not mentioned must, logically, be different. One of the problems with the concept of 'only' in this exercise is, however, that it emphasises the similar characteristics very positively. Many children will, therefore, follow the two similar parameters in drawing a new figure but ignore the differences.

In the first exercise a typical response is for a child to draw in the first frame a triangle with the same size and form. This would be wrong. The correct answer is two or more triangles of different colour. The full implications of the concept 'only' would have been missed and this type of partial reading of instructions is a very typical failure of many children in tests.

The procedure to be followed in this task is to look at the sample figure, then at the ringed parameters, to construct the

Look at the sample. In each of the two frames, make a drawing that is different from the sample in those aspects indicated by the encircled words.

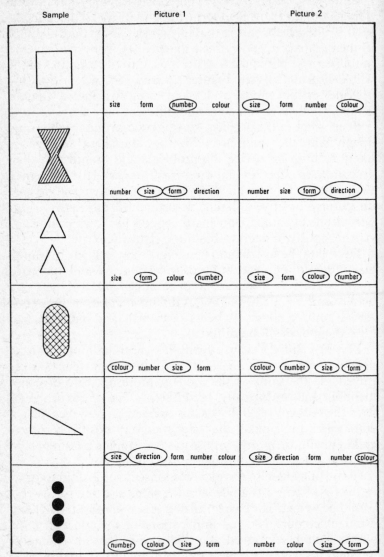

Fig 29 Comparisons. Mobilising parameters II (from Feuerstein, 1978).

new figure mentally, and then adapt it according to the differences *before* any attempt is made to put pen to paper.

A yet more difficult variation of this is found in a task (see Figure 29) where the instructions are more ambiguous because they do not include the world 'only' and there are no other cues. In fact the concept of 'only' is implicit in the task which is still governed by the model figure. In the first frame the square must still be the same form, size and colour but its number must be different. In the second line the model's form and size cease to be important because they are the criteria which must be contradicted. The direction of the model and its number are what must govern the new drawing's restraints.

As in other exercises, the 'adult' vocabulary and concepts used here should be followed in class and children should be encouraged to apply such words as 'class' (of object), 'ambiguous', 'contradictory', 'govern', 'assumption', 'synchronous' and so on.

Discrimination, Deduction and Induction

The rôle of deduction and induction in comparisons is explored in a series of exercises where children are asked to deduce specific objects from a given class, such as 'citrus fruits' and given colours of yellow and orange to the specific objects of lemon or grapefruit and orange or tangerine.

Another problem is where the class is vehicles, location is in the air and on the water, and the deduced answers are ship and aeroplane. Moving from the general class to specific objects is, it can be explained, a process known as *deduction*. The reverse process of moving from specific object to a set, family or class is *induction*.

In Figure 30 it is necessary to induce the class to which the sample object belongs by locating two other objects which share attributes. It would be wrong to call the hoe in line 3 simply a 'tool' because that could include the pick, the rake and the broom, which is used as a tool by a sweeper. 'Garden Tool', or 'Tools with wooden handles and metal heads' would be a classification that would exactly include two other objects. Similarly 'shoes' is better than footwear because the latter could include socks.

In the exercises that follow deduction is required. Children

Mark a + under the two pictures which are most like the sample.

Write the numbers of the pictures you chose, and explain the basis on which you made your choice.

The following words will help you to categorise the pictures:

furniture curved forms drinking utensils
shoes tools five-angled forms

I have chosen numbers 1 & 5 because they are also _____

I have chosen numbers __&__ because they are also _____

I have chosen numbers __&__ because they are also _____

I have chosen numbers __&__ because they are also _____

I have chosen numbers __&__ because they are also _____

I have chosen numbers __&__ because they are also _____

Fig 30 Comparisons. Induction (from Feuerstein, 1978).

must assign a class to a given word, such as piano, and deduce the words in the same class. Using the verbal modality makes children represent attributes in their minds and, therefore, the tasks are more abstract than those using pictures. The superordinate, 'class' concepts that provide the comparable relationships, albeit at a very abstract level, are, vocation, geometric shape, emotion or language. The use of classifications in real life is a natural bridging point, as is the rôle of deduction and induction and the importance of choosing exactly the right word for the purpose.

Children tend to enjoy this instrument greatly and, believe it or not, derive great pleasure from the organisational capacity their improved skills in comparison provide. The instrument can dramatically improve analytical perception, which is formally addressed in the next instrument, and their willingness and ability to adopt a reflective and creative attitude to their environment.

ANALYTICAL PERCEPTION

Culturally-deprived children tend to find themselves bemused, buffeted and even victimised by situations and by systems which they can neither accommodate nor systematically challenge, since they lack the intellectual analysis to do either. Such children often have no interest in how things work or are made, or why certain events happen when they do. They lack a spontaneous need to analyse the world around them and fail to distinguish clearly between their subjective response to experience and the objective, external forces or stimuli that affect them.

In severe cases such children develop behavioural problems in which they seem unable to overcome intensely selfish, egocentric and wildly irrational reactions to their environment. Or they might become 'born losers', the pathetic individuals who always seem to be the victims of circumstance. In more run-of-the-mill cases children might have low levels of curiosity and problem-spotting and solving skills, and find it difficult to reflect on what they see, thus adversely affecting such skills as reading and comprehension.

To be effective actors on the environment, rather than its victims, children must have an internal frame of reference, a series of rules with which they can differentiate reality into its component parts, so that information can be processed and situations analysed and restructured. Sadly it is often disastrously missing or, if it is present, is not used spontaneously in day-to-day experience.

The instrument Analytical Perception seeks to 'operationalise' some of the basic cognitive functions learnt in the earlier instruments and forge them into an altogether higher level of intellectual skill—that of systematic analysis. At the heart of the instrument and of the process of analysis is the ability to break down a whole into its constituent parts. The instrument is basically about different strategies for locating and identifying parts of a whole and working out their relationships.

The skills which the instrument targets, are precision and focused perception, the conservation of constancies, systematic exploration and the search for logical evidence, the ability to use more than one source of information simultaneously, and the all-important ability to represent abstractly changes in relationships, between elements in an object or situation, and to hypothesise alternative configurations.

Children tend to find Analytical Perception quite difficult because the strategies seem very sophisticated when learnt consciously, and when set against the immediacy of the visual stimuli of the various shapes. The strategies are, however, applicable and necessary to virtually every activity in life and school. It is vitually important for teachers, if they are to catch their pupils' interest, to bridge the skills of analytical perception to other areas of experience, such as following instructions, household management, mechanics, and all school subjects.

The instrument does address the most basic skills and children will not become great politicians or scientific analysts after completing it. But it is integrated into a series of other instruments which also elicit the processes of analytical perception, reaching a high overall level of skill. These include the Organisation of Dots, Orientation in Space, Comparisons, Categorisation, Instructions, Syllogisms and Representation Stencil Design.

Figure 31, the front cover of the instrument, provides an opportunity for laying down some of the ground rules of Analytical Perception while, at the same time, engaging in some very philosophical discussion. It shows a circle or ellipse with different parts slightly extruding to show they are the parts that make up the whole, that is the component parts. In class, calling the circle a cake would be a useful analogy but it would also be imposing a perception on the figure which would then dominate our approach to it.

The number of divisions need not be permanent, pupils should be told. It depends entirely on the number of people we want to serve. Nor need the pieces always be the same size, as babies might want less or someone might only want a small piece. Here are two principles: we divide a whole into parts to

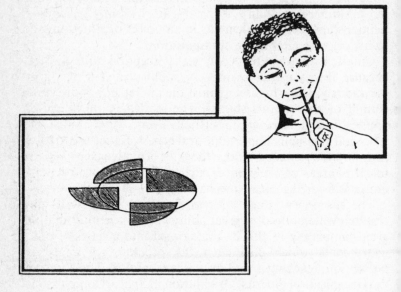

JUST A MINUTE ...
LET ME THINK !

Fig 31   Analytical perception. Instrument cover.

answer a specific need and according to the criteria we set, or which are set for us.

As part of their passive relationship to their environment children often assume without thinking that divisions occur naturally, and are pre-ordained by some super-being without rhyme or reason, rather than for practical usage. Divisions like those of time and space, it can be pointed out, are quite arbitrary and vary from culture to culture. They are man-made, even when they do not seem to be. Night and day seem at first to form a natural divide. But is it always so? In practice they often do not correspond to light and dark.

Some schools, to take another example, have lessons lasting 30, 40 or 50 minutes. These divisions are made by others. However, if you are not at school you can divide your own day into half for chores and half for play. Whoever makes the divisions of wholes into parts, it is important to be able to recognise, identify and label them in order to be able to use them. We need to know the labels given to the days of the week in order to use them to make arrangements and order our lives.

Why do we bother to divide wholes into parts? Enter another principle. It makes for easier organisation and breaks down complex tasks and structures into easier, smaller parts. Creating the sequence of stages in constructing a road or in making a cake can be much more efficient than a slapdash try-it-and-see approach. In fact the making of all major structures involves both complex structural (materials, amounts, locations) and operational analyses (how and when constituent elements are put together to make a whole) before anything is practically started.

In bridging to other areas the teacher can briefly run through how analysis (the dictionary definition is 'separating, breaking up of anything into its constituent elements') works in other school subjects. In history, for example, we use events, periods and dates, as well as different areas, such as economic or social history and levels, state, region, town or individual, as basic divisions before these are further broken down into forces, events, personalities, changes and so on.

Language is broken down into parts of speech and other grammatical elements. Words often have basic roots and common groups of letters and written texts have paragraphs, pages, chapters, parts, volumes. The sense of anything you read—a comic story, for example—is made up of many parts, frames, words, pictures, meanings which together make a whole. Some elements are more crucial than others and careful examination of the parts can often help us to a much better understanding and appreciation of the whole.

In mathematics, fractions and percentages of whole numbers are key features, indeed the whole science of maths is concerned with arbitrary but commonly accepted systems of division. Science, in general, proceeds by analysis, in breaking things down into constituent parts, the better to understand the whole, or slowly uncovering the elements in a problem or phenomenon that builds up to a new discovery. The part-whole relationship, it can be explained, is basic to human thought.

The first phase of analysis is learning how to extract the parts from the whole. The process of analysis is completely dependent on children acquiring a habitual need to seek and recognise constituent parts (see Figure 32). Here the instrument repeatedly asks children to break down various shapes into their constituent parts. Children are also asked to colour and number the various parts and to count the totals. Simple though this seems, the practice opens up numerous areas for discussion about the techniques of systematic analysis.

The rôle of colours as codes for easier differentiation of the parts can bridge to the use of colour as communication codes in electric wiring, traffic lights, etc. If colours are not available an appropriate substitute would be different patterns of black on white. Where shapes overlap and form new parts, the collision of two patterns would make a third.

Numbers are another and more useful communication code for separating the parts. If they are used in sequential order, the last number assigned to a part will also be the total number of parts to a whole. A principle, therefore, has emerged about numbers; they can be used as labels, as indicators of sequences and as indicators of quantity.

Colouring or using patterns for the simple overlaps is easy. But children need to be aware of the different interpretations that can be put on the figures. For example, the answer to the first frame in Figure 33 can be three if the shapes are viewed as discrete transparent plates laid on top of each other. Another

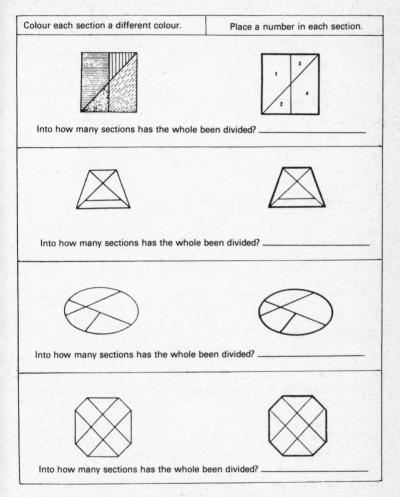

Colour each section a different colour.	Place a number in each section.

Into how many sections has the whole been divided? _____

Into how many sections has the whole been divided? _____

Into how many sections has the whole been divided? _____

Into how many sections has the whole been divided? _____

Fig 32   Analytical perception. Constituent parts (from
Feuerstein, 1978).

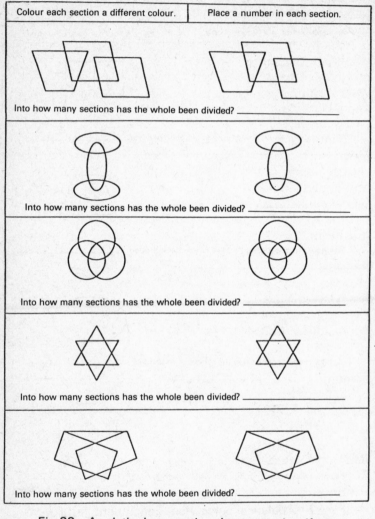

Colour each section a different colour.	Place a number in each section.

Into how many sections has the whole been divided? _____

Into how many sections has the whole been divided? _____

Into how many sections has the whole been divided? _____

Into how many sections has the whole been divided? _____

Into how many sections has the whole been divided? _____

Fig 33   Analytical perception. Interpretation (from
Feuerstein, 1978).

answer is five because the overlaps of the figures create new shapes. But are the two side figures overlapping the central one, or vice versa? The answer can be both. Children are being taught to interpret the same whole in different ways, even though all its characteristics remain constant.

Actually to assign a label, particularly if it is a pattern or colour, to the parts in these figures, children must make an arbitrary decision about which are dominant or subordinate shapes. Numbering the parts need not indicate such a hierarchy and is certainly much the easier way of doing it when it comes to the complex figures like the trio of interlocking circles in line 3.

To introduce a sense of amazement and even disequilibrium into children's understanding of perception, partly to combat a rigidity in their reactions to what they see, and partly to show how analysis can change one's perspective, the Star of David, the Israeli national symbol, is provided for analysis in Figure 33 in a task that sums up much of what these initial pages of the instrument are about.

Irrespective of his level of ability, every child will have an immediate perception of the figure at a global level. But looked at more carefully it can be seen as a hexagon with six triangles stuck on, or two triangles placed on top of each other. Even then each triangle can alternatively be viewed as the dominant or subordinate one. Says Feuerstein:

> The capacity to articulate an object or event in a great number of ways according to need induces divergent approaches. The whole and its parts are not viewed as rigid or stable but as entities that can undergo change while still conserving their constancies.

Perception and Logic

The precision of perception required in the early tasks is reinforced in the next exercises (Figures 34 and 35) which require children to identify and number sections embedded in broader designs. They must search systematically for a section or sections that correspond to a model along two parameters —size and shape, although orientation can change. Some of the shapes within the designs are like the model, but in fact have small differences, so it is necessary to break down the

On each line indicate the number of times the section next to it appears in the design.

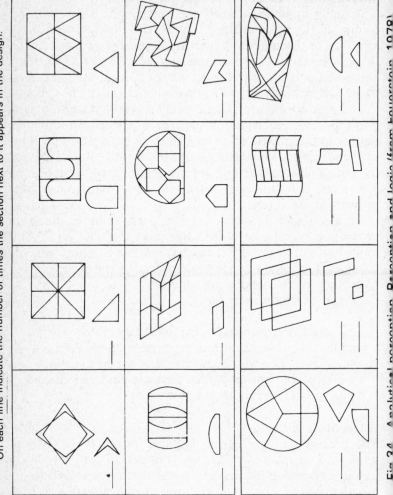

Fig. 24. Analytical perception. Perception and logic (from Feuerstein, 1978)

parts of the whole into even smaller parts to look for very fine differences. Logic and hypothetical thinking can also be employed as aids to efficient perception.

A typical answer to Figure 34 second task, third row, is four of the set-square shapes and two rhombuses. There are only two of the set-squares, although logic should show that, since an object that contains another must be larger, then the various set-squares differ in size and shape and therefore not all can be correct.

To fight low-achieving children's tendencies to sweep randomly over a large figure in order to find parts which correspond to a model (see Figure 35) the rôle of logic and hypothetical thought, as a basis for a systematic search, is emphasised before children are asked to carry out the task. If we are looking for a large irregular figure with straight and curved lines, we can use these cues logically to eliminate small, regular shapes comprising totally straight lines. The work must be systematic, from top to bottom or left to right, transporting the numbered image in one's mind until a possible correspondent is found, whereupon it becomes necessary to check it against the model. This procedure must be spelt out to many children whose immediate instinct is to sweep randomly over the large and dominating image of the complex design to try to find shapes that fit the models, which themselves have not been very carefully perceived. This break-down into steps represents an operational analysis of the task in hand.

The principles involved in this search-and-label operation are: determining in detail the characteristics of the object of search, using those characteristics to narrow the field of search, planning a strategy of systematic search, checking against a model using hypothetical thinking (if this shape changes orientation it would obviously be the same as the model), rechecking using finer discrimination to verify your find.

The act of putting together the parts to create the model design is one of synthesis, accomplished with the help of analysis. In doing this, however, one is creating a qualitative change in the parts that are being manipulated; they are no longer discrete but joined in an integral whole which, by virtue of its particular arrangement, is more than simply the sum of its parts. A cake is much more than the sum of its ingredients, and

The numbered sections are hidden in the design which appears within the frame. Find each section, number it appropriately, and darken its outline.

Fig 35   Analytical perception. Logic and hypothesis (from Feuerstein, 1978).

Correct the errors
Do the separate parts in each frame fit together so that they form the complete design? If they do not, correct.

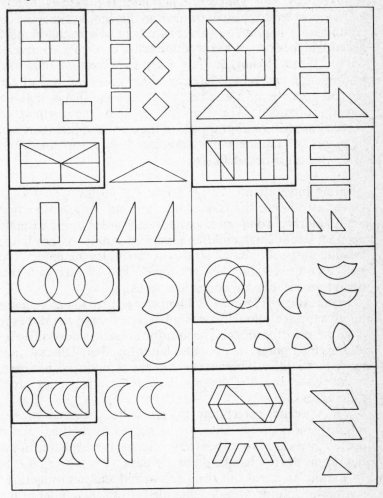

Fig 36   Analytical perception. Discrepancies (from Feuerstein, 1978).

this difference is caused by the way the parts are put together, the order; the proportions of ingredients, the quantity; and the process by which they are interrelated, such as baking. Alternative configurations of these three elements would produce, with the same ingredients, puddings, pancakes or biscuits.

The most sophisticated problem in this block of exercises is contained in Figure 36 of the instrument, where children are asked whether or not the separate parts construct the model design. If they do not, they are asked to correct the situation, but are not told how. They can either cross out one of the shapes, add one or a number, or change the shapes that are already provided. The principle is that the method of correction must be appropriate to the error and that there can be errors of commission or omission. In order to correct an error one must first define it.

Abstract Integration

Once introduced, the task of synthesising designs after first analysing their component parts is reinforced at increasingly abstract levels. First, children are asked simply to draw in the missing parts of a design so that it resembles the model (top half Figure 37). But they are then asked to carry out this operation without any motoric actions.

In the tasks of Figure 38 children are required to superimpose purely representationally two figures, one from each side of the page, to make the model. The solution must then be codified by joining the figures' number and letter together. The tasks are made more difficult because each of the components has parts of its own and the shapes have fine rather than gross differences.

Very precise perception is, therefore, required of the internal and external lines of the shapes, as well as careful overall analysis of the model and what parts are missing in the figures on the left hand side of the page.

A complex process of comparison and analysis using three sources of information is demanded, from the model to the design which needs to be completed, to the possible alternatives and back to the model. The children must visually transport one figure to another and then project the relationships formed by the two superimposed figures. And if they are to avoid

To the left of each section you will find a design.
Finish each of the drawings so that, when completed, each is the same as its model.

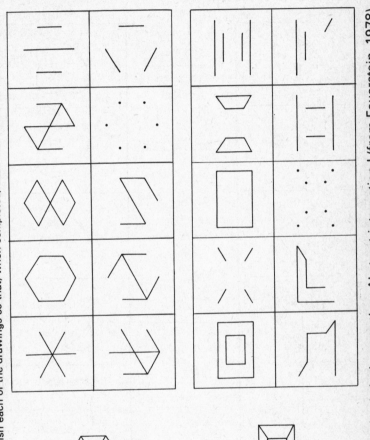

Fig 37 Analytical perception. Abstract integration I (from Feuerstein, 1978).

Look at the figure at the top of the page.
For each drawing in the left column,
there is a drawing in the right column
which completes it. Write the number
and the letter of the two drawings you
combine to make the complete figure.

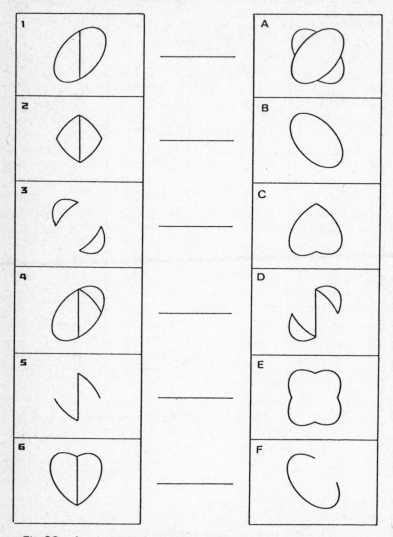

Fig 38   Analytical perception. Abstract integration II (from
Feuerstein, 1978).

painstaking testing of every possible combination they must use hypothetical thinking and logic to draw conclusions about which of the figures to try and combine first. Even when they have reached a conclusion, the only way it can be checked is through a representational comparison with the model, so it is not an easy task. One way to begin is to ask children to discuss the different ways the model can be seen.

By asking the class what is missing in the figure A it is possible to show how we can use words to aid the search for the complementary shape (dictionary definition of complement is something making up a whole). Two small curving lines which make up the middle sections of the external lines of one of the rugby balls are missing. So is the middle radius. The answer is therefore No 5.

If children find the representation needed in this exercise too difficult, they can be allowed to trace or scratch the missing lines in. But teachers will quickly discover that those children who do this without adequate hypothetical thinking to reach a suitable figure will make a terrible mess of the basic figure and find it increasingly hard to get the right answer.

There are several principles which can be extrapolated from doing the exercise on the page and which can lead on to bridging examples. When one has a model and some parts of it are given, the other can be deduced. If we have a pattern of a dress but the part for the arms is missing, it can be calculated from the rest of the pattern's dimensions. Objects taken out of their context often look very different. It would have been hard to believe that some of the shapes in the exercise were ever embedded in the design. A mountain taken out of context is no longer high; it is the elevation of the land around it that makes it high or not. Some of the things we learn in school seem sensible in the context of school but ridiculous outside it. Two other principles, touched on before, are that it is necessary to identify an error to correct it and that a whole, say a building, is more than the sum of its parts.

In subsequent pages other cognitive principles are explored, such as the way the fusion of parts can create a whole with completely new and different characteristics from its components—the fusion of two colours or two chemicals. Orientation and direction are often critical factors in integrating a part to a whole, and the relationship must usually be conserved. When we are not given a reference point or a starting point one must choose one's own—and the cautionary lesson is that it is easier to recognise something than it is to construct it. By the end of the instrument children will have acquired many of the principles of analytical perception which more privileged children take for granted. Watching the instrument progress and seeing how previously inert children become smitten by the bug to take things apart and put them back together again, often in different but still valid ways, is a great experience. They have started off on the road to becoming critical thinkers.

THE OTHER MAIN INSTRUMENTS

Categorisation

Leading on from Comparisons, this instrument seeks to train children's control of information by giving them the skills to organise it into general, superordinate categories. This is a vital prerequisite for logical thinking and enables children to move on from constructing links between objects to making relationships between concepts. (See Figure 39.)

Categorisation is quite a complex skill and is based on comparison, differentiation, discrimination and analytical perception. Typically, low-performing children will try to categorise according to very primitive forms of association, with their memory and senses ruling their intellect. Confronted with a red ball, a tomato and a banana, such childen might group the ball and tomato on the basis of colour and shape, instead of using the concepts of fruit or food.

Moreover, because the mediationally-deprvied child finds it hard to use more than one source of information at a time, or to order things into hierarchies, he has difficulty in creating appropriate categories.

The instrument attacks these deficiencies and trains children to gather information systematically, to distinguish between relevant and irrelevant information and to seek out attributes which could form the basis of groups or sets. It teaches children to draw conclusions based on the common attributes they have found between objects and then apply conclusions to create general categories. This involves inductive and deductive reasoning. For example, the induced relationship between trees, wheat and grass is that they grow from the ground. This is then applied to deduce that other items like flowers and shrubs can be incorporated into the category.

An important aspect of the instrument is its goal of training

Here are four stars marked A, B, C, D. Classify them according to size and colour and write the correct letter on the appropriate line.

Subject of classification: STARS

Principles of classification: *size*: (1) large (2) small
                              colour: (1) black (2) white

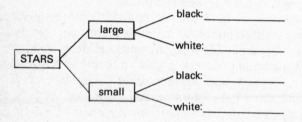

Put a circle around the words that describe the colour and size of each star:

	colour	size
Star A	black/white	large/small
Star B	black/white	large/small
Star C	black/white	large/small
Star D	black/white	large/small

Fig 39   Classification of stars according to size and colour

flexibility in thinking. Once they have acquired the basic categorisation skills, children are trained to re-categorise objects according to different criteria.

Family Relations

The family as a system is used in this instrument to instil in children a need to project relationships onto objects and people. As systems go it is ideal because there are so many different types of relationship within families: hierarchical, horizontal, vertical, temporal—the list is enormous. Children are asked to use and construct genealogical maps which explain these various relations. (See Figure 40.)

The instrument constantly requires children to use a number of sources of information, such as sex, status, age and rôle, and to encode it into symbolical representations before they place individuals in their genealogical map.

They are also required to represent abstractly transformations of individuals' rôles and relationships to others in the system as they move through time. A daughter becomes an aunt, becomes a mother, becomes a mother-in-law, and so on. They are trained in the course of the instrument to infer and deduce, to make analogies and to draw upon logical evidence to determine, through planning, various relations. They are also taught to use various modalities of representation, verbal, symbolic, diagrammatic. And they are constantly asked to follow instructions and construct their own maps based on limited information. In this way the instrument seeks to instil in passive children an understanding that they can generate new information beyond what has been given to them.

Temporal Relations

Time is a highly abstract idea and the more sophisticated the society the more important it becomes. (See Figure 41.) It is abstract because it is a relation between two things or events and this characteristic of time—that it is a relationship rather than a concrete object—makes it difficult for deprived children to grasp in all its aspects. As a result, they cannot use time to impose order on a chaotic existence and this inhibits rational planning or even control over personal behaviour.

The instrument explains to children the various aspects of

Look at the diagram and write the relationship between Joseph and the members of his family as indicated by the direction of the arrow.

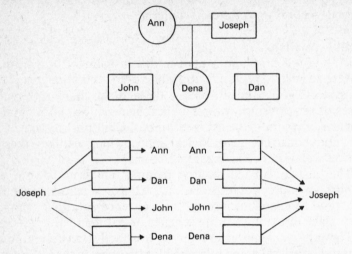

Write the names in their proper places.

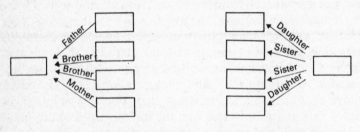

Write your names in the rectangle on the right of each diagram.

Write the names of four members of your family and the relationships, as indicated by the arrows.

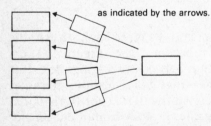 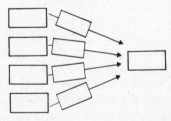

If you prefer, you may substitute the name of a famous person, either living or dead, in place of your name. Then, you may list the names of four members of his/her family and the relationships, as indicated by the direction of the arrow.

Fig 40   Family Relations.

Jack ran a distance of 5 miles (8 kilometres) in one hour.

The following day Jack ran a distance of 7 miles (11 kilometres) in one hour.

Explain the difference: _____

_____

Give several possible reasons for the above: _____

_____

A lorry travelled at a speed of 40 miles (64 kilometres) per hour.

A car travelled at a speed of 60 miles (97 kilometres) per hour.

Which one travelled faster? _____

Both the lorry and the car travelled from San Francisco to Los Angeles and arrived at the same time.

Explain why: _____

_____

_____

_____

Ann and Sarah rode home from school on their bicycles. They travelled at the same speed yet Ann got home about half an hour later than Sarah (without any problems or accidents en route).

Explain: _____

_____

_____

_____

_____

Fig 41   Temporal relations (from Feuerstein, 1973).

time: how it is employed as a form of standard division and measurement of experience, through the use of seconds, minutes, hours, etc., and how, when combined with other factors such as distance, it can produce a measurement of speed. Subjective time is covered, too, and the instrument looks at the way it differs from standard or objective time, and the way emotional factors can affect our perceptions of time. There is also uni–linear time—the movement from the past through the present to the future.

An understanding of cause and effect is one of the goals of the instrument, as is an insight into the way time can be well or badly used, a friend or foe. Hypothetical thinking, the use of logical evidence and the use of various sources of information are reinforced in the exercises.

Numerical Progressions
Training children to deduce relationships between objects and to find the governing principle, is the objective of Numerical Progressions (see Figure 42). Encouraging children to see themselves as generators of new information on the basis of certain limited facts is the important secondary goal. The instrument is not about teaching arithmetic but about how to use relevant information, logical evidence, comparison, deductive and inferential thinking to find the principles behind a numerical sequence.

Instructions
A range of deficiencies are attacked in Instructions, which basically asks children to follow exactly explicit and implicit information given to them to carry out certain tasks (see Figure 43).

Children might find it difficult to follow instructions, written or verbal, because they have never been taught to look for the key words telling them who, what, why, when, where and how. The when and where elements in Instructions might also require children to operate spatial and temporal arrangements and this might be a source of failure, as might blurred and sweeping perception which causes children to misread instructions.

Inadequate planning behaviour and an impaired ability to

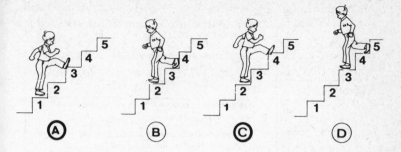

1 Fill in the relationships between the numbers with the help of the formulas; then continue the progressions.

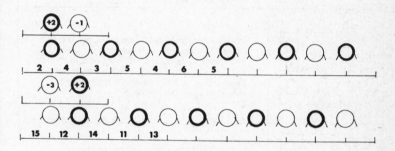

2 Continue the progressions; then write down the formulas.

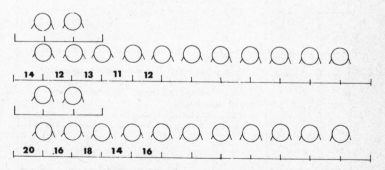

Fig 42 Numerical progressions (from Feuerstein, 1973).

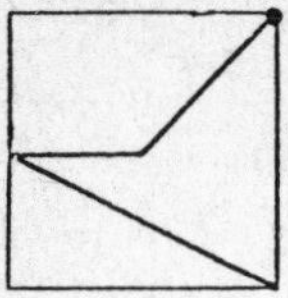

The line starts from the upper _____ corner, reaches the _____ of the square and continues from there to the _____ of the _____ side. The line reaches the _____ corner.

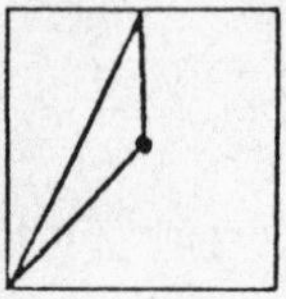

It is possible to describe the drawing of the line in two ways:

a. The line starts from the _____ of the square; reaches the _____ of the _____ side, and continues from there to the _____ _____ corner, returning to the _____ _____.

b. The starting point of the line is in the _____ of the square. The line reaches the _____ _____ corner, and continues from there to the _____ of the upper side, returning back to the _____ _____ .

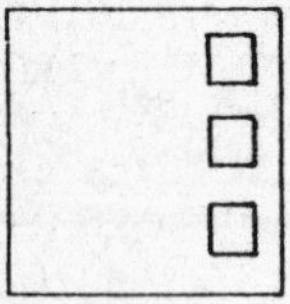

Draw a line which starts from the upper left corner. The line will cross between the upper and middle squares, and touch the middle of the right side. From there, the line should pass between the bottom and middle squares and reach the lower left corner.

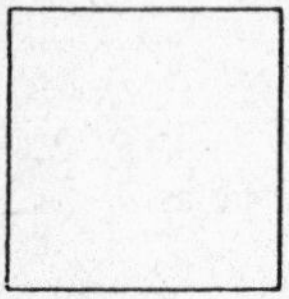

The centre of the square will be the starting point of three lines:

1. To the middle of the upper side.
2. To the lower left corner.
3. To the lower right corner.

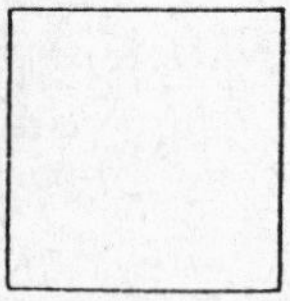

Draw a line which passes through the centre of the square. The line should start from a corner and end at a corner. Describe the line you have drawn.
_____

_____

Fig 43   Instructions (from Feuerstein, 1976).

Fill in the blanks.

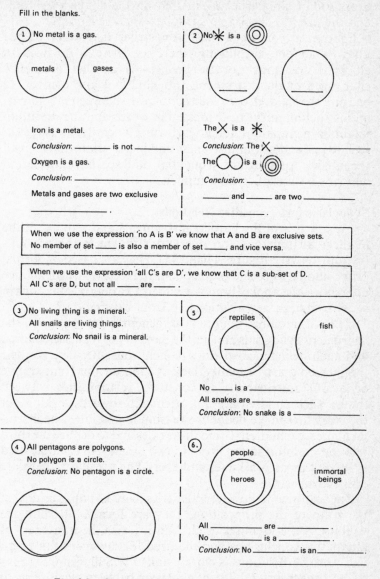

1 No metal is a gas.

metals   gases

Iron is a metal.

Conclusion: _____ is not _____ .

Oxygen is a gas.

Conclusion: _____

Metals and gases are two exclusive

_____ .

2 No ✳ is a ◎

The ✕ is a ✳

Conclusion: The ✕ _____

The ◯◯ is a ◎

Conclusion: _____

_____ and _____ are two _____

_____ .

When we use the expression 'no A is B' we know that A and B are exclusive sets.
No member of set _____ is also a member of set _____, and vice versa.

When we use the expression 'all C's are D', we know that C is a sub-set of D.
All C's are D, but not all _____ are _____ .

3 No living thing is a mineral.
All snails are living things.
Conclusion: No snail is a mineral.

5 reptiles   fish

No _____ is a _____ .
All snakes are _____ .
Conclusion: No snake is a _____ .

4 All pentagons are polygons.
No polygon is a circle.
Conclusion: No pentagon is a circle.

6. people / heroes   immortal beings

All _____ are _____ .
No _____ is a _____ .
Conclusion: No _____ is an _____ .

Fig 44   Syllogisms (from Feuerstein, 1976).

sequence their actions might cause children to fail in the execution of an instruction, or they also might lack the tools and the need to check their progress and their product.

Egocentric communication—the belief that other people know what one is thinking, therefore there is no need to elucidate too much or be precise—is another deficiency challenged by the instrument. Inflexibility is also confronted because the children are required to move between modalities; an instruction might be expressed in words and the execution might be in graphic or numerical form. Generally, the exercises seek to undermine impulsiveness and imprecision, and to instil the ability to integrate sequential and spatial information which is both explicit and implicit.

Syllogisms and Transitive Relations

These are two of the hardest instruments and require all the intellectual functions and operations taught in the previous instruments (see Figures 44 and 45). They are based on formal propositional logic and require children to carry out deductive inference—the application of a rule to a variety of situations in order to infer a new relationship from existing ones.

Since it requires children to generate information, the instrument Syllogisms attacks the passivity of retarded children and their reluctance to draw conclusions. Because of their fragmented grasp of reality, lack of spontaneous comparative behaviour and inability to construct relationships between things, such children are not orientated towards seeking out the rules that make deductive reasoning possible. The instrument presses children to find these rules and to deduce the third relation on information given in two others. An example used is: 'Every razor is a knife, and every knife is sharp, therefore every razor is . . . ?'

The instrument, however, also tries to make pupils critical of the truth of the propositions they are formulating and the validity of the premises used. And it trains the awareness of alternative conclusions and the need for divergent thinking.

Transitive Relations is closely linked to Syllogisms. Transitivity is the transferability of a relation between two objects or terms to a third. 'If A is smaller than B and B = C, then C is . . . than A.'

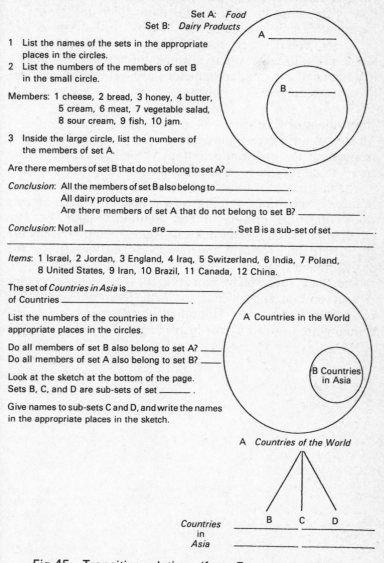

Set A: *Food*
Set B: *Dairy Products*

1 List the names of the sets in the appropriate
 places in the circles.
2 List the numbers of the members of set B
 in the small circle.

Members: 1 cheese, 2 bread, 3 honey, 4 butter,
 5 cream, 6 meat, 7 vegetable salad,
 8 sour cream, 9 fish, 10 jam.

3 Inside the large circle, list the numbers of
 the members of set A.

Are there members of set B that do not belong to set A? _____.

Conclusion: All the members of set B also belong to _____.
 All dairy products are _____.
 Are there members of set A that do not belong to set B? _____.

Conclusion: Not all _____ are _____. Set B is a sub-set of set _____.

Items: 1 Israel, 2 Jordan, 3 England, 4 Iraq, 5 Switzerland, 6 India, 7 Poland,
 8 United States, 9 Iran, 10 Brazil, 11 Canada, 12 China.

The set of *Countries in Asia* is _____
of Countries _____ .

List the numbers of the countries in the
appropriate places in the circles.

Do all members of set B also belong to set A? _____
Do all members of set A also belong to set B? _____

Look at the sketch at the bottom of the page.
Sets B, C, and D are sub-sets of set _____ .

Give names to sub-sets C and D, and write the names
in the appropriate places in the sketch.

A Countries in the World

B Countries
in Asia

A *Countries of the World*

Countries
in
Asia

B C D

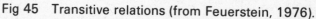

Fig 45 Transitive relations (from Feuerstein, 1976).

To execute the problems in Transitive Relations successfully, children must be precise in their perception and gathering of data, they must be able to use more than one source of information simultaneously and be able to understand and apply sequential order, spatial relations and directionality. Other crucial skills taught through the instrument include hypothetical thinking, comparisons and categorisations and accurate definition of problems.

Illustrations or Cartoons

This instrument (see Figure 46) is used partly as light relief throughout the programme but, as you might expect, it also trains some very important cognitive functions.

The instrument is full of cartoons which present a series of humorous situations leading to a crisis. This crisis and its causes must be recognised and solutions found. Because children must follow and link one frame to another they are required to think logically and to explain cause and effect as the story line unravels.

They must spot which elements in the frames change, which remain constant, and which factors in the frames are responsible for the transformations. Hypothetical, analogical and logical thinking are instilled by the instrument.

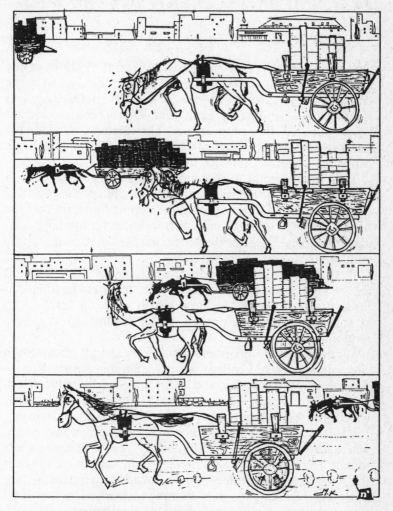

Fig 46   Cartoons (from Feuerstein, 1973).

TRAINING AND EVALUATING TEACHERS

One of the most common, almost universal, findings of the international trials of Instrumental Enrichment has been the enthusiasm of teachers for the new skills of teaching and insights into learning that it can offer. This is not an accidental by-product of the programme. The theory of Mediated Learning provides theoretical underpinning for a rigorous, one could say scientific, practice of teaching.

The Instrumental Enrichment exercises are at once a structured and progressive attack on children's cognitive deficiences, and a series of organised opportunities for the type of teacher-pupil interactions which will transfer thinking skills and principles. Without the latter, the former does not apply with anything like the same effect.

Be they professional or non-professional teachers, it is vital for the instructors of Instrumental Enrichment to be trained in mediational styles of teaching, which need, in turn, to be established upon a thorough understanding of cognitive modifiability.

Within Israel the theory and practice are already integrated in some university and college teacher-training courses. For in-service training Feuerstein and his colleagues, Mildred Hoffman and Yaacov Rand, have developed a training programme which they have attempted to see replicated in other countries. It is based on an initial workshop of a minimum of two weeks, where the theory and approximately four instruments are taught, followed by up to five week-long workshops to cover the rest of the programme. A special workshop is provided for those experienced enough to become trainers of Instrumental Enrichment teachers. For all those teachers beginning to teach for the first time, there is regular in-class supervision and collective discussion meetings, plus careful evaluation of each teacher's prowess.

One of the interesting and surprising aspects of this

supervision and evaluation is how positively it is viewed by teachers. This is confirmed in the reports of every one of the research projects quoted in the next section. It stands in sharp contrast to the anxiety and resentment occasioned by the normal supervision of student and probationary-year teachers.

Traditionally, students and probationers are required to perform for their supervisors who sit in passive judgement at the back of the class. They are supposed to have acquired a methodology for teaching their subjects at college, and this, together with their personality and vocation, is assumed to be able to train them to control and teach children a syllabus. Yet the inadequacy of teacher-training courses in giving teachers the basic teaching skills is legendary, and this failure is premised partly on the assumption that teaching ability, like intelligence, is something that you either have, or have not, got. The emphasis is, therefore, on straightforward academic knowledge of the chosen subjects for teaching, with a little academic theory on child development and behaviour which is largely inapplicable to day-to-day teaching.

In Instrumental Enrichment training a supervisor, who is an experienced practitioner, works with the class and the teacher on the instruments and helps in the difficult, very rigorous business of preparing a lesson. (Team teaching is in any case used in many Instrumental Enrichment classes in Israel, particularly for organically handicapped children.) Rather than a superior sitting in judgement, there is an assumption that teaching Instrumental Enrichment involves difficult skills which must be shared between experienced and inexperienced staff. After all, it is one thing to be told how an Instrumental Enrichment task can strengthen a cognitive deficiency and another to find the right questions and examples to guide children into carrying out the skill or operation on their own, or to bring them to the point of intellectual vigilance where they are highly receptive to acquiring a principle from a teacher.

Interaction is the key concept—teaching by invoking comparisons, by requesting more sophisticated categorisations, by eliciting precise discrimination. It is through interesting and involving children by using their own responses, even when wrong, to draw out cognitive principles or strategies, and by bridging to areas of life they know well and which can expose the need for certain intellectual principles and approaches, that certain intellectual operations become habitual.

Feuerstein points out that good teachers already do much of this in class intuitively. But whereas a good teacher's interactions might stimulate the class and keep them involved, the teacher might not be directed to mediating the precise cognitive skills and operations which the children need. A lack of theory and training about cognitive functions and the common deficiencies manifested in children inevitably make the interactions less intentional and focused.

Also, in academic subject teaching, content tends traditionally to dominate the conveyance to children of the cognitive prerequisites that they need to understand and manipulate the information they are being taught. Feuerstein maintains that it might be too much for the teacher, under pressure to clear a syllabus, to keep one eye on the content of a lesson and, at the same time, use the lesson to rectify some of the children's cognitive shortcomings. That is if the teacher is disposed to think of his pupils in that manner, rather than in fixed 'level of ability' terms, and has the knowledge to interpret what the children's cognitive problems are.

The repertoire of interactions, even for the excellent instinctive teacher, might also be restricted—certainly the attitudes of teachers involved in experimental projects suggest the ways of relating to children, and the ability to stimulate and create different types of thinking through such interactions, has been greatly enriched. And one should not forget that not all teachers are good at the intuitive level and (often in contrast to their personal values) their style is sterile and authoritarian —one of dispensing knowledge.

Moshe Egozi, one of Feuerstein's colleagues at the Hadassah Wizo Institute, responsible for the implementation of the Instrumental Enrichment programme into Israel's state schools, uses a system of teacher evaluation based on the various types of interaction which qualify as Mediated Learning Experiences. (*See end of this chapter for evaluation scheme.*)

Although designed for the Instrumental Enrichment programme, the evaluation system's theoretical basis is that of mediated learning as a whole and not just of Instrumental Enrichment. As previously stated, Feuerstein insists that

Instrumental Enrichment is only one operationalisation—to use an ugly word—of the theory, and that there are many other ways of mediating to children. If the theory of Mediated Learning Experiences were to become more widely accepted, Moshe Egozi's teacher evaluation system could become a widely used measure of teachers' skills. It is, of course, a form of evaluation which is not at all dependent on children's current levels of ability and achievement.

Teachers' subjective enthusiasm for the skills Instrumental Enrichment can proffer has been confirmed in a study carried out in the USA, by Dr David S. Martin, of the Gallaudet College for Deaf Children in Washington DC. He found that 14 experienced teachers improved their teaching skills considerably after being trained for six days in Instrumental Enrichment.

The 14 teachers and a control group were assessed before and after training by independent supervisors, using a standard USA rating form which lists 12 different categories of teaching behaviours, such as 'Communicating' and 'Facilitating', each with its set of performance indicators. A number of categories were selected because they were thought to be most relevant in assessing changes resulting from a cognitive improvement programme like Instrumental Enrichment. They were:

COMMUNICATION. Considering students' comments and suggestions. Giving directions in a clear concise manner.
FACILITATING. Using strategies which involve the students in high level thinking. Using strategies which involve students in decision making. Phrasing questions to encourage students to respond appropriately.
PRESCRIBING. Making teaching decisions based on evaluation of students. Accepting and using students' feedback in planning instruction.
EVALUATION OF STUDENTS. Identifying the reasons why students have or have not met objectives.

A specially developed Teacher Self-Rating Scale was also used to assess any perceived changes in teachers' approaches to planning and solving problems which are involved in day-to-day teaching.

The results are very interesting because the supervisor's ratings show significant improvements in the Instrumental

Enrichment teachers in all but one of the indicators, while the control group only fared better in two of the indicators—the giving of clear and concise directions and the phrasing of questions. Moreover, this improvement tallied with the Instrumental Enrichment teachers' own self-reported perceptions of the changes in their approach and skill.

Those indicators which related to efforts to improve students' thinking skills, such as considering students' comments and phrasing of questions to encourage appropriate responses, showed much greater gains for Instrumental Enrichment than control group teachers. This corroborates the findings of Orme and Wakesman from the Toronto-based Ontario Institute (in 1977 and 1978) that teachers trained in Instrumental Enrichment were found to have developed a much better use of probing questions in classroom discussions.

Instrumental Enrichment teachers performed significantly better on deploying strategies to involve students in higher-level thinking and involving students in decision-making. Martin claims this stems from the pervasive method of 'discussion for insight', which is such an important part of Instrumental Enrichment. Also, the basic awareness of cognitive development should enable teachers to move students on to increasingly higher levels of thinking.

Improvements in teaching skills are directly related to the requirement in Instrumental Enrichment to give clear, precise and increasingly complex directions. The greater ability to identify reasons why students have, or have not, met objectives can be linked, says Martin, to the requirement in the Instrumental Enrichment training to practise analysis as a skill. This, however, has to be set against the inability of teachers to improve their evaluation of students' deeper cognitive problems, or to change their teaching for individuals to any great extent. It suggests that the teachers had not been given an adequate grounding in the theory underlying Instrumental Enrichment and in the theory and practice of the Learning Potential Assessment Device to diagnose learning blockages in depth in individual children, and target the remediation accordingly.

The study is important not so much for its 'scientific' findings—the sample was small and the Instrumental Enrichment teachers were particularly interested in the programme and in self-improvement, which could colour the results—but in the fact that it confirms the views of teachers who have worked on the experimental programmes around the world. The introduction to Instrumental Enrichment is the first time many teachers come into contact with a theory and a method that can give them an understanding of the development of children's thinking, a diagnostic tool and a theorised style and practice of teaching.

In a report on the training of teachers for Instrumental Enrichment by Ruth Arbitman–Smith of Vanderbilt University in Tennessee, a teacher is quoted as saying after a training workshop: 'The most interesting experience since I became a teacher'. This is quite a common reaction, she notes:

> Most teachers' reactions to the workshops have been very positive . . . Many teachers who have gone through numerous workshops and have completed their training in all the instruments keep coming back to workshops. Sometimes they are repeating the training they received but they state, nevertheless, that they continuously learn new aspects of the programme and improve their understanding of it.

But the staff at Vanderbilt University found that not all teachers are capable of learning how to teach Instrumental Enrichment. Teachers who see their goals as 'making learning a positive experience, who encourage original thinking, who develop positive self-regard, who emphasise co–operation, who have respect for divergent thinking and who have few disciplinary problems, tend to be more successful in teaching the Instrumental Enrichment programme.' Such teachers also score well on the Minnesota Teacher Attitude Inventory. There is a correlation between poor Instrumental Enrichment teachers and those who score low on the Minnesota Inventory.

Teachers who found it uncomfortable to work in such an unconventional classroom atmosphere of intellectual collaboration between pupils and teachers, and students (with the latter prepared to defend their opinions) often failed to implement the programme after training and also tended to score poorly on the Inventory. Instrumental Enrichment lessons require a lot of preparation and those teachers unable to find time for this and who were, therefore, forced to spend much of the lesson actually working out the problems on the worksheets, also tended to be unable to master the programme. Because such teachers reduced the amount of time in a lesson left for discussion, Ruth Arbitman-Smith said they,

> deprive their students of possibly the most important part of the lesson—the mediational aspect. It is through the discussion of how the problems should be solved, and through the generalisation from the exercises to new situations, that students develop awareness of the cognitive processes they need and how to use them efficiently.

The training programme outlined by Feuerstein and Hoffman cannot be curtailed, even for experienced teachers, she reports. Indeed, one of the lessons the organisers of the project said they had painfully learnt while teaching Instrumental Enrichment was not to assume any level of classroom skill in teachers.

> We initially offered very little training in actual didactical issues, such as questioning styles, how to structure a lesson, and how to get students actively involved in discussions. We have found over the years that teachers appreciated such teaching. It is quite obvious that our assumption that all these issues were well familiar with experienced teachers was erroneous. Whereas some teachers have acquired such didactic skills over the years, many others grope for them and are thankful for the opportunities to improve in their general teaching skills.

Ruth Arbitman-Smith reports that training colleges in the States emphasise behaviour-modification approaches when it comes to teaching children with special needs, and this assumes low levels of ability and requires low expectations.

> In order to teach Instrumental Enrichment many teachers need to modify their expectations as to what levels students may reach in their development, and have to learn new and quite different techniques by which to teach their students. Our accumulated experience suggests that many teachers felt ill-prepared for such an approach to

teaching, but are willing to modify their own behaviour and expectations.

QUESTIONNAIRE ON MEDIATIONAL ACTIVITIES OF TEACHERS
Directions for Completing the Questionnaire

You will find it difficult to complete the questionnaire on mediational activities in classroom situations while observing the actual lesson. You are asked therefore to take detailed notes during the course of the lesson, and to fill out the questionnaire immediately after the lesson, relying on your fresh impressions and your notes (please attach notes to the questionnaire).

Coding:
Rate each activity in main questionnaire according to the following code:
  0 = No opportunity for activity in the lesson
  X = Missed opportunity for activity in the lesson
  – = Activity in contradiction to given Mediated Learning Experience activity
  1 = Infrequent use of activity
  2 = Some use of activity
  3 = Frequent use of activity

Summary of answers

Criteria	Rating	0	X	–	1	2	3	Row/Total
1								
2								
3								
4								
5								
6								
7								
8								
9								
10								
Column Total								

QUESTIONNAIRE ON MEDIATED LEARNING
ACTIVITIES IN THE CLASSROOM
(items are organised by main criterion of Mediated Learning Experience related to activity)

1   INTENTIONALITY AND RECIPROCITY
   a) The teacher arrives in time for lesson and is ready to stay on after it, when necessary
   b) The teacher comes well prepared
   c) The classroom is well organised
   d) Recent students' work is exhibited on the walls
   e) The teacher establishes and maintains an atmosphere of learning
   f) The teacher arouses students' interest and motivation in subject matter
   g) The students listen and respond to the teacher
   h) The teacher invests time in checking students' work
   i) The teacher reveals his interest in the students and their work
   j) The teacher reveals his pleasure when students succeed and make progress
   k) The teacher is ready to explain again when something is not understood
   l) The teacher takes special interest in slow learners and passive students

2   TRANSCENDENCE
   a) The teacher connects the subject of the lesson to previous or future subjects
   b) The teacher reveals the relationship between subject-matter and general goals
   c) The teacher selects subject-matter according to structural importance for following stages
   d) The teacher ensures proficiency of students in basic skills and working habits beyond present needs
   e) The teacher prefers 'why' and 'how' questions to 'who' and 'what' questions
   f) The teacher explains the reasons for his actions and decisions
   g) The teacher asks the students for rational explanations of their answers and behaviour

h)   The teacher teaches facts, concepts, principles and relationships, beyond the needs of the present situation
i)   The teacher fosters use of higher cognitive operations (representation, categorisation, etc.)
j)   The teacher fosters problem-defining and problem-solving activities

3   THE MEDIATION OF MEANING
The teacher enhances the importance or value of certain subjects by:
a)   Transformation of stimuli (selection, framing, changing frequency and/or intensity)
b)   Changes in his own behaviour (positive, facial expression, level and inflection of voice, etc.)
c)   Giving positive or negative feedback to certain student behaviours or responses
d)   Causing changes in classroom atmosphere and students' behaviour (anticipatory behaviour)
e)   Conveying explicitly the importance or value of certain subjects to students
f)   Implicit, hidden cues to the students ('the hidden curriculum')

4   THE MEDIATION OF FEELING OF COMPETENCE
The teacher arranges opportunities for success for students through:
a)   Transformation of stimuli according to their level of competence: Selection of appropriate material, restructuring, division into easy stages, simplification, addition of cues, slowing down, repetition
b)   Phrasing questions according to students' level of competence
c)   The teacher interprets to the student the meaning of his success, using standards relative to his level of competence
d)   The teacher makes the student aware of his progress

5   MEDIATED REGULATION AND CONTROL OF BEHAVIOUR
The teacher makes students aware of their need and ability to adjust their investment of time and effort to the

complexity of the tasks and the circumstances through:
a) Restraining impulsiveness of students:
    1) Asking them to concentrate on a certain subject
    2) To reread a certain paragraph
    3) To think before answering
    4) To check own work
b) Planning work according to priorities
c) The teacher demands orderly and organized work from students
d) The teacher demands orderly appearance and behaviour in classroom
e) The teacher models regulated and controlled behaviour, through
    1) Not interrupting students' answers
    2) Reflecting before answering
    3) Admitting own impulsiveness as reason for mistake
    4) Structuring lesson and using blackboard in an orderly fashion
    5) His own appearance and behaviour

6 MEDIATED SHARING BEHAVIOUR
a) The teacher models sharing behaviour—relates his experiences as child or at home to students
b) The teacher encourages students to share their experiences with others
c) The teacher encourages students to help each other
d) The teacher encourages students to listen to each other
e) The teacher fosters empathy of students to feeling of others
f) The teacher arranges opportunities for group activities
g) The teacher applies group-teaching methods
h) The teacher selects subject-matter which emphasises importance of co-operation

7 MEDIATION OF INDIVIDUATION AND PSYCHOLOGICAL DIFFERENTIATION
a) The teacher is ready to accept divergent responses
b) The teacher encourages independent and original thinking and activity

c) The teacher holds the students responsible for their behaviour
d) The teacher distributes responsible tasks to students
e) The teacher encourages self-government of students
f) The teacher lets students choose part of their classroom activities
g) The teacher enhances positive aspects of cultural pluralism
h) The teacher encourages diversity in students' use of free time
i) The teacher maintains the right of a student to be different
j) The teacher gives opportunity for individual work
k) The teacher refrains from insulting the students
l) The teacher respects the students' right for privacy in certain areas
m) The teacher demands from the students to respect his own right for privacy
n) The teacher refrains from asking for total identification with his values and beliefs
o) The teacher refrains from asking for total obedience to him

8   MEDIATION FOR GOAL-SEEKING, GOAL SETTING, PLANNING AND GOAL-ACHIEVING BEHAVIOUR

a) The teacher models goal-directed behaviour: setting clear goals for each lesson and for learning in general
b) The teacher persists in his efforts to achieve his goal
c) The teacher demands from the students an effort to attain the goals set for them
d) The teacher encourages perseverance, patience and diligence in pursuit of goals
e) The teacher fosters need and ability of students to set realistic goals for themselves
f) The teacher fosters need and ability of students to plan how to achieve their goals
g) The teacher fosters need and ability of students to review and modify goals according to changing needs and circumstances

h)   The teacher fosters an autonomous attitude of the students for their future and destiny

9   THE MEDIATION FOR CHALLENGE: THE SEARCH FOR NOVELTY AND COMPLEXITY
a)   The teacher makes available to the students challenging, novel and complex situations in accordance with their competence
b)   The teacher encourages intellectual curiosity
c)   The teacher encourages originality and creativity
d)   The teacher imposes unconventional tasks on students
e)   The teacher encourages students to create their own exercises and to present them to the class
f)   The teacher makes the students aware of the feeling of satisfaction on completing a novel and complex task
g)   The teacher presents to students models of excellence in confrontation with challenging, novel and complex situations (scientists)
h)   The teacher encourages students to initiate discussion

10   COGNITIVE FUNCTIONS NOT MENTIONED ELSEWHERE
a)   The teacher fosters sharp and discriminatory perception
b)   The teacher fosters the need for accuracy and precision in gathering information, processing information and communicating information
c)   The teacher teaches methods of data collection and data organisation
d)   The teacher fosters the ability and need to deal at the same time with several sources of information
e)   The teacher fosters the ability to discriminate between relevant and irrelevant information
f)   The teacher fosters summative behaviour
g)   The teacher fosters the need and use of logical evidence in arguments and conclusions
h)   The teacher imparts to the students strategies for hypothesis-testing.

The above questionnaire © Moshe Egozi.
Reprinted by permission.

PART 3:

INTERNATIONAL RESULTS

A QUESTION OF INTERPRETATION

A vast amount of research has been undertaken on Instrumental Enrichment and on the Learning Potential Assessment Device in North and South America, Europe and Israel, virtually all of it producing evidence to support most of the claims made for Instrumental Enrichment. In the researches on specific populations, such as the deaf and the prison populations of the Canadian penitentiary system, the result appears to offer striking new opportunities for advance.

But the transfer of Feuerstein's work from Israel to foreign countries has been fraught with problems of interpretation and implementation, nowhere more so than in Britain, as we shall see. Because of these obstacles, much of the research on Instrumental Enrichment in particular is viewed as partial or unsatisfactory by the Hadassah Wizo Institute in Jerusalem.

In the majority of cases the research has been carried out on unstable sample groups of children over too short a period to include all the 15 or so instruments for the two-to-three year course. Between two-to-three hours of Instrumental Enrichment instruction is thought by Feuerstein to be the minimum requirement to effect substantial and visible changes in children.

Teacher training, particularly in theoretical aspects of Feuerstein's work, such as the rôle of inadequate Mediated Learning Experiences in producing cognitive deficiencies and the use of the Cognitive Map for analysing individual children's responses, has often been inadequate or completely absent. Consequently teachers on experimental Instrumental Enrichment programmes have often not fully appreciated the importance of their own mediating rôle and simply used the instruments as simple exercises to be ploughed through as quickly as possible. Using the cognitive principles of the exercises to 'bridge' to other areas of life and school work disappears with this type of approach to the material.

In the British case it is quite clear, in my view, that many teachers not only lacked any real grasp of the theory involved, but were reluctantly dragooned into the programme, often in schools which did not seem willing to put themselves to any trouble to fit enough Instrumental Enrichment classes into timetables.

Since the rôle of teachers is crucial in producing substitute mediated learning experiences through the Instrumental Enrichment exercises, teacher indifference or ignorance is bound to have very damaging effects. It is hard to see how a teacher who does not believe in cultural deprivation or the hidden potential of pupils can use the programme to any advantage. Almost by definition, and certainly by design, Instrumental Enrichment is not teacher-proof.

The tendency of traditionally-trained teachers to reduce Instrumental Enrichment to simple exercises is, one suspects, a major problem for any research project, even in Israel. To teach the programme properly requires a change in objectives —the process rather than the product becomes more important —and also in style because the programme relies on continual interactions between teacher and class and between the pupils in the same class: the teacher becomes a guide (albeit a very forceful one) and a participant in problem-solving rather than a donor of knowledge.

Any natural proclivities among British teachers towards a technical reduction of the programme to 'a worksheet job' has been strengthened by Feuerstein's use of a commercial dissemination company to carry out the teacher-training in Instrumental Enrichment in Britain. Feuerstein refuses to take any money for seeing individual children at his Institute, which is entirely funded by voluntary subscription and fees from training workshops and Instrumental Enrichment materials.

Not unnaturally, the American company which has the dissemination rights on Instrumental Enrichment for Europe —handled with acknowledged skill by its chief agent in Britain—has organised the training in accordance with practical business requirements.

Some teachers and educationalists, however, found that there were more instruments covered in the workshops than they could assimilate, and they would have welcomed more time to examine the theoretical basis. They would also have liked some discussion and practice of the Learning Potential Assessment Device which is responsible for providing an important ideological challenge to prevailing views about intelligence and for giving teachers a diagnostic insight into children's thinking problems.

The degree and importance of the ideological shift in Feuerstein's theoretical and technical work seems to have been underestimated, too, by many researchers when designing their research projects. Inadequate teacher-training is one sign of this, but another is the interpretation of results. In a research project involving three USA universities, very significant results were found in children with socially determined learning disabilities. In the write-up of the research, however, this was rather down-played in relation to the less satisfactory results with mentally handicapped children who 'only' benefited from a much more protracted and intensive Instrumental Enrichment programme.

These comments suggest the researchers had failed to distinguish between children who were merely educationally retarded, due to cultural deprivation, and those who suffered from fundamental mental handicaps—a crucial demarcation in Feuerstein's theories. In fact this failure to make such a demarcation is a common and tragic conflation in the West caused by the simplistic view that low intelligence is low intelligence, whatever the origins.

Actually, Feuerstein insists that Instrumental Enrichment is much more immediately effective with children retarded through social factors, and they are the main target group for the programme. Handicapped children require much more intensive investment to overcome the deficits caused by organic damage.

Yet despite the immense problems of transferring Instrumental Enrichment across countries and cultures (which, incidentally, are common to all new educational innovations) the research results remain remarkably positive and exciting. Although questions remain, the three long-term studies of Instrumental Enrichment carried out by Feuerstein and his colleagues in Israel, one in Venezuela (unfortunately not yet available in English) and Mogens Jensen's project in the USA, all show evidence that Instrumental Enrichment can produce structural cognitive changes in low-performing school children.

THE ISRAELI STUDIES

In one vitally important respect Israel offers a unique opportunity for the study of the long-term effects of Instrumental Enrichment. Universal military conscription means that all children who have undertaken the programme can be re-tested and compared with other groups by a completely independent authority, using tests applied for its own purposes.

The original research report was published in 1977 and describes the achievements of a group of 218 children, aged between 12 and 14 years, who were on the border-line or actually classified as having 'educable mental retardation' and were three to four years behind their school peers.

The sample was split into two halves: those who were given Instrumental Enrichment and those who were given a programme of General Enrichment consisting of extra tuition in school subjects. Both of these groups were divided equally into students from residential settings and those who learned in day centres in their own towns.

The Instrumental Enrichment programme lasted for two years. The Instrumental Enrichment group was given tuition five days a week for one hour a day as part of their school curriculum. An equivalent, if not greater amount of time, was given in additional tuition in ordinary school groups for the General Enrichment group.

Tests were administered to the groups at the beginning, middle and end of the period, and were followed up two years after the programme ended with tests by the Army. The Instrumental Enrichment groups achieved higher scores on Thurstone's Primary Mental Abilities Tests than the General Enrichment groups. There was some slight evidence to support the view that children in residential care did better than those in day centres, although this lead disappeared in the follow-up.

Included in the Primary Mental Abilities Tests are separate

scores for verbal, numerical and spatial relations, reasoning, perceptual speed and an overall score from which an estimate of 'tested intelligence' can be made. On this total score the Instrumental Enrichment group enjoyed 'significantly greater' gains than did the General Enrichment children at the same sites. If, as Thurstone claimed, his tests were equivalent to intelligence, then the children given Instrumental Enrichment seemed to acquire a deal more intelligence during the two years.

In the eight separate scores in the Primary Mental Abilities Tests the Instrumental Enrichment group, after completion of the programme, fared better on numerical and spatial relations and figure groups. In addition to seeing whether cognitive abilities would improve, the researchers wanted to know if basic educational skills were more developed as a result of Instrumental Enrichment. So a special battery of 12 tests was compiled on general knowledge, nature study, antonyms, the Bible, geography, part-whole, geometry, reading, comprehension, addition, subtraction, multiplication and division.

The children were also tested before and after the Instrumental Enrichment programme with the Classroom Participation Scale which measures non-intellectual aspects of personality characteristics and behaviour in class.

On ordinary school subjects the Instrumental Enrichment group maintained an equality on most subjects and outperformed the General Enrichment group on geography and the Bible. This was despite the latter children being given extra instruction in mainstream curricula subjects and the Instrumental Enrichment group losing time from such conventional schooling to fit in two-to-three hours of Instrumental Enrichment. This suggests the transfer of skills to areas not touched upon by the Instrumental Enrichment exercises.

It is an important part of the claims for Instrumental Enrichment that it enables children to assert much more cognitive control over their behaviour in relation to schoolwork and towards their peers. Poor motivation, unthinking impulsiveness and the inability to recognise another point of view, are as harmful in personal relationships as they are in academic work.

Such claims were strikingly borne out by the results from

the Classroom Participation Scale. The children given Instrumental Enrichment made better gains than the control group in the following areas: interaction with classmates, deportment in class, level of disruptive behaviour, willingness to take turns, ability to start and finish work independently as well as under supervision, persistence, pride in work, efficiency in moving from one type of work to another, helping other children, caring and sharing school materials, taking pride in schoolwork and co-operative working.

In one important test, however, Instrumental Enrichment produced no improvement. Despite all the other gains, a test to show changes in self-image registered no change—bearing out Feuerstein's belief that poor self-image is the most difficult product of inadequate mediated learning experience to rectify.

The results of the study on the use of Instrumental Enrichment in different educational settings surprised the research team. They had believed that residential pupils would benefit more from Instrumental Enrichment because the intervention was administered in a 'total care' environment rather than through the relatively limited contact of a day centre. But, in fact, there were only very slight gains for children in the residential Instrumental Enrichment group in cognitive abilities and less favourable results in some conventional school subjects. Residential pupils also scored less on the part of the Class Participation Scale which measured unsocialised behaviour. Apparently they were more depressed, withdrawn, hypersensitive and shy than their counterparts from the day centres.

What astonished everyone outside the programme was the extent of the changes in the students when they were re-tested by the Army two years later. The Army test (called Dapar) showed that the better performance of the Instrumental Enrichment group was maintained and increased! The effects of intervention programmes usually diminish over time: in the case of Instrumental Enrichment, however, effects were more pronounced over time. The students' improved cognitive abilities appeared to have enabled them to learn and become modified by exposure to direct experience. As a result of this they were able continually to expand their intellectual organisation of experience.

This had been one of the hypotheses of the research programme because the theory of structural modification states that cognitive changes provide the intellectual infrastructure for children to acquire skills to think in increasingly elaborate ways. Even so, the results from the Army tests proved far more conclusive than Feuerstein and his colleagues had hoped.

As we have seen, there had been three sets of scores taken over the course of the experimental programme and so the Army results made a total of four sets of figures taken at various intervals. The original pre-test scores, taken before the start of the programme were used as the basis for analysis of the scores from the Dapar and Primary Mental Abilities Tests, and the changes over time were plotted on a graph. This clearly established that the process of change becomes self-propelled. Once in place, the child's cognitive system becomes more efficient, their scope for learning becomes larger and the level of their functioning develops at a higher rate.

At two points in the research the Instrumental Enrichment and General Enrichment students were also divided into two further groups of relatively high– and low-performers: at the beginning of instruction and again after the two-year follow-up tests by the Army. It was found that 46 per cent of the original low-performers in the Instrumental Enrichment group moved across the median line of average ability in the Army tests in comparison with only 13 per cent of the General Enrichment group. From the lowest part of an already low-performing category of children, this group had moved to an above-average position in the whole Army population, and were now offered a chance to break the cycle of cultural deprivation. Test scores are used by the Army to allocate duties to soldiers, and those with the more complex duties automatically become better placed in the job market after military service.

Of the relatively high-performers in the Instrumental Enrichment group, 88 per cent crossed the Dapar median line and were, therefore, considered by the Army to be of above-average ability. However, only 53 per cent of the original high-performing General Enrichment group made it into this category. This, suggests Feuerstein and his colleagues, is a little alarming since it implies that without intervention there is a likelihood of further subsequent deterioration in cognitively low-functioning individuals.

FEUERSTEIN and RAND. *Redevelopment of Cognitive Functions of Retarded Early Adolescents. Instrumental Enrichment.* Hadassah Wizo Canada Research Institute, 1977.

RAND, MINTZKER, MILLER, HOFFMAN, FRIEDLANDER. 'The Instrumental Enrichment Programme Immediate and Long Term Effects'. In: P. MITTLER (Ed), *Frontiers of Knowledge in Mental Retardation.* Vol 1. University Park Press, Baltimore, 1981, pp, 141–152.

RAND, TANNENBAUM, FEUERSTEIN. 'The Effects of Instrumental Enrichment on the Psycho Educational Development of Low Functioning Adolescents'. In: *Journal of Educational Psychology.* 1979, pp, 71–75.

YALE UNIVERSITY COGNITIVE MODIFIABILITY PROJECT

The Yale Project, directed by Mogens Jensen, represents the largest and most elaborate long-term study to have taken place outside Israel. It has involved the careful, extended training of both teachers and psychologists in Instrumental Enrichment and the accompanying theories, and great care has been taken to match students in the experimental project with those in control groups, according to age, sex, ethnicity and level of functioning. Moreover, the number of student participants was very large, 275 in the experimental group and 174 in the control group.

In addition to full-length Instrumental Enrichment workshops, the 32 participating teachers in Hartford and New Haven education authorities were given field coaching and follow-up sessions in Instrumental Enrichment teaching. Before the children were started on the Instrumental Enrichment programme, all were measured on the Raven's Standard Progressive Matrices, Primary Mental Abilities and WISC-R (the Wechsler Intelligence Scale for Children). After two years a sample of students was tested in an attempt to provide early documentation on the efficacy of the Instrumental Enrichment programme and some highly-significant results emerged.

The effects of Instrumental Enrichment were assessed in both intellectual and non-intellectual measure. The first measures were divided into three: 'acquisition' of cognitive skills; 'near transfer', meaning the ability to complete similar but previously untried tasks; and 'far transfer', meaning the ability to complete tasks completely unlike those already attempted during the Instrumental Enrichment programme.

The object was to assess whether the cognitive skills acquired during Instrumental Enrichment could be used creatively by students to solve problems that became less and less familiar. Such things as motivation and self-concept—the non-intellectual measures—were also assessed with the Piers Harris Self-

Concept Scale and the Haywood Mazes (designed to test children's intrinsic motivation).

Results were analysed separately for children who had one year or less of Instrumental Enrichment and those who had one year or more of Instrumental Enrichment. It was found that for children given the Instrumental Enrichment programme for less than a year there were significant differences in their favour from children in the control group, in terms of 'acquisition' and 'near transfer' of cognitive skills. But no differences for 'far transfer'.

However, the situation changed dramatically when the effects of Instrumental Enrichment were measured on those children who had been given the programme for more than a year. Statistically very significant differences were found in the 'far transfer' measure in favour of Instrumental Enrichment children. Additionally, the differences in individually compared cases were quite large. Those students with a year or less of Instrumental Enrichment had a half standard deviation difference from control group students, while those with more than a year had a full standard deviation difference. In psychological terms this represents a considerable advance.

On the non-intellectual measures the data indicated a tendency for experimental Instrumental Enrichment subjects to exhibit more intrinsic motivation in their work and both statistically significant and very sizeable differences between cases and controls in self-reported self-esteem and self-perception.

Overall the analysis of the mid-point data suggest that the experimental Instrumental Enrichment programme may produce meaningful upward changes in the intellectual functioning of low-functioning children and adolescents and that, moreover, involvement with this programme is associated with positive changes in the youngsters' perception of themselves and their effectiveness.

SINGER, J., JENSEN, M. R. *Cognitive Modifiability Project Yale University*. Narrative Progress Report: Executive Summary.

NASHVILLE, LOUISVILLE AND PHOENIX RESULTS

A wide variety of children from the Southern States of America have taken part in an extended research project into the effects of Instrumental Enrichment, carried out under the auspices of Vanderbilt University. The children in the project were categorised as being Learning Disabled, Emotionally Disturbed, Educable Mentally Retarded (in Britain these children would be called mentally handicapped and would probably be found in special schools for children with severe learning difficulties), and Varying Exceptionalities—children with particular difficulties who were withdrawn from class for special tuition but not placed in special education. The Instrumental Enrichment programme was also given to regular classes of relatively low-functioning children in ordinary schools and to some gifted children.

Nashville was where the bulk of the research was carried out. In Louisville the children tested were emotionally disturbed and learning disabled, and in Phoenix children of Mexican-American immigrants in a migrant education programme were included. Many in this last group were poor school attenders and low-achievers, and had low predictor scores on standard tests of intelligence and school development. Finally, several high school classes of Navajo Indian children, as well as emotionally disturbed and Educable Mentally Retarded groups were later added to the Phoenix sample.

Volunteer teachers were given about 80 hours of training in the initial instruments, with special emphasis on 'mediational styles' of teaching in a workshop and follow-up training, as well as in-class supervision, before they began to teach in classes monitored for the experiment. All the children were given initial tests on Raven's Progressive Matrices:

> . . . because according to some theorists that test is the best measure of exactly the kind of thinking that many of

our subjects are not supposed to be capable of doing, that is, abstract reasoning.

The researchers pointed out that the theory of cognitive modifiability predicts an improvement in children's learning processes, problem-solving and even their enthusiasm for learning, after focused training in cognitive functions and mental operations. But there is no reason to expect that in the short run such gains would be reflected in school achievement gains or in changes in predictor measures, such as intelligence scores.

Nevertheless, it was precisely this type of gain that school administrators, teachers and research-funding agencies were interested in. So measures for these were included in the research project and represented 'the most severe tests' of the programme. Some of the school achievement measures were the Peabody Individual Achievement tests, the Wide Range Achievement tests, the KeyMath Diagnostic tests, the California Test of Basic Skills, as well as ordinary school tests. The measures for general intelligence included the Lorge-Thorndike Non-verbal test, the Primary Mental Abilities test and the Woodcock Johnson Psycho-educational Battery.

Although Nashville was the main site for the research, 'upheaval' in the public school system meant that the planned second year of the programme was not given to most students, so the data were based on one year of Instrumental Enrichment only, and provision in the 15–20 Instrumental Enrichment classes participating was as little as 50 hours a year. In Louisville and particularly Phoenix it was 80 hours a year and sometimes much more.

This seems to have had a profound effect on the results of Instrumental Enrichment. But even in Nashville they remain very interesting. Data from Nashville and Louisville sites show IQ gains of seven to eight points over one year of Instrumental Enrichment, compared to two points in control classes. Significant improvement was found on only some parts of the Primary Mental Abilities test, but on the total score and all the sub-tests of the Lorge-Thorndike Non-verbal Intelligence test. No gains were found in personality or motivation or in school achievement.

Another single-year set of data for the following year found that in Nashville most of the IQ gains were in the Varying Exceptionalities group—the low-achieving children with relatively mild learning difficulties. In Louisville there were 'promising gains' for emotionally-disturbed students (measured on the Woodcock-Johnson Psycho-educational Battery) compared to their achievement history. They usually achieved only .25 to .30 grade equivalents, but after one year of Instrumental Enrichment showed .90 to 1.75 grade equivalents in reasoning, memory, reading aptitude and the full-scale score.

The most dramatic one-year gains were in Phoenix. The bilingual children in the migrant education classes showed about a nine-point gain in IQ on the Lorge-Thorndike test compared with about two points in a control group and four points in a tutored comparison group. 'Dramatic gains' were recorded for these students on Raven's Progressive Matrices, with Instrumental Enrichment students increasing their mean scores from 33 to 44, compared with insignificant gains in the control and tutored group. There were 'small but encouraging gains' in task-intrinsic motivation.

When tests of cognitive functions were made in Nashville, using the Woodcock-Johnson Psycho-educational Battery (Cognitive Ability Sub-scales) Instrumental Enrichment children performed better in four of the five areas: broad cognitive ability, verbal ability, reasoning and memory. The only exception was perceptual speed because, said the researchers, Instrumental Enrichment teaches children to slow down in order to have time to think.

Children's ability to master cognitive skills and transfer them to similar but untried problems was measured with seventh-grade low-achieving children and sixth-grade high-achievers who either had or, had not had, Instrumental Enrichment. In both mastery and transfer of skills Instrumental Enrichment children performed better. The same students were also given the California Test of Basic Skills and Instrumental Enrichment children 'surprisingly' outperformed the non-Instrumental Enrichment children, absolutely, in all seven areas of the test, and significantly in two of the areas. The seven areas were: language expression, social studies, maths concepts, maths applications, science, reading comprehension and reference skills.

Using mazes to measure children's persistence and interest in continuing to process information, the researchers found that Educable Mentally Retarded children who had been given Instrumental Enrichment spent longer in the mazes and made more correct decisions per minute than did non-Instrumental Enrichment or minimal Instrumental Enrichment children— indicating positive changes in retarded children's motivation to engage with tasks and persist in them.

Generally the Phoenix children, whose exposure to the instruments was most extensive, showed more significant gains than did those in Nashville. The most extreme example of this was in 1982/83, when Instrumental Enrichment classes in Nashville made, for several reasons, very few gains over the control classes. Yet the tests in Phoenix, in the same year, showed that all six of the different categories of classes in the project, which were given Instrumental Enrichment, scored better than control and tutored classes in absolute terms, and significantly better in five of the six categories of classes.

Similarly, the two-year data for Nashville (very limited because of the breakdown of the implementation of the programme) shows little significant gains in favour of Instrumental Enrichment, while in Phoenix the two-year programme of Instrumental Enrichment appeared to produce a 15-point gain in IQ (Lorge-Thorndike) and the results on the Raven's Progressive Matrices were yet more dramatic—the mean rising from 31 to 49 (on a 60-item test).

The report went on to state: 'More important than the magnitude of the gains is the fact that both groups after two years are scoring in that range of the Matrices where it is not possible to score without abstract, sequential and analogical thinking.' In Louisville there were 'large gains in the same direction' and some evidence to support the 15-point gain in IQ in two years of the Instrumental Enrichment programme.

Such was the difference in results between sites, especially between Nashville and Phoenix, that it has prompted a further investigation. In addition to the significantly greater number of hours a year that Instrumental Enrichment was taught in Phoenix, along with the more successful implementation of a two-to-three-year programme, the Phoenix teachers were also involved in teaching other subjects to the same children. The mediational style of teaching could well have carried over into other subjects and reinforced the intellectual skills acquired. In Nashville Instrumental Enrichment was taught by teachers who taught only Instrumental Enrichment.

The interpretation put on this by the researchers was that 75–100 hours of Instrumental Enrichment is an irreducible minimum investment (Feuerstein says that it should be nearer to 300 hours) necessary to produce significant and generalisable changes in cognitive functions and in second order effects. They also maintain that Instrumental Enrichment is best taught by teachers who teach the children other subjects and that it is by no means teacher-proof.

Overall it is clear that Instrumental Enrichment works— at least for some of the people some of the time. It is equally clear that it works better for some than for others. Unfortunately for those of us whose interest in it derives from our interest in mentally retarded persons, it seems to work best for those who need it least, that is persons of average or above average intelligence whose learning difficulties may arise from environmental maladjustment, psychiatric disorder, specific learning disability, or related problems—and least for those who need it most—that is retarded and low-functioning children and adolescents. Our Educable Mentally Retarded have not made consistent gains, and the gains they have made have not been large. Retarded students in Phoenix have gained more than have retarded students in Nashville. One reason might be that in Nashville they have been given a 'stretched-out' programme of Instrumental Enrichment, that is many hours have been spent with relatively few pages of the instruments. Such a procedure appears to be promising, and should be tested systematically.

HEYWOOD, H. Carl, ARBITMAN-SMITH, Ruth, BRABSFORD, John D., DECLOS, Victor (Vanderbilt University). TOWERY, Jane R. (Louisville, Kentucky). HANNEL, I. L., and HANNEL, Maria V. (Phoenix, Arizona). *Cognitive Education with Adolescents: Evaluation of Instrumental Enrichment.*

THE VENEZUELAN EXPERIMENT

One of the boldest ventures ever undertaken in cognitive education, at least in the non-communist world, has recently taken place in Venezuela. With high-level political backing, a range of intelligence programmes was introduced into the state educational system in an attempt to increase the opportunities for the participation of the population in the rapidly developing scientific and technological sectors of the economy. They were one of the central features of the 1981–85 national plan.

Unfortunately very little comprehensive empirical data are available in English about the effect of the programmes, one of the chief of which has been Feuerstein's Instrumental Enrichment programme. But a description of the Instrumental Enrichment project and a field survey comparing teachers' responses to Instrumental Enrichment with those to Edward de Bono's teaching thinking programme called CoRT (after the initials of the Cognitive Research Trust in Cambridge where he is based) has been conducted by Mireya Gonzalez as part of a dissertation for a Master's degree in education at Manchester University.

To launch the Instrumental Enrichment project 19 Venezuelan teachers went to Israel for an intensive six-week training in all the instruments at the Hadassah Wizo Institute. Back in Venezuela they were to become the trainers of other teachers who initially were given a three-week training course in the first four instruments.

There were two main centres for the pilot study, the capital, Caracas, and Guayana. In the letter there were 1,454 students and 43 teachers from 12 'primary' schools involved in the two-year pilot study, while in Caracas there were 1,872 students, 40 primary teachers and 25 schools included in the scheme. This represented approximately 34 students per Instrumental Enrichment teacher in Guayana and a ratio of 1:47 in Caracas, which is very large. The age of the pupils varied from 9-17 years and many of the schools were located in *barrios*—the poverty-stricken and ramshackle suburbs of the big cities.

The children were given five hours of Instrumental Enrichment a week over two years, along with their normal curriculum. After the first training course for teachers, it was planned to hold a second for the next three instruments with the remainder being taught to teachers in a third training session in the second year. Unfortunately, in Caracas this rigorous preparation did not prevent the emergence of great difficulties. Industrial disputes and problems created by the resignation of five of the six training teachers, who also acted as classroom supervisors, created delays and disillusionment. Teachers also expressed concern about the lack of time for preparation of Instrumental Enrichment lessons and about the large number of students in each class, as well as doubts over whether the students they taught for two years would be given any follow-up tuition; if not, what was the point of it all? These anxieties impeded the programme in the capital and in the end only seven of the planned 12 instruments were covered.

In Guayana the research and supervisory team expanded rather than declined and the morale of the experimental project was maintained. As a result, teachers were given all three training workshops on schedule and managed to teach the 12 instruments to the children.

Edward De Bono's CoRT programme did not have such extensive training preparation, largely because he believes that his ideas and techniques are so simple they can be easily grasped through the manuals. De Bono believes that there are four different and complementary types of thinking, natural, logical, mathematical (all of which are claimed to be 'vertical' thinking) and lateral.

The difference between vertical and lateral thinking is that the former is selective, sequential in character and follows the most likely paths; while lateral thinking is generative, takes jumps and explores the least likely paths. In vertical thinking categories, classifications and labels are fixed, but with lateral thinking they are not.

De Bono recommends lateral thinking because it counteracts

the errors and limitations in the way the mind arranges information in ordinary vertical thinking. Lateral thinking restructures the information, often making different and better use of it, and is closely related to what we call insight, creativity, as well as humour.

According to De Bono, skills in thinking (which he distinguished from a rather unclear concept of intelligence) have much to do with perception and directing attention. They involve the exploration of experience, the application of knowledge through planning, decision-making, looking at evidence, guessing, creativity and many other types of thinking. His course of teaching thinking as a skill is designed to train perception and attention, rather than the processing of information. In fact, perception to De Bono is the processing of information for use—it is virtually the same thing as thinking.

Hundreds of schools in the Commonwealth and now Venezuela use his programme. It is based on six sections which cover a general theme: 'breadth', 'organisation', 'interaction', 'creativity', 'information and feeling' and 'action'. Each is split up into ten lessons and each lesson focuses on a single attention area, such as 'guessing', 'decision' or 'defining the problem'. Some lessons concentrate on a thinking operation which is condensed into a tool to assess situations. One typical 'tool', for example, is collecting the plus, minus and interesting points in a situation. It is an attention-directing device.

Comparing De Bono's programme with Feuerstein's, Mireya Gonzalez points out that there are no compulsory materials for children to complete, as there are in Instrumental Enrichment, no right or wrong answers in CoRT lessons, and improvement can only be judged by an outsider; it is up to the teacher to give pupils a sense of achievement. There is no way to analyse cognitive deficits in children or systematically to remediate them. In fact, in her opinion, De Bono's theory appears to operate at a more general and undifferentiated level in which 'intelligence' is mysteriously assumed as given and completely separate from thinking skills.

The survey of teachers' attitudes towards Instrumental Enrichment in Caracas, the least satisfactory of the sites, found that 50 per cent of the teachers agreed that Instrumental

Enrichment aroused interest in class while 36.3 per cent slightly agreed. Only 4.9 per cent disagreed. However, 86 per cent of teachers said they thought Instrumental Enrichment capable of obtaining changes in their students, and the same number said they had benefited in teaching skills from the programme.

Asked if Instrumental Enrichment had improved their students' analytical skills 90 per cent of teachers said it had. Of those, 27.2 per cent strongly agreed, 63 per cent said there had been improvements in children's organisation regarding school tasks, 13.6 per cent were uncertain and 4.5 per cent said there had not been improvements. A high proportion of teachers, 90 per cent, said that students' self-image had improved.

There were less positive responses from teachers when it came to the question of whether Instrumental Enrichment improved participation in the class. Only 59 per cent thought it did. The research suggests this could be linked to the age of the teachers and to their traditionally authoritarian relationship to their students who are expected to be passive in class.

With De Bono's programme, 86 per cent of teachers agreed that the major contribution of the programme had been in the emphasis of solving problems rather than in content. Nearly 50 per cent said there was some transfer to other subjects—a significant finding, said the researcher, since De Bono admits this is a problem with his work.

Also 52 per cent said that children became more co-operative in class, mainly due to the use of group-work techniques employed in the programme and the ability to give opinions. But 28.1 per cent of teachers disagreed with this and 18.4 per cent were uncertain.

In comparing teachers' responses to the two programmes important differences emerge. While the majority of teachers in the Instrumental Enrichment programme were secure in having learnt new skills and techniques, this consensus was not present with the CoRT programme teachers, 47.3 per cent of whom said they had not benefited in this way.

When asked if they wished to continue with the programmes 72.6 per cent of Instrumental Enrichment teachers said they did. Yet this enthusiasm was not present in the CoRT programme where 42 per cent rated it as only 'acceptable' with nearly 20 per cent saying it was poor or very poor. Some 31.57

per cent thought it was good and 5.26 per cent thought it was excellent.

Mireya Gonzalez concludes:

First, a consensus of opinion was observed among Instrumental Enrichment students regarding the programme's benefits for themselves as well as their students. However such a consensus of opinion was not possible to observe in the Learning to Think (CoRT) teachers. On the contrary there was a number who appeared to be negative towards the programme's benefits. Second, a general amount of enthusiasm and motivation was noted by Instrumental Enrichment teachers towards their work in the programme. On the other hand, such an enthusiasm and motivation was not the same in the case of the Learning to Think programme. They gave the impression that they were participating in it as a compulsory activity.

GONZALEZ, Mireya. *CoRT and Instrumental Enrichment in Venezuela*. Department of Education, Manchester University.

THE GUAYANA CONNECTION

A series of research projects were undertaken by Ruiz Bolivar and colleagues in Ciudad Guayana, the site in Venezuela where the most successful implementation of the Instrumental Enrichment programme took place.

The most recent has been a study of the effect of Instrumental Enrichment on pre-college students of general ability but needing remedial academic treatment to be admitted to an engineering degree at the Guayana Technological Institute. As with the other Venezuelan studies, only abstracts are available in translation.

The sample was 86 students split into control and experimental groups, both of which were tested before and after an intervention programme of 82 hours of Instrumental Enrichment given five times a week.

Consistent with earlier results, the programme 'had significant effects on the subjects' subsequent performance on general ability at pre-college level. In addition . . . the present study extends the research of intellectual development beyond the limits of adolescence.'

In 1983 Bolivar, together with de Sardina and Ortiz, measured the changes in 10–14-year-old children from high and low socio-economic groups following Instrumental Enrichment. A second objective was to observe any changes in the attitudes of teachers.

The children received five hours of Instrumental Enrichment a week, totalling 275 hours over two years—therefore meeting Feuerstein's recommended minimum requirements for creating significant changes. The control group underwent only the normal curriculum.

The results indicate that the treatment was effective in respect of the overall intellectual capacity, in the improvement of academic achievement, self concept and classroom behaviour and participation. The treatment was also successful regarding the change in attitudes of teachers.

BOLIVAR, Ruiz. *Effects of Feuerstein's Instrumental Enrichment Programme on Pre-College Students.*. Ciudad Guayana, February, 1985.

BOLIVAR, Ruiz, DE SARDINA, C., and ORTIZ, E. and A. T. *Efectos del Programa Enriuecimiento Instrumental sobre los Factores Cognoscitivos y No Cognoscitivos en Sujetos de Diferentes Estratos Socioeconomicos.* Ciudad Guayana, May, 1983.

THE NEW YORK EXPERIMENT

The Instrumental Enrichment programme was administered to 203 children ranging from fourth to eighth grade, in seven classes of four non-public schools in New York City. The objectives for Instrumental Enrichment were to increase children's reading or mathematics scores. The teachers were 'Chapter 1' remedial teachers of mathematics and reading.

The California Achievement Test and the Stanford Achievement Test were used to assess reading or mathematics achievement. A survey discovered students' attitudes and teachers' opinions were recorded.

The average gain in reading for second-year students of Instrumental Enrichment was 17.8 points on a special scale. The gain of non-Instrumental Enrichment groups of children over two years was 12.4 points.

On a test measuring the application of children to school work there was considerable improvement, as there was in mathematics, although the lack of control groups made scientific measurement of the changes impossible.

Seventy per cent of students indicated they were 'highly satisfied' with the programme and teachers were 'unanimous' in their enthusiasm for the programme.

WALKER, S., and MEIER, J. *Instrumental Enrichment Programme.* Office of Educational Evaluation. New York City Public Schools, New York, 1982/83.

MORE READING IMPROVEMENTS IN WESTCHESTER, USA

Twenty-six sixth-grade under-achievers from two remedial classes in Westchester, an East Coast town in America, were given 59 hours of Instrumental Enrichment training for one school year. The object of the study was to see what improvements occurred in reading achievement, reasoning abilities and task orientation.

The 59 children were matched with peers in a similar setting to provide a control group and the teachers were trained in Instrumental Enrichment by the researcher.

Children in both groups were pre- and post-tested on vocabulary and reading sub-tests of a standardised battery, a non-verbal reasoning battery of a standardised cognitive abilities test, and a criterion referenced test. Teachers were asked to record changes in task orientation on a student behaviour rating scale for both groups, and those teaching Instrumental Enrichment supplied written evaluations.

After the 59 hours of Instrumental Enrichment the findings showed no significant differences between the groups in reasoning abilities. Within-group analyses showed significant differences emerging between children in the Instrumental Enrichment group, but not in the control group. The Instrumental Enrichment children's gain on the criterion referenced tests was significantly greater than those of the control group.

Total reading gains were also significantly greater for the Instrumental Enrichment children. Findings on the task-orientation part of the research were discounted because of incompleteness and bias.

The teachers involved in the Instrumental Enrichment programme expressed:

a high estimation of its value for student learning and teacher professional growth.

Overall findings suggest that the Instrumental Enrichment treatment aggregate produced greater gains than conventional remediation and greater impact on reading achievement than previously studied Instrumental Enrichment programmes of longer duration.

BRAININ, S. S. *The Effects of Instrumental Enrichment on the Reasoning Abilities, Reading Achievement and Task Orientation of 6th Grade Underachievers.* (PhD Thesis). Teachers' College, Columbia University, 1981.

NEW PROMISE FOR DEAF CHILDREN

When the first major psychometric studies of the deaf were undertaken in America in the 1940s (by Pintner and colleagues), they were said to be mentally retarded by about ten IQ points compared to able-bodied people. Children born deaf, or who became deaf before they could speak, were found to have a relative mental retardation equivalent to two years, and a school achievement retardation of four to five years!

This view of automatic retardation has now been superseded by two competing theories about deaf children. The first claims that they are intellectually average, but have problems in communication as a result of deafness which superficially affects their performance. The second says that they are as intelligent as able-bodied children, but have a qualitatively different type of intelligence.

According to this latter view the loss of one of the senses causes a 'shift' in the cognitive structures which tend to make deaf children function less abstractly and more concretely, because they are so dependent on what is in their immediate visual field or within their touch. Language, necessary for the development of abstract thinking, is impaired in these children.

Another, more social, reason put forward for the cognitive difference of deaf children has been the lack of similar experience compared to other children. Numerous researches on deaf children show them to have characteristics remarkably similar to culturally-deprived children in that they are often highly impulsive, egocentric, selfish and immature for their age. As a result of 'educational and psychological malnutrition' they have been found to suffer from rigid personalities and social isolation. Like the culturally-deprived, they also manifest a general lack of reflection.

In this view—the 'experiential deficit model'—these differences from hearing children can be remedied by providing 'appropriate experiences' to deaf children, although what constitutes these appropriate experiences is never described. A form of general enrichment is all that is prescribed—a variation of the 'more stimulation' school of remedial education.

But, argues Kevin Keane, of Columbia University, New York, there are problems with both the theories of deaf people, as cognitively normal and as cognitively different. The first theory cannot explain why deaf children who score the same in non-verbal IQ tests as ordinary children continue to perform so universally badly at school. There is commonly a three-to-four-year lag in performance between deaf and hearing children and it seems unconvincing to blame this completely on inappropriate education systems.

The deaf, as the cognitively different theory suggests, do suffer from language and experiential deprivation and these need to be remedied for children to achieve more at school. But the failure to detail what the appropriate experiences are which need to be given to deaf children to raise their performance, means that the theory is of very little practical use, since it cannot form the basis of an intervention programme. The doubt in this area has been increased by studies which suggest that, in terms of quantity of experiences and stimulation, low-performing deaf children are often given much more than culturally-deprived children.

Kevin Keane used Feuerstein's Learning Potential Assessment Device to bear out his hypothesis that what causes low achievement in deaf children is not a general lack of experience but a lack of specific mediational learning experiences. He was able to show that in using the intense and targeted, short-term mediation of the Learning Potential Assessment Device, it was possible to improve significantly the cognitive functioning of deaf children.

Keane points out that there is evidence to support his hypothesis from studies of interactions between deaf children of deaf parents and those of hearing parents. Hearing mothers of deaf children with low communication skills were found to be more inflexible, controlling, didactic, intrusive and disapproving than is usual in mother-child relationships. Researchers have found in deaf children of hearing parents a passivity to people and the environment, and a lack of initiative which they have explained as 'learned helplessness'.

Hearing parents, traumatised by having deaf children, are prone to over-protect them and therefore restrict their range of experiences and their interactions with them. And because hearing parents use all their senses to operate in the world, mediating experience to their children visually is very difficult for them. This, obviously, is not the case with deaf parents of deaf children who should, therefore, not suffer from intellectual deficits to the same degree. Keane quotes studies which, sure enough, show that deaf children of deaf parents perform better than deaf children of hearing parents in written language, reading, vocabulary and finger-spelling. They also have a more positive self-image and social adjustment, and exhibit less impulsiveness and score higher on traditional tests of intellectual ability.

Over 90 per cent of deaf children are born to hearing parents. For a majority of these parents it is their first encounter with the handicap of deafness. Schlesinger and Meadow, 1972, and Mindel and Vernon, 1971, cite guilt, anger, grief, and repression as stages through which parents normally pass in coping with the reality of having a hearing-impaired child.

As the nurturing agents in the environment of the deaf child, the nature of the parents' coping mechanism may cause a significant disruption or reduction in the mediational learning process, where the organisation of environmental stimuli is not interpreted for the child. Also, as a hearing person, the adaptive response to the environment is through an integrated sensory network with hearing playing a central rôle in the orienting framework. Hearing parents are faced with the dilemma of trying to mediate the world to their deaf child visually when they are not singularly visually orientated themselves.

In terms of Feuerstein's overall theory of mediated learning Keane says that hearing parents of deaf children can be handicapped when it comes to the transmission of cognitive skills to their children. Poor communication skills, or difficulty in coming to terms with deafness, can adversely affect intentionality on the part of the parents, which is the key feature in the creation of mediated learning experiences. These children, therefore, can be culturally-deprived.

The Learning Potential Assessment Device examiner is supposed to assist children's performances during the training part of the test by regulating impulsive behaviour, improving impaired cognitive functions, enlarging the number of mental operations and trying to create reflection and insight. Keane hypothesised that, given this corrective mediation, deaf children would more nearly approach their intellectual potential. They would be able to perform better when finally compared with deaf children measured on standard psychometric tests (with neutral examiners) and those given tests with limited feed-back from the examiner.

So 45 severely to profoundly and pre-lingually deaf children, aged 9–13 years, of hearing parents and with no diagnosed secondary handicaps, were formed into a sample and randomly assigned into three different groups which varied in the nature of the examinee-examiner relationship. The first was the Learning Potential Assessment Device mediational group, where the children were tested, taught and then retested. The second was a limited feed-back group where the examiner orientated the student to the task, discussed the principles involved and offered positive reinforcement for behaviours considered valuable (like taking time before answering)—but never providing the correct response before the student had answered. The third was the standard, completely neutral rôle of the examiner.

The pre- and post-test measures used were Level B of the Non-verbal Battery of the Cognitive Abilities test by Thorndike and Hagen and the Kohs Block Design Test. Each group of children was also assessed on five instruments (used for the treatment of the experimental group) within the Learning Potential Assessment Device battery, but with the varying rôles of the examiners. The instruments were Raven's Coloured Progressive Matrices and the Learning Potential Assessment Device variations, Organisation of Dots, the Plateau test, the Associated Recall test, and the Representational Stencil Design test. In this last test the Learning Potential Assessment Device experimental group was not allowed to handle the materials while the other two groups were.

The results were highly significant and produced much more than expected gains for the Learning Potential Assessment Device group over the two other groups of children for all but the Associated Recall test. This exception is, Keane says, probably due to the nature of the test where only very limited mediation is possible. Some form of feed-back interaction with the examiner produced slightly more favourable results than in the standard, neutral, test condition, showing that deaf children's performances can be modified with even limited and unfocused mediation.

The Cognitive Abilities test result showed a significant difference between the experimental Learning Potential Assessment Device group and the standard group, but no significant difference between the experimental and the feed-back group. The Learning Potential Assessment Device children showed a significant increase in the number of designs they completed in the Kohs Block Design Test; but there was no similar increase for either of the other two groups. This suggests that the Learning Potential Assessment Device children were more able to transfer their cognitive skills to different but related tasks. There was a significant decrease in the number of trials used to complete the designs in the Learning Potential Assessment Device group but not in the others, suggesting more planned and less impulsive behaviour.

In previous studies researchers noted that deaf children find intellectual problems very difficult when they have to refer to two critical elements for a successful resolution. It is a level of abstraction which they find hard to encompass and they perform much worse at this level than hearing children.

In Keane's study, the Raven's and its Learning Potential Assessment Device variations require this ability to refer to two critical elements—at least!—and they also require the kind of abstract conceptual ability which Jensen and other researchers consider beyond the 'concrete' functioning of deaf children. The comparative performance, however, between the experimental and other groups, strongly indicated that 'although the ability to refer to two sources of data may not be available at a direct experience level, it is potentially evident through a mediated learning exposure.'

The results on the Organisation of Dots instrument, where

children must project relationships, lent credence to the concept that the prerequisite behaviours may be mediated. Stated inversely, the cognitive deficiencies that may impair performance on this task are modifiable for this deaf population. While 66 per cent of the children in the standard test group had to be discontinued before they completed the task because they were failing, and 40 per cent were discontinued in the feed-back group, none of the children in the experimental group were discontinued!

On the Plateau test, 60 per cent of the standard group and 27 per cent of the feed-back group were discontinued, while none of the Learning Potential Assessment Device experimental group were. This shows that with adequate mediation deaf children are able to internalise an operation requiring the transformation of stimuli.

The superior performance of the experimental group children in the Representational Stencil Design test, particularly since they were not allowed to handle the materials while the other groups were, was very significant, says Keane. It showed that they were able to carry out with mediation complex mental operations required for the intellectual transformation of the materials. The better performance of the Learning Potential Assessment Device children 'lends support to the hypothesis (of Feuerstein and others) that the deaf child population is *more* capable of demonstrating reflective thought processes when they are less able to rely on concrete forms and trial-and-error behaviour'.

Such dramatic differences, says Keane, suggest that the elaborational potential of deaf children can be significantly enhanced through a mediational approach. Deaf children are very much open to cognitive modifiability. But the striking differences between the standard and the experimental group also indicated that direct experience learning for this sample population was severely limited. This was supported by the enhanced performance of the feed-back group.

Anecdotally, the researcher found an extraordinary change in the level of motivation of those children in the Learning Potential Assessment Device group.

Most subjects entered the test situation if not negatively,

at least defensively. Dramatic changes in motivation were observed, presumably as a function of a recognition of their own success on tasks they knew were difficult. This was demonstrated by alterations in energy levels in approaching new tasks and even in requests for more tasks when the treatment procedure was finished. The subjects went back to their classes and discussed their experiences to such a point that their teachers became inquisitive and other students requested if they too could be tested. This shift in motivation appeared to be a powerful force in maintaining attentional levels, especially as the tasks progressed in difficulty.

The theory of mediated learning could, says Keane, reconcile the two hostile positions of the deaf-as-normal and the deaf-as-cognitively different. Feuerstein explains in specific terms the way experiential restrictions result in cultural deprivation and cognitive deficits that make deaf children 'different'. On the other hand, as the theory of mediated learning suggests, and the research on the Learning Potential Assessment Device shows, it is quite possible to modify this difference and allow the normal cognitive potential of deaf children to surface.

Important implications flow from this research. It suggests that the way in which hearing parents mediate the world to their children must be systematically improved, perhaps using the theory of Mediated Learning as a principle in the construction of any training programme. The implications for education are, as Keane says, the need to diagnose in children the cognitive deficiencies which are preventing them from achieving at acceptable academic levels, and to use Instrumental Enrichment, especially adapted for the deaf, as one of the means for their remediation.

Half-way across the world, in New Zealand, J. Thickpenny found very similar effects of Instrumental Enrichment with profoundly deaf students, when it was given to two classes of adolescent children at the Keseltone School for the Deaf in Auckland. However, the classes received Instrumental Enrichment at different times. In the first part of the experiment one class was given Instrumental Enrichment for 57 hours, while the second was instead given an ordinary remedial teaching programme. At the end of this initial period Thickpenny found that the Instrumental Enrichment class had made significant gains on the picture completion and picture arrangement sub-tests of the WISC-R test, and in the matching Familiar Figures' test which were not shown in the control group.

In the second part of the experiment the second class was given 110 hours of Instrumental Enrichment, while the first class had their hours increased to 167. Individuals from both groups then showed, in highly sensitive tests, that the training in Instrumental Enrichment had been transferred to other areas. But only the first class, with more hours of Instrumental Enrichment, showed a wider application of the cognitive skill taught in Instrumental Enrichment in low sensitivity tests. This suggests, as Feuerstein maintains, that the greater the exposure to Instrumental Enrichment, the wider the use of the cognitive skills that it teaches.

'The conclusion from these results is that Instrumental Enrichment can be successfully implemented with profoundly deaf students and appears to produce generalised application of Instrumental Enrichment-trained cognitive behaviours.'

KEANE, Kevin J. *Application of Mediated Learning Theory to a Deaf Population: A Study in Cognitive Modification.* (PhD Dissertation). Graduate School of Arts and Sciences, Columbia University.
—— 'Dynamic Assessment with the Deaf: Theory and Practice'. In: C. LIDZ (Ed), *Dynamic Assessment: Theory and Perspectives.* Guildford Press, New York.
THICKPENNY, J. P. *Teaching Thinking Skills to Deaf Adolescents: The Implementation and Evaluation of Feuerstein's Instrumental Enrichment.* (MA Thesis). University of Auckland, New Zealand, December, 1982.

CANADA'S PRISON TRIALS

Investigations into the way in which imprisoned convicts think, compared to the rest of the population, have found that the cognitive processes of low-functioning inmates are often quite different and deficient when compared to the population as a whole.

These differences and deficiencies show a remarkable affinity with those identified by Feuerstein in culturally-deprived children and adults. Prisoners in America and Canada have often been found to have perceptual difficulties which make it difficult for them to perceive and understand causal relationships. Additionally, some have been observed to have 'perceptual distortions'.

A tendency towards egocentric perception is one of these distortions. Prisoners, apparently, are often unable to understand and assume the rôle of others and, therefore, are unable to predict, anticipate or identify with their behaviour or feelings.

There is evidence of a high degree of impulsiveness among prisoners. This involves making ill-thought-out errors, replying without thinking, a disruptive inability to settle down and work and an inability to delay gratification.

Evidence also exists (although it is more inconclusive) that prisoners commonly lack temporal perspectives—that is, they are less likely to recognise the relevance of their behaviour to their future. Observed behaviour of prisoners suggests they have difficulty understanding the relationship between cause and effect in relating past activities to the present. The entire concept of time is said to be 'poorly perceived and poorly internalised by inmates'.

Many studies of prisoners' reasoning ability have suggested that the issue may not be a lack of morality *per se* among prisoners, but a much more generalised and profound cognitive deficiency. It has been suggested that prisoners' lack of moral reasoning is tied in to their poor hypothetical thinking and an inability to assess a social situation or understand social rules and values.

Prisoners, it is also claimed, often lack a clear sense of their goals and expectations in a given situation. They lack intentionality, and, linked to this, they have poor planning behaviour.

All this prompted academics from the University of Toronto, interested in cognitive education, to see if Feuerstein's Learning Potential Assessment Device could produce evidence of modifiability in low-functioning inmates of Canada's penal system. If evidence was found, a longer study on the effects of an Instrumental Enrichment programme would be instituted.

The Learning Potential Assessment Device study was carried out on two groups of high-performing prisoners (reading and mathematics achievement above grade 8) and two low-performing groups (reading and maths below grade 5), in two different institutions. In the event, the differences between the two high groups and between the two low groups was so small that the data were collapsed.

There were 28 prisoners in the high-performing group and 21 in the low, and they were given three of the tests from the Learning Potential Assessment Device, the Organisation of Dots, the Raven's Progressive Matrices and the Representational Stencil Design Test, with the Lorge-Thorndike Non-verbal Intelligence test as a pre- and post-test measure.

The results were quite striking. Despite the very significant differences between the scores of the groups prior to the Learning Potential Assessment Device training, the low group afterwards achieved results that brought them to the same level as the high-performing group's pre-training scores. The only difference was that the low-performing group took slightly longer to carry out two of the more difficult pages of the Organisation of Dots instrument.

The Instrumental Enrichment programme which followed was the first major attempt at a tested cognitive education course in various prison sites to have taken place in Canada, and perhaps anywhere in the world. In the six prisons involved in the programme 135 inmates volunteered for the course. The views of the prisoners, educators and evaluators were that, despite some problems, Instrumental Enrichment was an important intervention in terms of cognitive development and the improvement of inmates' skills in social interaction.

Statistically significant differences were found between scores in the Instrumental Enrichment prisoners' performance in two of the criterion tests used as measures before and after the Instrumental Enrichment programme. In the number of correct frames in the Organisation of Dots instrument and in the Representational Stencil Design test, Instrumental Enrichment inmates fared better than did a comparison group not given Instrumental Enrichment. However, on the Raven's Progressive Matrices, Organisation of Dots (number of correct shapes) and Personality Trait Value Scale advantage was not shown.

The researchers point out, however, that despite the 'fortunate' findings of improvements, a variety of unfortunate factors made the figures less than reliable. The main problem was that the small nature of the sample made the analysis insensitive to any changes that might have occurred. From the original 135 prisoners involved only 38 took part in the final post-intervention testing. Some were sent into solitary confinement, others transferred to better-paying prison jobs, others had changes of schedule forced upon them and others dropped out because they were interested in their mainstream educational activities or felt that early parts of the Instrumental Enrichment programme were too simple.

Although the prison administrators were supposed to ensure that all prisoners involved had a three-year academic retardation, this proved not to be the case and the groups were very heterogeneous. Some of the participants were far more able than the others and objected to the juvenile format of some of the instruments—although this did not mean they were always able to complete the tasks successfully.

In addition, the teachers were only given one week's training of 35 hours, during which they were introduced to the theory and covered the first seven instruments. This compares with the three weeks given to Venezuelan teachers to master the theory and first four instruments. The teachers all complained subsequently that the training period had been much too short.

Given these limitations, despite the promising statistical analysis of the effects of Instrumental Enrichment, the researchers were inevitably forced back onto more subjective evaluation. The teachers said that the students had gained most in communication and social skills, but had also demonstrated improvements in the articulation of ideas and tolerance of the opinions of others during group discussions. The exercises were viewed as helpful in reducing the egocentricity, impulsiveness and inflexibility of inmates when they responded to questions and problems raised by the teachers.

Despite the problems and the inadequate adaptation of the materials, the teachers said the course should be continued for 'the purpose of developing social skills, promoting self-confidence and increasing the inmates' ability to think effectively'. The course, resolved the teachers, should receive the full support of the administration, recognising its value as well as the importance of testing new educational methods in prisons.

The inmates, when questioned, all said some positive changes had occurred as a result of the course. Many thought their thinking had become less impulsive and they were now more cautious and methodical. Others felt they were more open to new ideas and more attentive to directions. One prisoner said there had been an improvement in his vocabulary and reading speed.

More than half the inmates who completed the course said there were no aspects in the programme which needed to be changed. But among the other respondents the most common recommendation was that the instruments should become more difficult, particularly in the early stages of the course.

Some inmates said that their problem-solving was now more effective and that this had been reflected in other school subjects. Some said their self-confidence had improved and they were better able to get along with other people. Overall, the view was that the course had positively affected their daily lives.

Although the hard 'scientific' evidence of beneficial effects from Instrumental Enrichment were slender, when taken together with the other evaluations for the project, the result is highly positive.

Common responses of prisoners when talking about their crimes are: 'I don't know what made me do it', 'I didn't think', 'I couldn't help myself'. These might seem like excuses which almost absolve people who commit such acts from personal responsibility; in fact, research is now suggesting that cognitive impairments or deficiencies could well be at the bottom of some people's seemingly incomprehensible inability consciously to control their behaviour.

The recent research on juvenile delinquency in the States and Britain shows that much of it is 'situational' in character. An opportunity for some sort of criminal act emerges and is taken by an adolescent on an unthinking impulse. Cognitive deficiencies seem to be strongly at work here, too, perhaps exacerbated by the personality confusions of adolescence.

If so, then Feuerstein's mediated learning through Instrumental Enrichment offers the opportunity for reinforcing offending adolescents' cognitive control over their actions. This, in turn, could save them from breaking into potentially disastrous patterns of behaviour which could cause them to become entrenched criminals. Exactly this type of project is now under way in California with recidivist juvenile delinquents. In Israel, interventions earlier on, at the point of chronic school failure (see Changing Environments, page 267), has resulted in children who were potential prison fodder altering their abilities, lifestyles and life opportunities.

WAKESMAN, M., SILVERMAN, Harry, WEBER, K. *Assessing the Learning Potential of Penitentiary Inmates: An Application of Feuerstein's Learning Potential Assessment Device.* Department of Special Education, University of Toronto and Department of Special Education, Ontario Institute of Studies in Education.

WAKESMAN, M., and VOLPE, Richard. *The Implementation and Evaluation of a Cognitive Education Course in Canadian Federal Penitentiaries.* Correctional Services, Solicitor General of Canada, Ottawa, Ontario.

GIFTED AND LOW-ACHIEVING CHILDREN IN TORONTO

Interestingly, one of the few areas in which it is wholly uncontroversial to talk about unrealised potential, and the misleading character of current performance, is with the education of gifted children. The phenomenon of the 'gifted under-achiever' is now a well-established concept in education literature, its entrance being smoothly facilitated by ideological connections with traditional elitist views of education.

Interestingly, too, educationalists' and psychologists' views of how the curriculum should be enriched for gifted children all revolve around improvements of thinking and problem-solving skills. J. J. Gallagher, one of the prominent American researchers in the field has stated:

> Special programming for gifted children should focus on teaching them skills for learning that will help them become independent of their teachers and instructors. Perhaps an efficient strategy can be devised once educators admit that the facts they present today will inevitably be replaced by the discoveries and intentions of tomorrow, and that more attention must be paid to teaching the child to seek knowledge on his own . . .
>
> All students, not only the gifted, should be able to solve problems and seek answers using search skills in the jungle of facts and ideas similar to the search skills they would need to survive in the natural jungle.

The fact that all children, and even perhaps educationally retarded and handicapped children, should be taught such skills seems rather an afterthought here. But, whatever the ideological imperatives behind the gifted child debate and the implicit (and sometimes explicit) desire to create little geniuses, it is certainly the case that 'obviously' gifted children do under-achieve in some cases.

Such children's exceptionally developed abilities in particular areas can make them resistant to mediation, points out Feuerstein, whose clinical cases have included several children who have combined great talents with academically damning inadequacies. Over-impulsiveness, lack of intellectual organisation, egocentric communication and impatience are commonly-found characteristics.

It is also true that, despite the recognised need for programmes solely, or at least primarily concerned with strengthening thinking skills of the gifted child, few satisfactory ones have emerged from professionals and teachers working in the area. Yet the desired objectives are precisely the same as those of Feuerstein's Instrumental Enrichment.

Recognising this, Mary Wakesman, Harry Silverman and Joanne Messner conducted an experiment in Canada in 1984 with gifted children and Instrumental Enrichment. Thirty-one children, aged eight to ten, with intelligence scores over 125 and achievement levels two years ahead of their ages and already on enrichment programmes, were randomly placed into an experimental and a control group. All the children stayed on the general enrichment programme, but the experimental group were given Instrumental Enrichment instruction as well.

The teacher responsible for the Instrumental Enrichment programme had a government qualification as a specialist teacher for the gifted. Before starting, she attended two formal workshops conducted by Feuerstein and his colleagues, totalling 80 hours.

The students' problems were discussed and appropriate instruments were selected. Although the children had a 'high level of verbal behaviour' the terms and concepts they used were often misunderstood by them, poorly defined and inaccurately communicated. The students were all highly motivated but some of their data-gathering skills were inefficient and imprecise, and some showed impulsiveness, erratic problem-solving strategies and an inability to stay with one task for long periods of time.

Eight instruments were used: Organisation of Dots, Comparisons, Orientation in Space 1, Analytical Perception, Instructions, Transitive Relations, Categorisation and Illustrations. These were thought to address best the main requirements of the children, summarised as follows:

1   The establishment of more systematic data-gathering skills.
2   The development of the need for more accurate and precise verbal communication.
3   The enhancement of the ability to follow a sequence of instructions systematically.
4   The reinforcement of impulsiveness control.
5   The further development of inferential and deductive reasoning.
6   The discrimination between relevant and irrelevant information.
7   The development of meta-cognitive awareness (that is, thinking about thinking).

The teaching procedures were different from those used when teaching Instrumental Enrichment to low-achieving children. Students were asked, within the context of the lesson, to form hypotheses and test and discuss them as a group; they were asked to research data and substantiate their arguments in great detail and were encouraged to respect other opinions and develop their skills in listening and flexibility. The instruments were expanded into related activities—discussion of the Illustrations' content was expanded into a story-writing exercise, and the students were asked to bridge the rules (principles) on a page to other areas that were interesting to them. Teacher-directed bridging was generally done with examples from advanced areas of computer programming, scientific experimenting and essay-writing.

The children were pre- and post-tested on Raven's Progressive Matrices (Adults) and the Representational Stencil Design test after receiving four hours of Instrumental Enrichment every week for a year. The Instrumental Enrichment students were able to use their cognitive strategies to gain better test scores when compared with their tested performance before the course, but there was a reduction in the control group scores. On the total scores for the Raven's Progressive Matrices they also improved, while the control group again reduced its overall score.

The research report by Silverman, Wakesman and Messner states:

> The improvement in their intellectual performance (as measured by Raven) indicates that the strategies they had been taught through Instrumental Enrichment training (systematic search patterns, comparison, relational thinking, summative behaviour) had improved their performance on most of the criterion measure's categories . . . In spite of the limited number of the criterion measures and the relatively small size of the sample, it is still possible to conclude that even high-scoring, above-average pupils are still able to be modified.

Similar results were found when Mary Wakesman, Harry Silverman and Harvey Narrol explored the effects of Instrumental Enrichment with a group of very low-achieving, vocational high-school students in Toronto. Children attending vocational schools in Canada are usually unable to cope with the academic demands of the elementary school system, and in the vocational schools 'a standard IQ of below 80 is already achieved'.

Teachers on this project were given a fifty-hour workshop, again by Feuerstein and his colleagues, while the subjects were selected by school staff as 'having a history of serious difficulties in coping with and benefiting from the instruction at school'. They were given Instrumental Enrichment, five times a week, in 40-minute periods—but only for one year.

Results of the Lorge-Thorndike Non-verbal Intelligence test showed that three out of five Instrumental Enrichment classes made significant gains compared to control classes. A fourth made gains, but these did not quite reach significance. All five classes showed results in favour of Instrumental Enrichment children on the Primary Mental Abilities test (Letter Series).

Teachers' anecdotal evidence said that the pupils had 'more positive personal development' and were less aggressive among peers and less disruptive. There were no measurable changes in Self Concept and Locus of Control scales. The authors suggested that this might be because measures were too 'gross' and, therefore, insensitive to the changes noticed by teachers. They also point out that personality factors are notoriously resistant to change and there could well be a significant 'lag', during which time the cognitive skills acquired become habitual and the individual grows in his self-confidence as a 'thinker' and consequently in his self-esteem.

The authors say: 'Except for the translation of some guides and instructions, it did not prove necessary to extend and revise Feuerstein's materials. Considering this, the outlook is most optimistic for the longer (two-year) application envisaged by Feuerstein and his colleagues'.

WAKESMAN, M., SILVERMAN, Harry, MESSNER, Joanne. *Instrumental Enrichment: Assessment of the Effects of a Cognitive Training Procedure on a Group of Gifted Students.* University of Toronto Education Faculty, Ontario Institute for Studies in Education, and North York, Board of Education.

NARROL, Harvey, SILVERMAN, Harry, WAKESMAN, Mary. *Developing Cognitive Potential in Vocational High School Students.* Ontario Institute for Studies in Education.

ENCOURAGING FINDINGS IN PARIS

The interim report of a large-scale study of Instrumental Enrichment in Paris, involving more than five hundred children, records a very high level of enthusiasm by researchers and teachers in the way that the programme is going. A translation of their provisional assessment finds as follows:

It seems in actual fact that, contrary to our initial opinion, an improvement in academic achievement may already be manifest in certain members of the experimental group, and this is in spite of the age and the chronic history of academic failure of all the children in our sample. This is a vital point which must give rise to optimism when confronted with situations where there are apparently considerable obstacles to academic achievement.

It does seem in effect that, with Instrumental Enrichment, we have at our disposal an instrument and a complete method of teaching, entirely new, which 'attacks' the mechanisms of habitual academic failure in a totally different approach. This new approach succeeds in destabilising the lack of motivation and the inhibitions and mental blocks obstructing learning, which up until now various other teaching methods have often helped to reinforce in pupils with learning problems.

The report goes on to say that the partial results achieved so far go some way to suggest that the programme can meet its goals of lastingly modifying learners, and 'justifies, so it seems to us, the enthusiasm of the teachers who are currently engaged in the second year of experimentation.'

DEBRAY, R. *Experimenting with the Programme of Instrumental Enrichment as Developed by Professors R. Feuerstein and Y. Rand.* Interim Report, 1984.

THE BRITISH ATTEMPTS

Of all the attempts to implement and evaluate Instrumental Enrichment around the world, those carried out in Britain have been, to put it mildly, the least rigorous. With some honourable exceptions, teacher-training, practical implementation in schools and evaluation procedures, have all been inadequate.

In contrast with virtually every other project there were no visits to Israel by British researchers or teachers involved in the official education authority experiments on Instrumental Enrichment, to see at first hand how the method operates in its country of origin. Instead it seems that senior administrators from several authorities responded to invitations from the American commercial company to visit the United States and examine Instrumental Enrichment in US schools. They then returned, full of enthusiasm, and set up, in my opinion, some very inappropriate schemes to institute Instrumental Enrichment in Britain.

At some point the then Schools Council was invited in to try to co-ordinate and evaluate the activities of five education authorities interested in Instrumental Enrichment: the Inner London Education Authority, Coventry, Sheffield, Manchester and Somerset. Its belated entry into the picture was subsequently cited by the Schools Council as a reason, perhaps a justifiable one, for the subsequent lack of monitoring, saying that plans had already been too far advanced by the education authorities to arrange any properly organised research.

In my opinion, by relying so completely on the Instrumental Enrichment materials, and in trying to skimp on the time and resources for training, the local education authorities achieved two disastrous effects which most of the other projects took great pains to avoid. The programme was reduced to a series of worksheet exercises, precisely what Feuerstein insists Instrumental Enrichment must never be.

This was partly because the authorities' schemes concentrated on the practical rather than theoretical aspects of the programme and partly due to the anti-intellectual traditions in British education.

The second effect was to implement the programme in schools where the head teachers were unsympathetic, or at least less than fully committed, and refused to give adequate timetabling opportunities for Instrumental Enrichment, and even with poorly trained teachers who were sometimes completely unenthusiastic about the philosophy and practice of the programme. Proper control groups to assess any effects were not established and even some of the psychological tests, used to measure the progress of the Instrumental Enrichment children, were inappropriate for the age groups involved and could not, therefore, tell the evaluators anything.

Initial workshops for Instrumental Enrichment in other countries were often of three weeks, or if a smaller number of instruments was introduced, between 50 and 80 hours. But the British teachers and psychologists were only given a four-and-a-half-day initial workshop where they were introduced to the programme and trained in four of the instruments. There was provision for teachers to receive classroom support, but this was by supervisors and psychologists who had not received the programme at first hand.

Most of the major projects around the world heeded Feuerstein's warnings about the minimum length of Instrumental Enrichment programmes—around 300 hours spread over two years. This works out at about five hours a week, and the majority of projects provided one hour a day. In Britain the evaluators produced their reports after only one year of Instrumental Enrichment had been taught—for as little as one hour a week in some schools!

Some of the comments of Instrumental Enrichment evaluators in the five local authorities, contained in a report by the Schools Council called *Making up our Minds*, are very revealing about British attitudes to educational innovation. The report, published in 1983, was billed as an 'exploratory report', but there has been no other and no plans appear in hand to produce one.

*   *   *

In the Inner London Education Authority two schools were involved, both single-sex. The boys' school had a large number of ethnic minority pupils. The Head of the Remedial Department was in charge of Instrumental Enrichment implementation but the teachers 'had understandable reservations at the prospect of Instrumental Enrichments' intrusions into their well-planned curriculum . . . there was no marked enthusiasm for Instrumental Enrichment work.' Notwithstanding this, some good results were noted, but both teachers left the school during 1982 and Instrumental Enrichment 'came to an abrupt and unsatisfactory end'.

In the girls' school two teachers had volunteered to do Instrumental Enrichment. One had a general interest in remedial work, the other was a Physical Education teacher 'who wished to develop skills in remedial work'. The Head of the Remedial Department was not, however, involved, there were no support arrangements within the school and the two teachers were isolated. Although they struggled with the materials the teachers 'found that their workload left little time for preparation, particularly for bridging issues. Instrumental Enrichment classes took place in rooms in general use, with the inherent difficulties of storage and portage of materials. Classroom facilities were very poor as the building was in the process of being run down for closure. Because of other pressures 'Instrumental Enrichment was a low priority on their time'. The two Instrumental Enrichment groups were drawn from 14 'lowest attainers' who had disturbed behaviour which, for the less experienced teacher, impeded her teaching of the programme.

*   *   *

In Coventry four schools took part, two comprehensive schools and two special schools. While some of the teachers had volunteered out of professional commitment, others were 'invited . . . [or] . . . requested by the headmaster' to take part. The local authority had expressed strong backing for the project, but in the two comprehensive schools there were problems timetabling Instrumental Enrichment, with the result that one school had Instrumental Enrichment reduced to once a week and the other curtailed its programme after just two terms.

The tests administered after the children had received Instrumental Enrichment for varying lengths of time did not show any general improvement, but 'unfortunately the test chosen did not have norms for children over 14 years 11 months, and this meant that comparison of standardised scores was possible for less than half of the Coventry pupils'. Had the tests shown anything else, given the level and manner of the implementation, it would have been a small miracle.

Nevertheless, the report stated that teachers felt that Instrumental Enrichment had 'helped some children to become more thoughtful and less impulsive in their approach to learning'. There was also a widespread feeling that teaching techniques had been improved by working with Instrumental Enrichment materials, and that the use of this approach had increased awareness of the strengths and weaknesses of various pupils.

In Coventry the special schools have continued to be interested in Instrumental Enrichment and have continued to teach it enthusiastically. But authority-wide the interest now seems to be declining. A similar phenomenon has taken place in Manchester in that the education authority is now ending its financial support to Instrumental Enrichment teaching in schools and it is up to schools themselves to pay for Instrumental Enrichment if they wish to continue it.

* * *

Manchester had one of the most sophisticated experiments, which was tried in four very different situations: a sixteen-plus community college containing some physically and mentally handicapped children, and its companion 11–16 comprehensive school; a suburban 11–16 high school, and a small part-residential special school for 11–16-year-olds.

The teachers received a one-week training workshop but also had extensive back-up from the city's Education Support Service. Initial scepticism from teachers was ameliorated when they 'experienced an unexpectedly good response from their pupils'. But staff changes, pupil movement between streams and timetable constraints meant that only the Further Education college group retained some membership stability over the two-year period.

Despite the wide range of disabilities in the Further Education college groups, this setting proved the most successful. A contributing factor, it was suggested, was the greater time spent on Instrumental Enrichment—some four hours a week. It was not stated how regularly children in the other schools received Instrumental Enrichment.

In many cases the teachers in the comprehensives stuck rigidly to the teacher's guides and produced teacher-centred lessons with little emphasis on pupil-pupil discussion. This strongly suggests that many teachers did not have an adequate theoretical grasp of the programme.

One of the main problems discussed by teachers, here and elsewhere, was the difficulty in coping with different levels of ability within class. Some children wanted to rush ahead on the worksheets, and in the case of one teacher this was remedied by producing extra cards for extending the instruments.

The evaluator found no obvious impact on attendance or on formal tests. 'However, for the Further Education group the teacher had never found materials capable of engaging and developing such pupils to the extent that Instrumental Enrichment was doing. Several of these students requested continuation of Instrumental Enrichment in the evening classes when they left full-time education.'

The report adds:

> There is virtual unanimity that the structured and progressive nature of Instrumental Enrichment has been helpful to many pupils in some of the following respects: reducing impulsiveness, developing analytical powers, improving behaviour and encouraging a sense of responsibility (probably a function of self-image). The structure of the programme also seems to have helped many teachers to plan work methodically and reflect on their objectives.

*   *   *

In Sheffield the staff in the two special schools involved in the experiment had been generally more interested than those in the comprehensive school, where there were yet again problems with timetabling and class organisation. Two of the teachers originally trained by the commercial dissemination company were unsympathetic towards the workshops and, although they continued teaching they dropped out after the first year for reasons unconnected with their attitudes. But two other teachers joined the programme because of their favourable experience with children who had been taught Instrumental Enrichment. Teachers generally found the theory difficult, and were initially sceptical, but increased familiarity with the programme produced greater commitment. The report went on:

> Teachers and evaluator noted that many children became more and more willing to engage in discussion and more confident in planning their activities. This was true for the older children but it must be said that a small group of younger children, all of whom claimed to enjoy Instrumental Enrichment and to have understood it, actually appeared to have gained little from it.
>
> The teachers felt that Instrumental Enrichment was helping them improve their professional skill; they liked the feeling of purpose the material and the project provided. They believed that their pupils were improving, and that this improvement generalised to other areas of the curriculum.

Overall, the evaluator in Sheffield found the experiment with Instrumental Enrichment 'not proven' and recommended more research with control groups. However he noted the following 'impressive outcomes':

* Teachers' perceptions that working with the material had made them better and more thoughtful practitioners.

* Improvements were noted with ESN(M) children to engage in discussion and in planning activities.

* Encouragement was given to art and other subjects by the

strategy of bridging. The teachers felt that Instrumental Enrichment could be an integrating factor in the curriculum.

* ESN (M) schools had begun to rethink their core curriculum in the light of this project and the secondary school was planning to offer Instrumental Enrichment as an option.

*   *   *

In Somerset three special schools, and a special unit within a comprehensive school, took part in the experimental project which saw 62 pupils, aged between ten and 14, being given Instrumental Enrichment twice a week. In the schools where the teaching was of a high standard, pupils and teachers reported that they had gained a great deal. In one special school, however, the teacher used the instruments in a question-and-answer fashion and found it impossible to engage or motivate her pupils. This school eventually withdrew.

The evaluator's highly favourable report says:

> There is no clear evidence to support the claims that cognitive skills are improved by the use of Instrumental Enrichment. However there is considerable evidence (observation, discussion, case studies and questionnaire) to support the view that pupils' and teachers' attitudes have changed. Teachers became increasingly aware of the learning capabilities of their pupils, and pupils gained in ego-strength as a result of their successes . . .
>
> The pupils appeared to learn the important rôle of 'learners'. Although there is no hard evidence about improvement in thinking skills, many pupils became aware of the processes and power of their 'thinking'. In three of the four schools, the level of involvement and pupil functioning was greater than any previously witnessed by this evaluator. Behavioural problems virtually did not exist in Instrumental Enrichment classrooms.

He then adds this extraordinary comment: 'It is nevertheless possible that these gains might result from using structured teaching with any materials.'

This remark says a great deal about the implementation of Instrumental Enrichment in Britain. Very many teachers struggled against inadequate training, frequent practical indifference of local education authorities and senior teachers, and almost insuperable obstacles of timetabling and classroom organisation. They were still able to report very important changes in themselves and their pupils.

Yet, in my opinion, their subjective experience has been squandered by an extraordinarily incompetent research programme. No control groups were established, Instrumental Enrichment was not tested against other remedial programmes, a basic number of hours of Instrumental Enrichment was not insisted upon and criterion tests, which could have compared performance on certain tasks before and after Instrumental Enrichment, were not widely used.

*   *   *

It therefore comes as no surprise to find that the implementation of Instrumental Enrichment in Britain is losing ground while it is gaining momentum in other countries. The cost of the Instrumental Enrichment materials, set against the 'not proven' verdicts, has encouraged local education authorities to wash their hands of Instrumental Enrichment.

Only two authorities, Somerset and Oxfordshire, are now trying to continue with more evaluations. They have sought to overcome the costs of the materials needed to carry out this further research in schools by producing their own materials and bridging manuals. Even here, however, the prospects for a proper scientific assessment do not look too good.

The educational psychologist supervising the teachers in Bridgwater, Somerset, (where the evaluation is being carried out), says that Instrumental Enrichment is not really getting a fair trial. Inadequate training in the theory and practice of the instruments has meant they have been viewed as 'worksheets' by many teachers whose 'eyes tend to glaze over when you talk of mediation. Only four of the teachers involved in Somerset could be said to have properly grasped the correct way to teach Instrumental Enrichment,' he explained. Also, the teachers' dispute and other organisational problems have prevented proper co-ordination and supervision.

The psychologist refused to discuss or show the new materials that had been produced in Somerset, and denied access to the teachers involved. The authority would not approve, he claimed. While there is certainly nothing wrong with people extending or changing the presentation of the instruments—Feuerstein would certainly not object in principle as he believes the theory is by far the most important thing—a question mark does hang over whether the supervisor and the teachers in Somerset really understand the theory enough to construct their own instruments.

They have not been to Israel and have not been trained in the theory and use of the Learning Potential Assessment Device, which is vital to building up experience in the diagnosis and effective countering of cognitive impairments. Building the instruments in Israel involved scientific evaluation and assessment based on enormous clinical experience with low-functioning children. Is this available in Somerset and Oxford?

Also questionable is the rationale put forward for constructing the new instruments. The Somerset supervisor said that some were inappropriate because they were too difficult and did not do enough to keep children interested. In my view, this smacks of reducing the instruments to the level of poor Instrumental Enrichment teachers and to the presumed level of unintelligent pupils. If the dispossessed children of the Latin American *barrios*, and the North American ghettos, can cope with the instruments it is hard to see why the children of Somerset cannot.

Patrick Leeson, an educational psychologist who is one of the key evaluators of the Oxfordshire Instrumental Enrichment programme, suggested that some of the difficulties lay with teachers, a number of whom 'did not respond to training' on Instrumental Enrichment. Apparently they had found bridging very difficult and the evaluators decided to try and build-in bridging ideas to the instruments. As a result they would be more content-based than Feuerstein's instruments and would not require the same level of teacher-training, financial outlay or pupil effort. It was entirely possible that this form of expediency could result in the instruments 'losing something' by way of effectiveness but he felt there was no practical alternative. He declined absolutely to show any of the new, redesigned instruments. There is no doubt that they are controversial even among Oxfordshire teachers. One committed Instrumental Enrichment teacher in the county called them 'good child distractors' and claimed they had little to do with Instrumental Enrichment.

One particularly interesting comment by Patrick Leeson laid bare the cultural obstacles to incorporating Instrumental Enrichment into Britain. The teachers who had shown most commitment had, in fact, been those who were more liberal and progressive in their attitudes and assumed the need for democratic values in class. However, Instrumental Enrichment was a very structured programme and required a great deal of teacher-direction, class discussion and interaction at the same time. This was exceptionally difficult for teachers to execute—they were either too liberal and allowed discussion to run away or were too authoritarian and not disposed to allowing enough effective pupil participation in the lessons. Then he went on:

> Theoretically, Feuerstein occupies the middle ground between teacher-centred and pupil-centred education. But in Britain we find this middle ground hard to find. We are finding that we need to pull teachers back from being a little over-liberal in the way they teach Instrumental Enrichment.

In Israel, education has always been highly directive because of the need to integrate children quickly from foreign and technologically far-removed cultures into a modern state. Economic and military exigencies have also required the need for a heavy emphasis on education and training, and this is generally accepted by the population.

On the other hand, the forms of Victorian authoritarianism which have accompanied professional teaching in Britain (according to which children were a lower form of social and intellectual life, to be seen and not heard in class—except when asked by the teacher to speak) has never surfaced in Israeli schools. Even the most rigorous and relentlessly demanding education in the Yeshivas—the religious schools—is based on debate and discussion, guided by teachers.

School students are treated with much more respect and have more relaxed relationships with their teachers, who are very directive, but not in a repressive way. Consequently, the middle ground Patrick Leeson finds so elusive in Britain is much more naturally occupied by Israeli teachers. If anything Instrumental Enrichment, which some British teachers find shockingly forceful and teacher-centred, only represents a slight liberalisation in the learning process in Israeli education.

Lack of funds is a real problem in British state education and the decision to hand over dissemination of Instrumental Enrichment to a commercial concern has, in my view, clearly weakened its future in Britain. There is some talk in Israel of radically reviewing the costs of the training and Instrumental Enrichment materials, so this disincentive can be minimised.

Many authorities have used government grants to buy the materials and then proceeded to waste teachers' commitment and public funds by not ensuring effective implementation or evaluation. It is now apparent that a majority of the authorities lurched into an Instrumental Enrichment programme with no thought of how to carry it forward in the long term.

While there remains interest in Instrumental Enrichment in Britain there will still be some hope that it can be properly assessed and evaluated with the same rigour as in other projects abroad. But if things progress as they are doing now, it is highly likely that an important opportunity for helping children in difficulties will be thrown away.

WELLER, Keith, and CRAFT, Alma. *Making Up Our Minds: An Exploratory Study of Instrumental Enrichment*. Schools Council, 1983.

SOME COMMENTS ON THE
INTERNATIONAL RESULTS

Transferring an educational innovation from one culture to another is always desperately difficult. It is hard to know what aspects of the innovation are culturally specific and which are general, and there are numerous pitfalls in the way an educational project can be misinterpreted and vitiated as it moves between administrative systems. The whole business becomes much more dangerous when the innovation is based on a fundamentally challenging view of intelligence and learning. The capacity for the receiving cultures to misinterpret or reinterpret work to suit their own ideological predilections becomes even greater.

Set against these obstacles, the international findings on Instrumental Enrichment can only be seen as very significant. Even in Britain, where implementation and evaluation was, in my view, the most amateurish, and the programme most debased, the overwhelming response of teachers was one of enthusiasm.

Some general features can be identified by the review of research. In the vast majority of experiments which used control groups, and which tested before and after Instrumental Enrichment performance, there were clear gains for Instrumental Enrichment children in cognitive skills. These were usually accompanied by improvements in self-confidence and classroom behaviour, and teachers' awareness of improved insight into their students and higher level of pedagogic skills. In some experiments, such as the Israeli studies and those at Vanderbilt University in the USA, standardised IQ tests showed improvements of up to 18 points after two years of Instrumental Enrichment.

Whether or not Instrumental Enrichment has clearly shown transference to other academic and non-academic areas seems to depend on the length and sophistication of the experiments, although this is not always the case. The Israeli, Paris, Vanderbilt Studies and the New Zealand study with deaf children, clearly showed this generalisation of skills. But so did the shorter studies in New York and Westchester which found improvements in reading and mathematics. The interim report of the crucial Yale study—one of the most rigorous attempted— found 'far transfer' in children who received Instrumental Enrichment for more than a year. This involved children trying to solve unfamiliar cognitive problems with the skills acquired from Instrumental Enrichment lessons, and was not yet, therefore, an application of skills to academic subjects. But this is a research area for the second part of the study and will be an important part of the full research report. Subjective indications from teachers suggest there is significant transfer to other school subjects.

The researchers at Vanderbilt expressed considerable surprise at the generalised effect of Instrumental Enrichment into other subjects. They point out correctly that Instrumental Enrichment seeks to remedy poor cognitive functions which are the prerequisite for abstract operational thinking skills. Changes could, therefore, be very real, but very subtle, and not immediately visible in other school subjects.

There are various reasons for this, which makes the Vanderbilt findings of transfer to other subjects and similar findings from other studies, all the more interesting. Firstly, the cognitive functions and operations which Instrumental Enrichment seeks to instil are not implanted in a mechanical way: one minute absent, the next in place and ready to go. They are the product of painstaking teaching and remain weak until they become embedded and habitual in children. This is a function of both time and practice.

Secondly, the emphasis in Instrumental Enrichment lessons is on discussion, looking at strategies and tactics in problem-solving, and the principles required to analyse situations and resolve problems. The process of thinking is more important than the product—whether a child is right or wrong, or whether he has been able to absorb large amounts of more or less irrelevant subject-matter. Needless to say, this does not happen in most ordinary subject lessons which do not try to engage children in thinking enthusiastically about their subjects. The teaching style is generally neither cognitive nor mediational, with no interaction between the children and no encouragement of pupil-to-pupil interactions; there is no attempt to give the lesson any human and cultural significance, or apply the principle to other areas of life. There is, then, no reason why children highly motivated in Instrumental Enrichment should cope better in such lessons.

Thirdly, the philosophy and theory behind Instrumental Enrichment warns teachers against too easily allocating children into fixed and immutable categories of 'bright', 'able' and 'dim'. It requires a teacher to look for cognitive weaknesses which can be strengthened, and insists on their keeping in mind the possible potential of a child rather than a cynical and jaundiced view of a child's current performance. One of the most damaging effects of inadequate mediated learning experience is a lack of a feeling of competency in children, and the need of a teacher to have a high degree of intentionality—to want children to improve their level of functioning and to believe that they can. This is not always present among teachers who have 'bought' the dominant Western psychological view of intelligence, or who have been worn down by years of routine and disillusionment with children who seem unable to learn, whatever is tried with them.

Finally, independent abstract thinking requires a system of cognitive functions which, in normal children, are interrelated and indistinguishable in normal use. They only become distinguishable when they are deficient and become susceptible to diagnosis. There is evidence presented in Instrumental Enrichment experiments that poor hearing, for example, establishes a range of cognitive impairments that prevent deaf children's cognitive systems from developing properly. As a result they show a tendency to become low achievers and require cognitive education to approach normal levels of performance. Even small impairments in the input of elaborational or expressive elements in thinking can have tremendous effects on a child's or adult's intellectual level and efficiency.

The ability to perform certain cognitive tasks might improve with limited exposure to the relevant parts of Instrumental Enrichment. But to have sufficient skills to organise, interpret and generate information, and to solve problems in completely new subject areas, depends upon a cognitive system which can assimilate new information and acquire new skills of its own accord. This can only be achieved through the whole or at least the major part of the Instrumental Enrichment programme.

All the research findings suggest that the transference of cognitive skills to new subjects happens when children have been given Instrumental Enrichment for a longer rather than a shorter time, by theoretically informed and, for want of a better word, 'democratic' teachers. Such teachers also tend to take the children for non-Instrumental Enrichment subjects as well, or to liaise with teachers in other subjects in order to co-ordinate teaching styles and to promote the cognitive emphasis in other lessons. Dramatic improvements in the generalisation of cognitive skills were reported by teachers and psychologists at the third International Workshop in Jerusalem when this co-ordination took place.

The training of teachers is obviously a crucial aspect of any implementation plan. This was the least successful part of the British experiments with Instrumental Enrichment, and the lack of theory in the practical execution of their work-shops is believed to be the main cause of the problem. It did, however, dove-tail into the traditional anti-theoretical bent of teachers which their teacher-training and acculturation in school staff-rooms has so entrenched. In Israel the teacher-training workshops progressively include more on the Learning Potential Assessment Device until the final workshop for Instrumental Enrichment which concentrates on analysing teacher performance, and on the Learning Potential Assessment Device, and more refined explanations of mediated learning experience.

This approach ensures that teachers are given the theoretical background to cognitive modifiability and an idea of how to diagnose cognitive impairments. As Feuerstein says:

> The division between teachers and psychologists must be broken down. Through knowledge of the Learning Potential Assessment Device teachers can become psychologists and can diagnose children themselves, and psychologists can diagnose and remediate children through teaching. And if parents learn how to use the Learning

Potential Assessment Device they can, if necessary, tell both teachers and psychologists that they are underestimating their children.

Yet the Learning Potential Assessment Device has been absent from the British experiments almost completely.

Despite the limitations imposed by an impoverished British educational system, I have to say that the workshops were serious and well organised, and probably gave teachers more food for thought than all their years of conventional teacher training. Many teachers said that, after the workshop, they 'felt the scales falling from their eyes'. It is not difficult to understand why a commercial company felt that it had to tailor its workshops to the time and resources that our education authorities would be likely to contemplate, and to the prejudices of the teachers taking part.

But this is just the point. Instrumental Enrichment insists on changing teachers' attitudes, powers of analysis and teaching styles. It is the opposite of a 'teacher-proof' method because it places human mediation, teaching in its widest sense, at the centre of all learning. To accept the *status quo* in terms of teachers' ideology and practices is antithetical to everything that Instrumental Enrichment and Feuerstein stand for.

It is fairly clear from the international reports that teachers, and British teachers above all others, need to be introduced to the theory of mediated learning and cognitive modifiability in their teacher-training courses if they are ever going to appreciate the possibilities that Feuerstein and cognitive education generally can open up. Once they have left college, the intellectual and administrative strait-jacket they are placed in within schools is just too strong for in-service training in Instrumental Enrichment to modify more than a few of the most committed and open teachers. It is only in Britain that timetabling rigidities, complaints about the theoretical nature of the programme and manuals, the high amounts of preparation for Instrumental Enrichment lessons, and lack of support from senior teachers, reached the pitch where it affected and, in my view, corrupted the Instrumental Enrichment programmes in schools.

PART 4:

CHANGING ENVIRONMENTS

SPECIAL TREATMENT GROUPS IN YOUTH VILLAGES

Interlinked with the development of Feuerstein's theories and Instrumental Enrichment was the creation of a whole series of imaginative placements for the re-education and re-socialisation of adolescents and younger children who were not, for a variety of reasons, surviving in ordinary schools and society.

Feuerstein was fortunate in that he worked for a voluntary organisation which was much more flexible than the State and was highly receptive to new ideas. Moreover, Youth Aliyah's style of provision allowed for controlled environments which facilitated the enaction of new but theoretically rigorous intervention strategies.

For instance, Youth Aliyah's creation of youth villages, where incoming Jewish children from various parts of the world could, under intense educational and ideological pressure, become Israeli in very short periods of time, were ideal communities in which to attempt the integration of very disturbed delinquent and educationally retarded children.

They were not predominantly care organisations, either for the deprived or the depraved, and hence were not dumping grounds for unwanted or orphaned children, along British lines, or containments for young trouble-makers. They were, above all else, educational institutions in which the values and skills required of young Israeli citizens were instilled.

They conformed to the pioneering tradition in Israel, which had started in the 1930s with the emigration of urban Zionist Jews from Russia and Eastern Europe straight into agricultural communities—the Kibbutzim—where they lived and worked, acquiring the new skills that they needed. The Youth Villages were based strongly on the ethos of the Kibbutz, mirroring its collective attitude to life, work and learning. As a result both of the Kibbutz and Youth Village, and perhaps of the exigencies of communities which had to endure separation as part of the process of emigration, Israeli education and child-care systems have had a strong residential tradition (very different from that of Britain) whose rôle and status remains unchallenged.

With a general population of more or less average new-immigrant children, an emphasis on education and accultura-tion and a highly controllable environment, the Youth Villages were an ideal setting into which to attempt to re-educate and re-socialise children who needed special help.

Fears of Contagion

Grave worries were expressed, however, at Feuerstein's plans to introduce backward and difficult children, terribly damaged from the Holocaust, or by rejection from their families, or from cultural and educational deprivation on a very severe scale, into institutions for run-of-the-mill immigrant children. Was there a risk of contagion?

Feuerstein argued strongly that if there was to be any hope of making them useful citizens and of rescuing them from their damaging past, the children had to be allowed the chance of regaining a place among their peers. He also reassured more traditional psychologists and youth workers that the last thing he wanted was simply to parachute children with such special needs into the mainstream of village life with the hope that the village regime would somehow magically affect the children. Their low self-image and poor competence in many areas of life were such that any uncontrolled competition with more highly achieving children would be counter-productive, producing very anti-social behaviour.

Feuerstein established an experimental trial at the Neve Hadassah Youth Village, where very low-functioning and disturbed children were placed in a treatment group which they could only leave if the psychologists felt they could survive and adapt to the majority of children. This experiment remains the best researched and theorised account of the now widely used Treatment Group provision.

During their time in the group the children were provided with intensive individual treatment programmes which were carefully controlled. Feuerstein and his team of Youth Aliyah psychologists assumed an unusually dominant and directive rôle—at least for the West—over the teachers and the preparation of teaching programmes. Teachers were not encouraged to attempt to deal with crises or serious bad behaviour themselves, but to report straight back to the psychologists, whose job it was to offer strong support and counselling through the tremendous trials that the Feuerstein regime placed upon them.

This theoretically rigorous regime was in complete contrast to the British *ad hoc* care and special school system. A basic element was the concept of 'unconditional acceptance'. No behaviour could be allowed to result in rejection of children who, precisely because of their early experiences of loss or rejection, had become so disturbed. As Feuerstein explains:

> With these children, a vicious cycle of rejection, disturbed behaviour and further rejection continues unabated unless adults, and environments constructed by adults, can intervene to break this compulsive repetition. Uncon-ditioned acceptance is an attempt to reproduce the child's lost experiences of total support from his or her mother in order to foster more self-confidence and security.

This was not done, however, in an over-emotional or soft way. Violent or deviant acts were met with discipline, but poor behaviour was never allowed to elicit a generally hostile response from the staff. If one teacher punished a child, another was encouraged to comfort him. This, of course, runs completely counter to the fashionable—and very mechanistic —rules of behaviour modification commonly used in children's institutions in the West, where reward and punishment systems are adhered to rigidly by the controllers of a regime.

In a real sense the children in the Youth Village shared control of their own regime. They insisted on certain conformity of behaviour but their fear of rejection, which was mobilised when any individual member of the group was in trouble or stood in danger of expulsion for extreme acts, produced a group solidarity which was itself a powerful socialising force.

Stopping teachers or other staff giving up on these children in the face of incredible provocation was a very difficult task, recalls Feuerstein, and required intensive counselling back-up by psychologists to the 'front-line' adults. The risk to any one child of rejection also carried the risk of damage to the whole group—only the most intractably violent children were removed. In the Treatment Group in the Neve Hadassah Youth Village, near Natanya, which was founded in 1960 (although Treatment Groups began in 1958), and on which much of the assessment studies were carried out, only one child was rejected out of 43.

Anxiety, particularly over learning where they had performed badly in the past, to the point of illiteracy, was common to all the children in the Treatment Group. So the regime constructed by Feuerstein devalued schooling in the sense that it became clear that academic criteria were not the only measure of their worth. Classes were organised around non-academic activities —a lot of them very regressive, like drawing and paper-cutting—and teachers were instructed to allow the children to be disruptive in the classroom. Feuerstein now comments rather sardonically:

> The therapeutic value in this was not easily recognised by the teachers or others in the immediate surroundings. On the surface it looked like a wanton explosion of aggression and unruliness. But the children could not act any other way: for their own sanity they had to undermine the area of performance which had caused them their greatest distress, frustration and sense of failure.

Inducing Regression

Regressive child-like behaviour, Feuerstein explains, was not only tolerated, it was encouraged, even induced, as a major part of their rehabilitation programme.

> Many of these children had learnt to control their behaviour in the wake of frequent unpleasant clashes with society. Unfortunately this control was achieved only by a means of total blockage of their intellectual and social capacities. There was really no ability to discriminate between areas of desirable activities and those leading to rejection and punishment, and this created symptoms of withdrawal or very submissive and conformist behaviour, which could alternate with extreme outbursts of disruptive behaviour.

This response to the world was deeply resistant to any type of change and, unless the defensive personality of such damaged children was broken down and reconstituted, rehabilitation was not considered possible. The children were encouraged to regress to being much younger—almost, as it were, guided through 'a breakdown', whereupon they received a host of gratifying and positive experiences, in contrast to what had happened in their real childhood. This induced regression should in no way be confused with what is, in my opinion, the 'break-their-spirit' ideology of British penal establishments and some regrettable children's homes run on certain behaviourist lines. It was brought about by 'unconditional acceptance', a reduction of anxiety and close supportive relationships with counsellors. To a great extent it was an attempt to control constructively the regression that deeply-damaged children go through when forced to confront their first caring relationships with adults and peers.

As much for the teachers' sanity, one suspects, as for anything else, much of the time was spent outside the classroom on excursions, cultural events and interesting field trips. Academic competition between the children was minimised and not allowed at all between the Treatment Group and their better adjusted peers in the Youth Village. In this way the children's delicate egos were protected and nurtured, and their anxiety about learning reduced. Instead of classroom ordeals, 'real' or more formal education was undertaken by individual tutors who doubled as special counsellors. The hours of private tutoring took place in a relaxed and supportive atmosphere where educational attainment, although considered important, was subordinated to the relationship between the child and his counsellor.

Once the child began to value himself independently of his performance in school, anxiety about learning declined and learning itself took place. An indication of the success of this policy was that when some contact was allowed with the non-treatment group children and the inevitable cruel jokes were made about their lack of brains, the children were able to shrug it off good humouredly. The eventual academic results of these children were very surprising, as we shall see.

The self-confidence of the children in the Treatment Group

was also based on their privileged access to games, sports and cultural events that allowed them to excel in non-academic areas. The ordinary children in the village often became intensely irritated at the repeated victories of the children in sports, carpentry, drama and other activities which were 'high-status' activities. The 'self-image' of the children rapidly improved, to the point that closer contact with their peers outside the group became possible.

The two powerful drives of adolescents—to disassociate themselves from their parents and the adult world, and to 'belong'—were used by Feuerstein and his colleagues to socialise the children by a very carefully-planned relationship with those outside the group. The Treatment Group and the other groups met in the grounds, sports field and dining hall of the village. Relationships that developed were monitored fairly closely by a relatively high number of adults who were on hand to intervene if a relationship looked as if it would become distressful to the weaker child. There were around four group-workers to 23–27 charges.

While the children in the Treatment Group had a different education and separate bunking facilities, these informal contacts provided a safe, relatively controlled means of mixing the children. But all children are obliged to carry out work in the Villages: this is a basic condition for living in any co-operative institution in Israel and, ideologically, is considered an activity which underpins the values of the society. It also liberates the potential of those involved and provides oppor-tunities for socialising disturbed adolescents.

The Power of Work
The duties placed on children in the Youth Village required responsibility, persistence and stability, and the ability to work with other children and untrained adults. It was clearly beyond the powers of the Treatment Group children. They were given, therefore, simple but enjoyable tasks under the supervision of their group workers. This was originally intended for a year, but after eight months the Treatment Group in Neve Hadassah rebelled and collectively demanded that they should share in the full, high-status work carried out by the ordinary children.

During the first stage the children were not even aware that other children of the same age functioned differently. Over time their maturing and the closeness of normal children changed their need for achieving social status. An extra incentive was that, while the treatment group were allowed to indulge in 'regressive' activities, they were not included in the rewards given to the children on the ordinary programme for their work. Most of these rewards were in fact symbolic and social—like being acknowledged—and their ability to need these rewards was a great step forward.

Work, in fact, became the first field in which the children within the Village were integrated, followed by school and other group activities. The children were continually reassessed so that they were only offered tasks within their emotional and intellectual competence. Gradually children left the group to join the ordinary Village programme and others joined in their place.

Although the graduation of children out of the group was destabilising, it was also a goal to be achieved. Equally important was the arrival of new, very disturbed children into the treatment community. This showed the 'veterans' that teachers were prepared to accept children who were even more low-functioning than they were and countervailed a tendency among the teachers to respond too quickly to changes in the group and individuals by lessening their tolerance of unacceptable behaviour.

Remarkable Changes
The results of the Treatment Group approach in Neve Hadassah were quite remarkable and formed the basis of Youth Aliyah's dramatic expansion of its intake of disturbed children as the numbers of immigrant children declined. Of the 43 children in the original treatment at the Neve Hadassah group, half were victims of the Holocaust and had been fully or partially orphaned; 25 of the 43 children had been subject to overt rejection from their families; 30 per cent had emigrated to Israel without their parents; only one child could read fluently and 62 per cent did not have an elementary grasp of addition,

subtraction, multiplication and division. On follow-up studies, some 30 per cent of the children reached tenth-grade level in basic subjects. In Israel children cannot move up the grades until they have reached a certain standard and tenth-grade represents the average ability for a 16-year-old. The majority reached grade eight level; a significant proportion, 20 per cent, reached grade nine, while something like 12 per cent went on to grade 11 and 12 standard.

These figures were confirmed by the fact that virtually all the age-eligible boys were accepted by the Army in ordinary units where average ability is required. There were no subsequent complaints from the military authorities concerning their behaviour or adaptation. This was a very different outcome from children who went into special residential settings. The Treatment Group children were also allowed back into the families and schools from which they were originally rejected after an average of two years and were successfully re-integrated. Another indicator of the programme's success was that the leader of the Youth Village and his staff felt there had been no 'contagion' of undamaged children and continued to accept the disturbed adolescents.

Considering the previous proneness of the Treatment Group to delinquency, the lack of subsequent delinquent behaviour was remarkable—only one graduate was involved in a minor illegal offence. This is a very different outcome from the children kept in British approved schools (now CHEs), borstals (now Youth Custody Centres) or children's homes, where the statistics of recidivism are very high. The academic success of the Treatment Group children also contrasts very favourably with that achieved by British children's homes with education on the premises. A recent report on these, conducted by Her Majesty's Inspectorate, found standards to be unacceptably low.

FOSTER HOME GROUP CARE

For younger children and even for adolescents with severe behavioural and intellectual problems and perhaps physical handicaps, too, any form of residential care poses insuperable 'survival' difficulties. Foster care would seem to be the answer for these children. But it is well established that the fostering of difficult children is prone to breakdowns which are profoundly traumatic for the children rejected by new sets of parents.

The Foster Home Group Care programme was developed by Feuerstein to try and counter the disadvantages of both residential and foster care while drawing on the strengths of both. Like all his changing environments, the programme is informed by rigorous psychological theory and beautifully simple, commonsense ideas. The programme is nevertheless, in my view, light-years in advance of Western practice and furnishes proof of the adage that it takes a clever man to find the simple solutions!

Pre-adolescent children require a sense of total belonging to a protective environment, and one of the problems of foster care is that it is a transient and conditional provision in which children, at least initially, feel like strangers on trial. They and the new family know that they will only be able to remain if they do not disrupt the family's balance too much and if they meet its members' needs and capacities. Feuerstein has a clear understanding of the problems that arise:

> Whether it is stated openly or not, the initial period of adjustment in a new home is a testing period when foster parents keep their new foster child at a distance, even when at the same time they are saying 'Call me mother', or 'Call me father'. I know of many cases where the parents have told of their struggle to overcome differences in the child's body odour before they could narrow the distance between them. This is natural but it sets up an estrangement

in the child and a reserve in the family that can leave a residue throughout the relationship.

This is the case with normal children. But imagine how much worse this estrangement can be with a multi-handicapped child or one with severe behavioural problems. For the child's part, he compares his new strange environment to the one which before gave him a sense of belonging and he does not allow himself to be fully 'present' in his new family. His mind is elsewhere. He can't function properly.

Matters can be equally bad outside the family, in the new school and in the street. It is usually parents who introduce their children to teachers, neighbours and social institutions. Foster parents' introduction of their foster children, as opposed to their own children, is fraught with uncertainty and anxiety, and even an excessive responsibility, and this is communicated to the child and heightens his feelings of estrangement.

A slightly different reaction is produced by a residential placement, argues Feuerstein. Here the child has been extracted from a damaging environment, inevitably creating a sense of isolation from the child's real world. This is not only accepted as an inevitable physical consequence of being placed in a home but is seen as part of the therapeutic or remedial programme. Although there is a sense of belonging for many children in residential homes, denied to foster children, because it is created by their identification with peers in the same predicament, the isolation from their family and communities is keenly felt by inmates anxious to end it. In some cases over long periods this sense of isolation becomes very serious and reduces children's ability to respond to the uncontrolled impact of real-life situations when they are finally 'released'. They are unable to benefit from contact with normal peers and ordinary social relationships.

So there are disadvantages and advantages in both types of placement. There is one major problem that they both have in common: foster families and residential settings willing to take very difficult children are in very short supply. It was this fact that provided the galvanising spark of Feuerstein's ruminations about the inadequate nature of placements for some children. Then, in 1962, a group of very disturbed and low-functioning children, deeply troubled by their separation from their parents during a secret flight from one of the developing countries, were referred to Feuerstein. 'They were considered very high-risk children and yet no suitable placement for them could be found,' he recalls.

Feuerstein and his colleagues established the Foster Home Group Care programme both as a response to the needs of the children and as a way of countering the lack of a traditional placement. Its key characteristics were that the children would be fostered to parents within a farming community but that the type of fostering would be much more limited than usual, and the foster parents' responsibilities much reduced.

The total burden for the care, treatment, education and regulation of the children was laid on the shoulders of the highly trained teachers and counsellors who ran the Treatment Group for the children inside the village. The aim of the programme was to use the strengths of fostering—the normality in relationships and environment—and the security and control of a highly structured group.

Strange Criteria

A controversial criterion for the selection of the village (an agricultural co-operative called a Moshav) for the trial run was that it had to need the work of the children and the financial reward for fostering them. A well-off community with a tradition of voluntary work was turned down in favour of a struggling village, and only adults who admitted they needed the income were allowed to be foster parents.

If a couple said to us they wanted to foster the child because they wanted to make an idealistic contribution, we didn't want to know.

Idealism has its place in child care. But in our experience it was not enough to sustain the relationship with very difficult children. Those parents who needed the money and the work to improve their life had an interest in stopping the placement from breaking down.

On the other hand, the child had a greater sense of

belonging, knowing he was a contributor to the family's financial well-being. These criteria of economic need proved the best indicators for stability in foster placements. And let me tell you, the financial relationship, and our insistence that the foster parents did not get too involved, did not stop love developing. Quite the reverse.

The foster parents were not allowed to assume the rôle of mother and father or to encourage their foster children to call them mum and dad. Their responsibility was limited to providing as much emotional support as possible during the few hours that the child spent in the foster home. The reason for this was the belief that fostering cognitively or behaviourally maladjusted children was a tremendous burden that was made untenable by very intimate relationships. These were liable to create daily frictions, unmet expectations, questions and doubts by the parents about whether the child was really for them, and whether they and their family were benefiting from the experience.

Foster children often do not feel any sense of belonging to a new foster family and resent attempts to try and make them feel that they do belong. They still identify with their real family or, because of repeated rejections, are unwilling to make new emotional ties.

In Feuerstein's view children who feel isolated and have difficulty adapting to their new home are prime risks for a placement breakdown unless they are given a great deal of support. The more difficult the child the greater the support needed.

For the children in the programme, says Feuerstein, it was necessary to establish a parallel environment that could support the foster family and 'take the strain', while offering the children a group environment to which they could belong.

The fact that the group is one of peers rather than siblings offers much greater strength to the child and creates a higher motivation for the child to adapt to group-life and to learn the rules of the group society. Because the child does not feel isolated in the group, but has a sense of belonging in this second society, integration in the family and the community is much easier.

From early morning the foster children are placed in the Treatment Group classes where cognitive development with Instrumental Enrichment is the main thrust of the remedial work. According to Feuerstein's general philosophy such development will not only attack areas of low intellectual functioning but will provide the child with more intellectual controls over behaviour. The class acts as an important tool for socialisation. But there are also one or two hours' individual tuition for the children, many of whom, on top of their 'trainable' or 'educationally mentally-retarded' classification also have communication, convulsive and motoric disorders. A number of the children also tend to show moderate signs of autistic behaviour.

From one o'clock to four o'clock there is a break for lunch and work at the foster home, after which the children return for various activities like homework preparation, dancing and singing. And then, after a break for supper, the children are gathered together again for supervised cultural activities. The time spent in the foster home is very limited indeed.

Stressful situations, such as a child's illness, are the responsibility of the Treatment Group staff. This comprises a house mother who is also the staff director (usually a teacher taken from the village and trained up), a youth leader who lives on site, too, and is responsible for extracurricular activities and counselling, a psychologist and a social worker who provide support to the foster parents and children and mould individual programmes within the group regime.

There is also a school head who assumes complete responsibility for the child's education, and it is stressed that foster parents should not feel responsible for the academic endeavour of their charges, so that they need not feel guilty about the child's failings. Foster parents are even discouraged from taking children on excursions or trips, such as to the swimming pool, where issues of control and levels of anxiety can reach crisis point very quickly.

Without the tensions involved in fostering a handicapped and disturbed child the relationship is relaxed and supportive to the foster child. Breakdowns are very, very rare. The intensity of the socialisation within the group has been very successful in reducing idiosyncratic and disturbed behaviour.

'We have observed that many autistic-like behaviours, echolalia (obsessive echoing of words spoken to the child), uncontrolled questioning and temper tantrums, are reduced by the reaction of the group which shows an unwillingness to accept such behaviours,' comments Feuerstein.

The temporary character of the placement at such Foster Home Group Care regimes is impressed on children and staff so that the orientation is to work hard to get out in the normal peer-group environment of the village school, or normal Youth Aliyah Village or the Army. It was found, however, that for children accepted at older ages or with too large a gap in their functioning, this was unrealistic. The final out-turn figures are nearer to 70 per cent. This is a reliable figure for the boys because it marks the number accepted into the Army on its quite rigorous criteria for admission. There is no similar concrete figure for the girls as entry into the Army is not so necessary, socially or legally.

But a large number of both girls and boys who do not go into the Army find jobs and live out lives previously thought impossible by psychologists and psychiatrists. A significant number of the graduates of the programme have even obtained rank in the Army.

Take Two Children

The case histories of Yitzhak and Avner show some of the ground that the children can cover with the help of the Foster Home Group Care programme. Yitzhak was referred to Feuerstein from a youth village where he had been placed as a new immigrant. At the age of 12, the boy was totally illiterate and apathetic, suffering from incontinence and covered in impetigo. He was listless and, when confronted with stimuli, responded only randomly. He had been diagnosed as severely mentally handicapped and neurologically and organically impaired. In one test, however, of the Learning Potential Assessment Device he did remarkably well and showed a glimmering of ability that had been assumed non-existent on the basis of all the other tests. In conventional psychometrics the significance of this one area of success would have been put aside in favour of the boy's overall performance. In the Learning Potential Assessment Device interpretation of results, it became the sign of a hidden potential which had to be helped in order to surface.

Yitzhak was placed at the Moshav Nahalim, the first Foster Home Treatment Group placement, in a foster family not considered altogether suitable because the father was felt to be a little too strict and emotionally involved for the severity of the boy's condition. The conflicts between the family and child were, in fact, very great and, had it not been for the support of the Treatment Group staff and the partial rôle of the foster parents, Feuerstein says that there is no doubt that the placement would have broken down disastrously.

Yet because the placement hung together—by threads, it seems—and offered the child some stability alongside his involvement in the parallel community of the group, Yitzhak made astonishing progress. He learned to read and write within a very short space of time and his incontinence subsided, apart from night-time bed-wetting which persisted until he was 20.

So rapid was his academic progress that he was moved into the village's ordinary elementary school—in the event a serious mistake. It removed Yitzhak too soon from the security of the group and allowed the control of the Foster Home Group Care programme to be diluted. Without its total support, conflicts emerged between foster child and foster parents that needed special intervention to keep them from boiling over.

Yitzhak remained disturbed for many years—all through high school, in fact—but although his emotional problems impeded his development he struggled on intellectually with some success. He eventually won a leadership position in a youth settler movement in occupied territories, and had a successful career in the Army, ending up as an army chaplain. He now occupies a senior financial position in a company, has married and had two children. Most interestingly, he has redeveloped his relationship with his foster parents and participates as an ordinary son in their lives.

Avner, at 14 years old, was considered so intellectually defective that psychiatrists felt he was not even trainable. At the time of referral he was being prepared for a permanent custodial care regime. Feuerstein's proposal to place him in an open regime was considered too dangerous by many who had known him. It took four years before Avner was able to express himself or to learn to read basic words. He did, however, manage to respond to instructions within the Treatment Group and took part in its activities.

Completely independent existence, in the sense of leaving the group and the Moshav to survive in open society, did not prove possible for Avner. But his work in the Treatment Group did provide him with the competency to work as a store manager's assistant within the Moshav. He has an affable way of dealing with customers, has shown surprisingly good organisational powers, seen in his arrangement of the merchandise, and is a respected member of the village community. The path mapped out for him before was to vegetate in a secure institution.

When Feuerstein shows visitors around Nahalim he tells them that in many ways the Foster Group Care programme is one of his proudest achievements. He points to the various children, all of whom he knows by their first names, and says: 'We took him from a hospital where they said he was an imbecile. This child, they said, had such a low IQ that any schooling was a nonsense, but in a year's time she leaves Nahalim for an ordinary residential school. Here is a child with autistic behaviour; before he just stayed at home and did nothing. Now he is very settled here and doing very well'.

In Britain difficult children are placed in foster homes often with little preparation and, in my view, little support either to the child or the family, other than weekly payments to take the children off Social Services' hands. The number of foster-home breakdowns for older children in care, according to recent research by the Social Services Research Group of Bristol University, is, on average, five per child. Although there are not the similar type of small co-operative village communities in Britain, this seems the least necessary element of the Foster Home Group Care Programme. There is no reason why similar programmes could not be set up to deal with very disturbed and handicapped children in Britain, where they can gain from the openness of a foster family and sense of belonging to a peer group, and be spared the traumatic experiences of placement-breakdowns and the destabilising isolation and estrangement of ordinary residential or foster placements.

PLASTIC SURGERY FOR DOWN'S SYNDROME CHILDREN

Giving plastic surgery to Down's Syndrome children to normalise their appearance does not, at first sight, seem to belong to an exposition of Feuerstein's changing environments. But the simple and speedy techniques used to alter these children's appearance changes their whole world. Following the operation, research has shown that other children and adults respond completely differently, and lose their prejudices and low expectations of the Down's children's abilities.

Even their own parents, no matter how devoted, have been found to lose their fatalism and become much more ambitious for their children after the operation has demonstrated that the effects of this genetic disorder are not insuperable.

The operations are immensely controversial because they question parents' often hard fought-for accommodation to their children's condition. A typical argument is, 'We love our child the way she is; why should she have to undergo painful surgery to appease the prejudices of the outside world? It is the world that needs educating rather than my child.'

Although understandable, Feuerstein and his colleagues maintain that parents' opposition is a reflection of the 'passive/acceptant approach' to handicapped children which dominates their care in the West and takes many different forms. Its basic premise is that children with genetic, physical or intellectual disabilities must be accepted for what they are. They need to be helped, but neither they nor their parents should be given too high expectations.

The whole of Feuerstein's theoretical and practical work stands in conflict with this passive acceptance. Instead, he argues for an 'active-modification approach', claiming that children, and indeed adults, can be modified far more than hitherto realised. The conflict surrounding Down's Syndrome children represents a strikingly clear example of this clash of fundamental ideologies.

Feuerstein argues that the notion that the world should change is a very nice one but, in the meantime, the children suffer from appalling stigmatisation which affects their self-image and every level of their performance. It is also asking too much that people, especially children, should not notice something so different as the highly distinctive facial character-istics of Down's Syndrome children. It is completely natural that other children should make these differentiations; if they did not, they would probably have some cognitive deficiencies, he insists.

Obstacles to Integration
Moreover, some of the physical characteristics of Down's Syndrome children make their integration into society very difficult. This, in turn, makes mediation with the child difficult and creates cognitive deficiencies, often assumed to be an incurable part of the condition but which are in fact highly remediable.

In a way the opposition to plastic surgery, once taken out of its social context, is very strange. The surgeon leading the medical team in the Israeli programme, Professor Manehem Wexler, head of the Plastic and Maxillafacial Surgery Depart-ment at the Hebrew University in Jerusalem, points out that everyone agrees with plastic surgery for Hypertelorism, where the eyes are much too far apart. 'In these cases vast cranial surgery is undertaken and everyone is very satisfied. Why deny the same right to Down's Syndrome children?'

For some reason, perhaps because of the comparatively high incidence of Down's Syndrome and its varying physical effects, the condition seems to have been peculiarly caught up in a protective welfarism, and a very strong passive/acceptant approach by both parents and professionals. When I first publicised this plastic surgery in an article in *The Sunday Times*, reaction to the idea was overwhelmingly hostile.

This is particularly strange when it comes from parents, because they know it is often their children's looks which play the largest part in keeping them out of ordinary schools or in causing their abilities to be underestimated.

It was precisely this prejudicial underestimation of Down's Syndrome children which prompted Feuerstein to consider plastic surgery as part of their active modification programme. Significant changes in children's performance after Instrumental Enrichment instruction were being rendered meaningless when they returned, or were placed for the first time, in ordinary schools. They were set low goals and it was assumed that their capacities were very limited.

This conformed to the generally unfavourable views of the potentialities of Down's Syndrome children held by professionals. Most of the research about the intellectual functioning was carried out in Israel in residential establishments where they did not lead normal lives. The upper threshold of ability was not considered very great. But their abilities do vary greatly and it is their looks more than anything else which falsely categorise many potentially able children.

Actually, other retarded children with the same cognitive problems as Down's Syndrome children do escape the stigma and labels that accompany their conditions. But Down's Syndrome children never escape.

Having reached a theoretical conclusion that it was necessary to 'neutralise' the damaging effects of their appearance in order to capitalise on their potential, it took Feuerstein a decade before he found the technical means. In 1981, however, he learned of the work of Professor Gottfried Lemperle, of the St Markus Hospital in Frankfurt-am-Main, Germany, who had successfully completed 250 plastic surgery operations on Down's Syndrome children.

Coincidentally, Professor Wexler, in Jerusalem, had read a German paper by a Professor Hohler, a colleague of Lemperle's, explaining the techniques used for plastic surgery on this group of children. Wexler then visited a large number of doctors to seek referrals. None came.

Professor Hohler turned out to be the main pioneer in the field and Lemperle was his collaborator. Only when Lemperle (Hohler having died) came to Israel and met Feuerstein and Wexler, did the Israeli programme of plastic surgery start.

So far, some 60 children have had the operation in Israel.

Generally their tongues are reduced in size, their ears are pinned back, excess folds of skin are removed from their eyelids, hanging lower lips are raised and cheek-bones and nose bridges are built up with silicone implants. In some cases implants are used to correct severely receding chins.

Parents were told that the operation was not merely a facial embellishment but a tool for integrating their children. They were also warned that it would not automatically make their children more intelligent. But it could make them much more receptive to change and open up opportunities in their interactions with society.

Some of the most fascinating aspects of the programme, led by one of Feuerstein's co-directors of the Hadassah Wizo Institute, Professor Ya'acov Rand, were the research findings. After the operation parents became much more enthusiastic about speech therapy for their children. Before the operation poor speech ranked third in the list of effects that parents found most disturbing, after protruding tongue and continually open mouth. After the operation, speech ranked first in their list. The research report comments:

> This change may indicate the increasing concern of parents with functioning in general and speech in particular. Many parents observed an amelioration in certain aspects of speech following surgery. We can hypothesise that confrontation with improvement—with the possibility of change, even if slight—would emphasise the impairment of speech, make it more salient, and perhaps, so we hope, render parents more demanding of speech therapy. According to our data, a considerable number of children did start speech therapy after surgery; they were not in speech therapy before, or had stopped it some years prior to surgery.

The parents' full responses to the effects of their children's condition before and after, were as follows:

As the results show, the parents were disturbed more by the facial characteristics of the child before the operation, and more with the functioning of the child, speech, gait, eating behaviour, running nose, after the operation. To Feuerstein and Rand, this is a healthy development since it focuses

STIGMATA	RANKING	
	BEFORE	AFTER
Protruding Tongue	1	6
Open Mouth	2	3
Speech	3	1
Slanted Eyes	4	7
Running Nose	5	2
Drooling	6	8
Eating Behaviour	7	5
Gait	8	4

parents' attention on the improvement of functioning.

Material collected from parents before the operations showed a very high sensitivity to the way that strangers, often well-intentioned, stared at their children and at them. Many parents stated that an ordinary trip in a bus, or to any public place, could be a traumatic experience and could provoke a series of negative reactions from the child. The extent and intensity of this sensitivity surprised the researchers.

In the follow-up research, 26 per cent of parents said that they felt strangers were staring much less than before, 42 per cent said they stared slightly less, and 26 per cent reported no change, although many of these said their children had only attracted a little attention before the operation.

The teachers of the children, when asked if they still looked as if they had Down's Syndrome, said that the condition could still be identified, especially by people familiar with it, but that surgery was very effective in removing the 'rejecting' traits, such as the protruding tongue. 'This helps the child in class,' said one teacher. Another commented: 'The eyes now appear more opened and a layman would not be able to discern anything unusual.'

Teachers had positive evidence, more so than parents, that the children achieved better social integration after the operation. Half of the 16 teachers felt that the operation had had a positive, though indirect, influence on the social relationships of the child within the peer group, due in their view to the diminution of physical characteristics such as drooling and the protruding tongue. The teachers observed an increase in confidence and participation in informal group activities, less hesitancy and reluctance to speak in front of the class and greater attention to their appearance. Improvements in clothes and hair styles were noted.

Of the 66 per cent of parents who felt that their children were not invited enough to friends' houses, 13 per cent said their children were now invited more often, and a quarter of these parents said that, after surgery, friends visited their child more often.

What did the children themselves think of the surgery? Thirty parents said they felt confident in offering an answer on this and 24 of them said they were sure their child was 'quite or very satisfied'. One boy told his mother: 'Now that my tongue is short I will not annoy you any more, and you will not get mad at me.' Another little girl spent a great deal of time in front of the mirror admiring her eyes.

Four parents felt that their child was not satisfied, and two ranked their child's satisfaction as medium. The parents who could not provide an answer said that their children were too young to know.

For one-fifth of the subjects some negative effects of surgery were reported. This included short-term regression to infantile patterns of behaviour and one case of bed-wetting—which had also occurred previously. Parents and teachers said the regressions were short-lived and minor effects.

Generally, the parents' reactions to the operations were overwhelmingly positive. Despite some initial trepidation, 77 per cent said they were 'very satisfied', 21 per cent were fairly satisfied and 2.3 per cent or just one parent, felt dissatisfied. There were no parents who felt 'not satisfied at all'. The vast majority recorded improvements in a range of behaviours, such as drooling and snoring, which had previously been distressing. Eating behaviour also improved as did breathing through the nose instead of the mouth, and there was a reported improvement in intelligibility of speech by 80 per cent of the parents.

When asked if they would recommend a friend to let their child have the operation 64 per cent said they would recommend it 'whole-heartedly', 23 per cent said they would recommend it and 13 per cent said they would but with reservations. None said they would advise against it. The main complaint from the parents was that their children's faces still contained vestiges of their condition. The parents with specific goals for surgery were much more highly satisfied than those who held vague, and also higher, expectations. These fell into the 'medium' satisfied category. There was a consensus among this latter group, perhaps also representing the aspirations of most parents, that the surgery 'was good, but not good enough'.

A Developmental Strategy
Partial plastic surgery is increasingly carried out on Down's Syndrome children, mainly in the USA, where the tongue is usually reduced. However, in the Israeli programme plastic surgery is part of a wider development strategy for the children. With Instrumental Enrichment and possible special placements, many of the Down's Syndrome children are cognitively advanced, and the intellectual effects of poor social interaction overturned.

The success of both prongs of the attack—several of the children whose records stated they were mentally defective are now in religious and technical higher education—has strengthened Feuerstein's criticism of those psychologists and parents who argue that Down's Syndrome children's faces offer protection for mentally handicapped children. It is their facial characteristics and their belonging, as a consequence, to a group, that has socially constructed a blanket assumption about the severity of their mental handicaps.

The inevitable conclusion, which Feuerstein and his colleagues draw, is that the operations should be performed on Down's Syndrome children as soon as possible after birth, so that they never develop a poor self-image and are not denied the type of social interactions and expectations that could save them from such profound retardation.

THE PREPARATORY CLASSES

In the West, children who reach adolescence and have acquired labels as school failures are effectively abandoned. Within the main school system they are placed in low-achieving groups and given low-status vocational courses which equip them to do very little in the world outside school. They leave at the age of 16 with no qualifications whatsoever—their only 'gain' a very low self-image.

Those that slip into the separate special-school system as children with 'moderate learning difficulties', those usually without serious organic or genetic conditions, are probably treated with more sympathy. But the educational outcome is the same. Low expectations are placed on them, the curriculum is reduced to the assumed ability of pupils and they usually leave with very low levels of intellectual performance.

The majority of these children would be said, by Feuerstein, to be educationally retarded by virtue of their cultural deprivation, and therefore capable, given the right intervention, of reaching at least average levels of ability. In the late 1950s and early 1960s he was instrumental in helping to formulate, within Youth Aliyah, a programme which saw adolescence as a prime point of intervention for rescuing educational failures and dramatically improving their performance so that they could be re-inserted back into mainstream society and education.

The programme not only challenged the pessimistic expectations of educators for such children, but also questioned the whole 'containment' ethos of the special-education system. It was based on 'preparatory classes' which would take severely educationally retarded children and, in just one or two years of intensive educational and social rehabilitation, try to ensure that they would be performing at levels more appropriate for their age group.

A Major Breakthrough

Although simple in conception, the preparatory classes mark a critically important breakthrough in the administration of services for educationally retarded children, and are the most important of Feuerstein's changing environments. At one and the same time they stress the importance of focused specialised teaching to restore children to normal ability, while undermining the whole notion of autonomous special-education systems which take rejects from the mainstream never to return them.

The preparatory classes are residential and set within Youth Villages inside Kibbutzim. During their stay in the classes the children lead very structured lives; they are only given two free hours a day, apart from short breaks. There are also concerted efforts by educators, youth workers and psychologists, to reform the children's whole personality, so that they can slough-off the negative attitudes and behaviours they have acquired to protect themselves during their period of educational failure.

The atmosphere of Ramat Hadassah and Kyriat Yearim, two Youth Villages with preparatory classes, is one of intense endeavour and privilege. This might seem a strange word to use, but the environment of the classes is exceptional in order that the children who go there should be envied rather than stigmatised. It has both work and recreation resources, and living accommodation that would be the envy of most teenagers anywhere.

Despite the population of children formerly unable, emotionally or intellectually, to sustain any educational activity for any period of time, the work rate and commitment in the preparatory class regime are extraordinary, as Feuerstein explains:

> The fact that these classes only operate for a year or two years at the most is of great significance for the children and the staff. The children are told in a forthright manner when they come here that they have fallen behind and are being given a limited time in which to recover lost ground. They have a firm goal—which is to get out—and it is a goal shared by every other child. It gives them a sense of urgency and commitment.
>
> The staff also have a goal they know they must reach.

They are not allowed to have the attitude found in special schools that there is plenty of time and progress needs only to be relative to where the child started. They also do not have the view that the child only has a limited intelligence and nothing very much can be done. If I could have had my way, special schools for this type of child would all be closed down and re-opened instead as preparatory classes. But preparatory classes are still a controversial concept—there are some strong interests in special education that are for the *status quo*.

The children enter the preparatory classes between 13 and 14 years of age on average. They are referred by schools, youth workers or social workers, or by parents. Attendance is voluntary and parental consent is a necessity.

The classes are particularly for children whose educational backwardness is social in origin; theoretically those with retardation caused by non-social factors are not selected, and the same applies to children with mental illnesses which are not linked to their educational failure. In practice it has been impossible to operate such criteria because the causes of low functioning and mental illness in children are so complex and inter-connected. The population with behavioural problems comprises the largest category of children thought to be educationally subnormal or, to coin the new euphemism, to have moderate learning difficulties.

Over-ambitious Origins
It took a long and painful process of trial and error before the preparatory classes came to resemble their present form. Originally, they had a strong Zionist ideological underpinning. It was hoped that after one year's intensive re-education the children would be able to resume an educational career within a youth group on a Kibbutz for a further three years and so finally become Kibbutz members. In this manner, Youth Aliyah hoped to re-socialise alienated and deprived children from immigrant groups with the Israeli values epitomised by the Kibbutz.

These goals were found to be over-ambitious. Many of the children from poor urban backgrounds failed to acclimatise to

Kibbutz life after the year in the preparatory classes and dropped out of the Kibbutz youth group before the desired four years were up. Even fewer became Kibbutz members.

But independent research, carried out by the Henrietta Szold Institute in Jerusalem into the classes at Ramat Hadassah, found that educational gains for 93 children in the first two years of the programme was far in excess of what could have normally been expected for the children who had graduated from the preparatory classes. This was true for both the children able to stay some time in the Kibbutz youth group and for the drop-outs who returned home after the preparatory first year was over.

This research, which provides the best account of the early regimes in 1960/61, showed that the population had, at the ages of 13–14, an education level of seven to ten-year-olds. (In the Israeli school system the children chronologically should have been in the seventh or eighth grades but had academic levels of the first to third grades.)

The majority of the children came from large, and poor, oriental Jewish families; in some cases one of the parents was mentally ill, in others the parents had separated.

Some of the children had already been caught in delinquent acts, others were reported by their parents to be mixing with young delinquents. The whole population was considered by Youth Aliyah psychologists to be fodder for teenage gangs and eventually custodial regimes.

Despite the directive that children with mental problems, unconnected with their failures in study, should not be admitted, the Institute found that 25 per cent of the children suffered serious mental problems and 40 per cent had moderate psychological problems. Just under half, 43 per cent, functioned at the level of first-graders although, because of the policy of not keeping children behind other children their own age, many had progressed up to the sixth, seventh and eighth grades. Needless to say, the gap between their classmates and their own performance was horribly wide and had led to severe psychological difficulties.

Once in the preparatory class regime the adolescents, to remove their sense of failure and frustration, were placed in small classes where the educational level of all members was similar. Great stress was laid on their cognitive development using Instrumental Enrichment exercises. In other subjects care was taken to choose educational materials which were at the right level, but not so juvenile in content as to be offensive. Apparently, this was no easy task and showed, by way of contrast, how unusually appropriate the Instrumental Enrichment exercises are for remedial work.

Feuerstein insists that such a homogeneous group of low-performing children is considered tolerable only because of its short duration. But in it the child once socially ostracised as backward can regain confidence and can acquire friends on a basis other than the formation of protective bonds between failures.

Within the regime children could compete as equals among peers instead of spending intellectual energy in avoidance strategies. The class was seen, as in other changing environments established by Feuerstein and his colleagues, as an important instrument of social and educational rehabilitation.

This was reinforced by intensive social activities, a collective approach to work, and by the exemplary rôle of the House Mother or Madrichim, a highly trained youth counsellor, who becomes a dominant figure in the emotional lives of all the children.

Although more than 70 per cent of the children in the first experimental regime dropped out before they had completed their third year, the learning programme had been completed. And it was found that the one year of intensive study in the preparatory classes had produced academic achievements beyond one normal year's study. More than half the pupils achieved fifth-grade level, even though less than one third of the children entered at fourth-grade level.

The Henrietta Szold Institute produced the following figures for education achievements—in terms of grade level—after one year of the preparatory classes.

After the year of preparatory classes, two-thirds of the children entering the Kibbutz youth group were at fifth-grade level. Three years later they were at eighth- or ninth-grade—which was a more rapid advancement than in normal school years, and was especially outstanding since the Kibbutz youth group did not place the same intensive stress on studies

GRADE LEVEL ON ENTERING AND LEAVING THE VILLAGE

Time Period	1st–2nd Grade	3rd Grade	4th Grade	5th Grade	Total Per cent	N
On entry	42.6	27.0	29.5	—	100	91
On leaving (A year later)	—	7.4	39.7	52.9	100	91

as the preparatory classes. For those who stayed the course of four years, there was a gain of up to eight grades in that period. The average was around six grades. As regards the drop-outs, some of whom stayed for 18 months in the youth group in the Kibbutz, the Madrichim reckoned that 60 per cent had reached sixth, seventh or eighth grades. These estimates were treated with great caution by the study, but they indicated above-average progress.

Greater Expectations

There were other very significant changes in the children, both in those who stayed and those who left. Eighty-two per cent of all the wards aspired to higher economic levels than their parents, which is in sharp contrast to other studies of slum children (particularly Adler, 1965) which found that such children assumed that their status would remain the same. Their experience of the high standard of life in the Kibbutz, and the education, work and social activities were held responsible for this rise in expectations.

This was true for the drop-outs as well. The study found that, in these cases, the causes of wishing to leave the Kibbutz environment were not always negative and did not mean that the wards had failed to benefit from their preparatory classes. An extraordinary number—86 per cent of the boys—were found afterwards to be working in permanent jobs requiring some skills. And 85 per cent of the girls had jobs with some defined professional content. Even though there has been a desperate shortage of labour in Israel for many years, this profile differs greatly from the expected career profiles of educationally low-achievers who were not referred to the preparatory classes and who tended to drift into marginal service jobs.

This was clearly a product of the change in their self-image as much as the educational advances brought about by the preparatory classes and the Kibbutz Youth Group. Many stressed that, on return home, they attempted to find a more 'positive' peer group and abandoned their old 'criminal' friendships. More than a third managed to break out of their immediate environment of family, friends and neighbours to make relationships outside. However very few joined youth clubs or youth movements, and sadly, one-fifth suffered from serious social isolation.

Although the more formal ideological goals of creating good Kibbutzniks from potential street urchins, delinquents and school drop-outs proved too ambitious, the research proved beyond doubt that low-achieving children with low IQ scores could make major advances. The study actually found significant gains on tests like the Raven's Progressive Matrices after the preparatory classes; the longer the children stayed on in the Kibbutz Youth Group the larger these gains were.

The conclusion of the study was that the preparatory classes and the Kibbutz Youth Group regime had shown that modifiability was possible and that the programme was worthy of expansion. This was carried out by Youth Aliyah, but some changes were made.

One of the reasons for the high drop-out rate after the first year of preparatory classes was located in the children's poor attitude to work, which, in turn, was linked to whether they had the ability to pick up a vocational skill fairly quickly once they had moved to the Kibbutz Youth Group.

A sizeable number of children found this difficult and objected to the too informal approach towards vocational education in the preparatory classes and Kibbutz Youth Group. It was also found that the high rate of drop-outs and failure to integrate with ordinary youths in the Kibbutz, or to join youth groups or movements on the outside, was due to inadequate socialisation. In this respect the educational rehabilitation was seen as more successful than the social and behavioural rehabilitation.

The preparatory classes were, therefore, extended to two years, the second year having a much greater stress on vocational training. Following this, the normal route was a further two years in a vocational institution rather than in the Kibbutz Youth Group. The re-orientation of the educational programme towards vocational training and a job was considered highly successful by Youth Aliyah staff.

The intensity of the programme operating now can be gathered from the daily schedule, which begins at 6.30 a.m., with washing and tidying rooms and morning exercises. Tuition starts after breakfast at 8 a.m., and there are five classes (with quite a long break) till 12.15, when there is 45 minutes for tuition or therapy for individuals and small groups.

From 1.45 p.m., to 3.45 p.m., there is work in the gardens, the workshops, or in the services to the Kibbutz and, after a light snack, at 4 p.m. there is preparation of homework supervised by the group leader. There then follows an hour of free time when children can read or take part in various interest groups. At 6 p.m., there is supper, followed at 7 p.m. by compulsory evening activities in the residential quarters. Two or three evenings are devoted to film or other communal activities for the whole institution. From 8 p.m. till 9 p.m., there is free time and then lights out.

The full timetable is designed to give children a strong sense of stability which is thought to promote self-confidence in those who have often led very irregular lives.

The curriculum stresses language. Using specially-constructed material which is simple enough for their level, but not so juvenile in content as to be insulting, there is much drilling in reading, writing, spelling, functional grammar, and discussions and debates. Other subjects include arithmetic, bible, geography, nature study, craft and singing. Emphasis is not on the quantity of information imbibed, but on the process of learning—skills and thinking ability. This provides a very fruitful general educational environment for the use of Instrumental Enrichment and its bridging into mainstream subjects.

Children who exhibit special difficulties are given intensive tuition and therapy if necessary—it is one of the great virtues of Kyriat Yearim and Ramat Hadassah that youth leaders, social workers, psychologists, teachers and the Madrichim work very closely together and monitor the progress of individual children.

There has been no research comparable to the Henrietta Szold Institute's study of the 1960s. But the outcome figures for the two-year preparatory classes are quite impressive. Some 80 per cent complete the two-year course (those who leave do so because of acute educational unsuitability, homesickness, the families' need for the child to work, or through sickness). Sixty per cent take the desired route into residential vocational colleges for courses varying from one to three years. They enter either at their own age grade level or a year behind, and 20 per cent return to their communities where they start working or enrol on courses.

The preparatory classes manifest all the main characteristics that Feuerstein and his colleagues in the Youth Aliyah psychological service constructed, often in direct contravention of received opinion and professional practice. They refuse to accept a child's low functioning as a permanent characteristic; the rehabilitative institution is educational rather than welfare based; they emphasise the need for controlled and planned re-entry into normal education and society, and for specialised tuition for backward children—particularly in cognitive development—while maintaining a principled opposition to institutionalised and segregated special education systems.

The lessons for the West are numerous. But there are many professional, cultural and ideological obstacles to reproducing these changing environments in Britain. Not the least of these obstacles is the refusal of the education system to take seriously the possibility of educational and social rehabilitation for adolescents, or to accept that there is a fundamental difference between children who are retarded because of cultural deprivation and those who have organic handicaps. Leaving the British social services and the penal system to carry out 'rehabilitation' has been, in my view, a disaster of profound dimensions. Feuerstein and Youth Aliyah have offered a way forward, but is there anyone in Britain prepared to take it?

PART 5:

FEUERSTEIN IN CONTEXT

THE RUSSIAN PARALLEL

Feuerstein's distance from mainstream psychological and educational opinions about intelligence has left him vulnerable to suggestions that he is an intellectual maverick with new and improbable theories. This view was typically canvassed by a senior British educationalist at a 1984 Oxford Schools Council conference on Instrumental Enrichment. While praising Feuerstein's 'practical teaching techniques', he found their theoretical basis a little too hard to swallow.

In fact Feuerstein's presumed theoretical isolation is more a function of the myopia of Western psychology and pedagogy than of anything else. His intellectual roots are in Piagetian thought. In humanising the Piagetian processes of child development through his notions of cultural deprivation and mediated learning, and explaining by them the causes of low functioning in children, Feuerstein did indeed make a clear break with much of Western educational psychology. But he at once moved uncannily closer to the educational traditions of Eastern Europe.

The Vygotskiian School

The similarities between Feuerstein's theoretical system and that of the great Russian psychologist, Lev Vygotskii are remarkable. Like Feuerstein, Vygotskii had been confronted after the October Revolution with the need to raise dramatically the levels of functioning of the culturally-deprived children of the workers and peasants of Russia, as well as those of the nationalities and social groups. Like Feuerstein, he found the application of psychometric tests on children from some communities produced absurdly low results, even when the tests were 'adapted' to their cultures. In one of the Soviet Union's republics only 16.8 per cent of the children were found to be normally endowed, while 63.4 per cent were mildly retarded and 19.8 per cent were severely retarded. Whole peoples were being intellectually placed at the levels of five-to seven-year-old children.

And like Feuerstein, Vygotskii was driven by political necessity (in his case to bring the backward peoples of the Union into the general economic and cultural development of an advanced socialist state) to construct an active form of psychological practice. It was this pressing imperative that required and produced his theoretical transformations.

Vygotskii believed in the ability and necessity of even the most backward nationalities to accomplish 'grandiose leaps up the cultural ladder' in a matter of years rather than in long historical stages. Feuerstein, for very interesting reasons which will be discussed later, never aspires to this wider historical analysis. But his clinically-based belief that low-functioning, culturally-deprived children can assume the skills of culturally-sophisticated people in a matter of years through education is highly analogous. The emphasis on the overriding influence of the cultural environment in human development and the possibility of dramatic intervention are the same for both.

For Vygotskii, mental functions—memory, perception, thinking—develop in the process of the child mastering social-historical experience. This is very similar to Feuerstein's conception of the acquisition of cognitive functions through the transmission of culture from the older to younger generation. In fact, Vygotskii said that children master social relationships and activity as a result of constant directive interaction with adults. His concept of teaching is a complex and not a simply didactic one: it corresponds very closely to Feuerstein's notion of mediation.

In Vygotskii's system, teaching is accomplished through signs, symbols and speech which mediate people's activity. They are a chief means through which culture is transmitted to children— and so the mastery of speech and certain types of activity *is* the process of individual development.

Feuerstein claims that Vygotskii's emphasis on langage as the basis of cognitive development is much stronger than his and is a distinguishing feature in their theoretical systems. In his view some basic cognitive functions are mediated at pre-verbal ages in the interactions between a child and its parents and siblings. If this is truly a difference, it is one only of degree.

Throughout the instruments of the Instrumental Enrichment programme, signs, symbols, codes and new words are accorded the greatest importance in facilitating the development of abstract thought, especially for children with poor literacy skills. Feuerstein claims, with some support from research, that the basic cognitive skills needed for reading, like focused perception and spontaneous comparative behaviour, are taught or strengthened by Instrumental Enrichment, and that this allows reading to become a possibility for children with previously chronic difficulties.

On the other hand, the key concept in Vygotskii's theoretical constellation is teaching—not, as is often thought, language. And teaching can, of course, take non-linguistic forms. However, for both Feuerstein and Vygotskii, verbal skills are the prerequisites of abstract formal thought. Vygotskii's disciples, it is worth mentioning, went on in any case to stress this non-verbal part of learning—for example, Leont'ev's Activity Theory—in which the internalisation of practical activity by the child plays the essential rôle in the creation of individual consciousness.

Zone of Next Development

There are two other fascinating correspondences between Feuerstein's theory and Vygotskiian psychology; the concept of the Zone of Next Development is analogous to Feuerstein's concept of hidden potential, and the notion of temporary retardation is similar to Feuerstein's insistence on the fundamental difference between the culturally-deprived child and the organically handicapped.

The Zone of Next Development represented Vygotskii's attempts to theorise the enormous plasticity of child development, in order to treat better individual children. This is where Feuerstein began. One of Vygotskii's basic formulations of the Zone of Next Development, with very minor changes in terminology, could have been spoken by Feuerstein:

Psychological research connected with the problems of teaching has usually been restricted to establishing a child's level of mental development. But it is not enough to define the state of the child's development by means of this level alone. How is this level usually defined? Problems that the child solves on his own serve as the means to define it. We can only learn from these what the child can do and what it knows today, since we pay attention solely to those problems which the child can solve on his own: it is apparent that by this method we can only establish what has already ripened within the child at the present day. We determine only his present level of development. (Manifest level of functioning in Feuerstein's terms.)

But the state of development is never defined only by that part of it which is already ripe. Just as the gardener who wants to determine the state of his garden will be wrong if he takes it into his head to evaluate it solely on the basis of the apple trees which have ripened and been picked of fruit, so, too, the psychologist, when he is evaluating the state of development, must inevitably take account not of the present level but also of the zone of next development.

The way in which Vygotskii set about establishing the nature of a child's zone of next development bears a striking resemblance to the procedures of the Learning Potential Assessment Device. Vygotskii suggested that if you took two children with the same present mental ages and then tried to show each how to solve problems above their age level, by offering help in the form of co-operation, a demonstration, a leading question, the start of a solution, etc., then it might be observed that one child solves problems up to a mental age of 12 years, while the other reaches only a mental age of nine.

Despite the similarity of their present development, there are great discrepancies between the children's real mental levels. The difference is measured by the number of years above their present mental age that the children can reach, four in the first case and one in the second. The significance for Vygotskii was that teaching should, for real effect, direct itself not at the child's current performance—for example, on an assumption of ability based on fixed IQ scores, which lower teacher and teaching aspirations for 'unintelligent' children—but always towards the Zone of Next Development.

The greater or lesser the child's ability to transfer from what he knows how to do on his own to what he can do in co-operation proves to be the most sensitive symptom that characterises the dynamics of the child's development and school progress. It wholly coincides with the zone of his next development . . . Education must be orientated not towards the yesterday of child development but towards its tomorrow.

This is exactly the philosophy of the Learning Potential Assessment Device and Instrumental Enrichment. In the Learning Potential Assessment Device the child's manifest level of functioning is of interest only as a starting point—and the child's points of strength, isolated and weak though they may be, are far more important than averaged-out low scores on tests. The Learning Potential Assessment Device procedure is designed to see how far children can move with co-operation and teaching from what they know, to what they do not know, and to add to their repertoire of cognitive skills in order to facilitate this transition.

The Instrumental Enrichment exercises move relatively rapidly from fairly simple to complex tasks, so that the child continually realises the Zone of Next Development. It is the teacher's job to assess the present levels of development of classes and individuals, and the higher thresholds of their potential. It is also the teacher's job to use the instruments flexibly within the range where teaching has the most impact on development.

A rigid and programmatic use of the instruments is completely inappropriate and gives rise to the types of comments from some British teachers that the tasks were either too complex or too simple. If used flexibly the instruments can be, indeed are, used to good purpose with such widely different groups as college students and brain-damaged young children. This is why the theory behind the method—rather than just the method itself—is so important. In Vygotskii's terms, Instrumental Enrichment is a system which requires teaching to be in advance of development in children and to draw development after it.

Vygotskii's work with the backward groups and individuals

in the Soviet Union led him to differentiate between children retarded by social or peripheral causes, which produced, in his view, children who were potentially only 'temporarily retarded', and those with central cerebral damage. The two groups were thought to have very different educational needs.

Two of Vygotskii's collaborators, A. Luriya and Ya. Yudovich, carried out an experiment in Moscow in the early 1930s which illustrated the reversibility of retardation. Twin boys very retarded by their upbringing, were separated and transformed under the influence of rich verbal interaction with adults. Their previous symbiotic and sealed existence had prevented adequate 'teaching' or mediated learning experience from taking place.

This experiment was part of a very different tradition in the USSR for the definition, assessment and education of unsuccessful school children, in which there is an official distinction between the temporarily retarded child and the mentally handicapped. An identical position is held by Feuerstein. The culturally-deprived are retarded as a result of their social and historical experience and, given adequate Mediated Learning Experience, or 'teaching' of the Vygotskiian kind, can be *expected* to function at normal levels.

Included within Feuerstein's culturally-deprived group are children with physical or emotional problems that prevent adequate interaction with their parents, relatives, peers or teachers. Deafness can obviously be a block to effective mediation, as can blindness. But such apparently minor things as squints or stutters can also profoundly affect cognitive development. Feuerstein's clinical work shows that mentally-handicapped children—such as those who experienced ataxia at birth or those with Down's Syndrome—can develop beyond all expectations with Instrumental Enrichment and lead almost normal lives. His achievements are truly astonishing. But there is no theoretical expectation that Mediated Learning Experience will produce completely normal cognitive functioning. Apart from the certainty that an investment in mediated learning will produce changes, the possibilities are much more open-ended.

The Twin Study of Luriya and Yudovich was repeated in Birmingham, by Andrew Sutton and Jo Douglas in 1976, with the same sort of results produced. But the implications of the experiment—that there is a fundamental difference between types of causes of retardation and the possibility of dramatic remediation of the socially caused variety—were ignored. Britain still lumps together the culturally deprived and the mentally handicapped under the broad banner of 'children with learning difficulties'.

The theoretical similarities between Feuerstein's and Vygotskiian thinking are so great that it seems strange that there was no direct confluence of streams. Feuerstein says he did meet Luriya, but only after he had elaborated his theoretical system. Some have speculated that the French psychologist, André Rey, may have been influenced by Vygotskii's thought and in turn influenced Feuerstein. But as with Vygotskii, very little of Rey's work has so far been translated into English, so it is hard to trace any common elements.

There are, in any case, other explanations for the similarities in their theories. Unlike most Western psychologists with their need to test, measure and classify intelligence as part of a neutral discipline analogous to the natural sciences, Feuerstein and Vygotskii were both teachers first and psychologists second. At critical historical upheavals they were concerned with actively changing, through education, the life prospects of children and communities thrust into new, rapidly developing, social change.

They operated with an ideology of teaching—of the power of teaching to transform the processes of child development—rather than with the ideology of the fixed and static nature of hereditary intelligence.

Vygotskii, like Feuerstein, also came from a Jewish background and shared the same preoccupations with history and the possibility for human betterment, which underpinned the writing of Vygotskii's philosophical mentor, Karl Marx. Both Vygotskii and Feuerstein were able to see first-hand, and in very extreme ways, the differential impact that social environment and history have on child development.

It is here, however, ironically, that their great theoretical difference lies. As a Marxist, Vygotskii drew upon a much larger philosophy of social development in which historical stages were defined and analysed. He was not afraid, therefore, of looking at whole societies and groups of people within the USSR and stating that they existed at an earlier, lower historical stage of development, with a correspondingly lower cultural level. One of the features of this low cultural level was a 'situational' (Feuerstein would say 'concrete') form of thinking appropriate to limited social organisation and experience. More abstract forms of thought were absent.

Vygotskii was not a liberal and did not believe in any notions of cultural relativism. As far as he was concerned, backward cultures were backward cultures; they had to be dramatically changed if they were not to become museums within the larger, more advanced society. Feuerstein, one suspects, developed his theories from the other end, beginning with his experience as a teacher in Bucharest, then as a youth counsellor in Youth Aliyah and, finally, as a psychologist trying to understand why North African Jewish children were performing so badly. A cultural theory grew out of this clinical experience.

One of the imperatives of the theory was to explain why learning failure was so widespread among Moroccan and North African Jewish children, without falling into reactionary and racist views that they were a people with a genetically-impaired intelligence. This view was actually being canvassed in Israel where traditional Western psychology still held sway. The theory of cultural deprivation achieved two goals: it explained a general phenomenon and slapped down the racist assumption of Ashkenazi Jews that the Sephardi Jews were inferior.

Feuerstein called attention to the cultural supremacy of the Moroccan Jews in the Middle Ages. There was no doubt that Moroccan Jewish culture had subsequently been undermined by colonialism and further affected by the migration to urban centres. The victims of this upheaval could be said to be deprived of their own natural culture—but for how many generations can one be said to be deprived of a culture that no longer exists and is purely historical?

Deprivation from a 'historical' culture (Feuerstein does not actually use this term, but it is implicit in his theory) is a useful notion in that it reminds one of the way forces of history, rather than of heredity, affect people's fortunes and levels of social and cultural organisation—the Holocaust or the enslavement and shipment of negroes from West Africa immediately spring to mind as extreme examples. But at the practical psychological level, a child's deprivation from a culture that ceased to exist for all practical purposes two or three generations back, or even earlier, is an idealistic concept.

If a culture has been destroyed, diluted or left behind general social development, or if it has never reached an advanced stage, there is no alternative but to say that it is a comparatively low-level culture. But Feuerstein, for political reasons, could not countenance this analysis. It would have placed him at the mercy of the racialists back home. Even now he is extremely wary of talking about the problems of the Moroccan Jewish community.

None of this negates Feuerstein's notions of being deprived of one's own culture. Far from it. Many children are so deprived: through circumstances or inadequate upbringing they have been denied the types of mediated learning experience which could allow them to take part in and contribute to their own culture. The notion of cultural level is entirely compatible with Feuerstein's theory of cultural deprivation.

The same compatibility can be claimed for Feuerstein's concept of cultural difference. It is a real theoretical advance. But at the same time it operates as a shield preventing the emergence of the politically-difficult concept of cultural level. On one hand Feuerstein has proved conclusively that some technologically primitive but rich and intact cultures—like those of the Yemenis and the Ethiopian Jews—can bestow upon their children more learning and social skills than those bestowed upon culturally-deprived children born in Israel.

Yet despite their much lauded speed of learning, it is also true that the Ethiopian Jewish communities have required highly intensive teaching in some cognitive functions which they now need in Israel. This is because their previous, much more limited social experience in Africa did not equip them for life in Israel. (Analytical Perception and Temporal Relations, and sometimes Orientation in Space, are typically weak and need improvement.)

The concept of cultural difference alerts us to the richness of the culture and the skills it bestows upon its children, while

Vygotskii's concept of cultural level reminds us that these qualities are not always enough to enable people to operate effectively in a more sophisticated society. Israel, with Feuerstein's early involvement, has sought to teach the skills that the Ethiopian Jews need for cultural integration in Israel. This has been done with a great deal of 'strong' and intensive direction and teaching, while seeking to bolster the main structures and elements of Ethiopian Jewish culture.

All three concepts, cultural deprivation, cultural difference and cultural level, would seem to be compatible. Together they make up a powerful analytical armoury for advancing upon presently-held beliefs about working-class and black under-achievement. They offer an ideology of teaching based on the premise that the most severe environmental obstacles to academic achievement can be overcome. Both Feuerstein and Vygotskii agree that, by utilising the type of teaching which forces the pace of development in children and which equips them with the cognitive skills to overcome their cognitive deficiencies, socially-handicapped school failures can become intelligent thinkers and operators in the world.

BUDAPEST

The two main underlying assumptions of Feuerstein's work, that children can be radically modified and that intelligence can be taught, form the ideological basis of many educational enterprises, although such enterprises are not always explicitly theorised in this way. One that is, and bears many similarities with Feuerstein's work, is the system of Conductive Education used in Hungary which teaches children to bypass their disabilities.

It has now been repeatedly reported by psychologists and educationalists, and a host of visiting parents and professionals, that the Hungarians have found a way to make the majority of their motor-disordered children, such as those suffering from spasticity or athetosis or spina bifida, walk and achieve functional independence. In Britain these children would remain in wheelchairs and often lead dejected and frustrated lives because they cannot control their limbs.

Conductive Education was developed by Andrea Peto who reasoned that children could be taught to build up small skills into complex movements in much the same way that Feuerstein believes that cognitive functions can build mental operations. New functions could thereby be created in the brain, bypassing damaged motor areas in the cerebellum. This conforms to what we now know in the West about how the brain re-organises itself after experiencing traumatic damage.

In Hungary, motor-disordered children must be prepared to work tremendously hard under the dedicated and rigorous direction of 'conductors' who teach them movements and functions, like walking and continence, which ordinary children acquire through cultural transmission. The work is carried out in a residential setting, so that close contact with their peers can provide a powerful group dynamic and ethos towards 'orthofunction'—the level of independent functioning necessary to integrate into Hungary's education system.

The success rate for children treated by the Budapest Institute for Motor Disordered Children is around 70 per cent integration into Hungarian schools, all of which require walking and independent functioning as strict criteria for admission.

The parallels between Feuerstein's theories and those of Conductive Education are extensive, as has been recognised by Feuerstein himself. 'It is,' he says, 'something of a shock to come across a system which modifies children in a more extreme way than my own.'

This is, of course, the first and major parallel: Conductive Education, like the theory of Structural Cognitive Modifiability, is based on an 'active modification' approach rather than on one of 'passive acceptance'. The children in both methods are the active participants in their own treatment rather than passive consumers of services. In Britain, children with cerebral palsy are given some exercises and very limited physiotherapy and speech therapy, and are usually placed in special schools where the main objective is to help them to cope with their handicaps through aids, gadgets and smothering care. The passivity of this approach is based on the assumption that nothing can be done to modify or master the underlying condition.

So strong is this passive acceptance in Britain, perhaps because so many professional interests are involved in maintaining the *status quo*, that the discovery of Conductive Education 20 years ago by British physiotherapists, linked to the Spastic Society, failed to dislodge traditional practices and 'treatments'. In effect the method was stifled from lack of commitment. A continual flow of parents are now travelling from Britain to Hungary, and insisting on their return that a qualitative leap in the treatment of cerebral palsied children has been achieved in Budapest.

Peto's and Feuerstein's systems both insist on children's conscious desire to improve their functioning. The objectives of Instrumental Enrichment are spelt out to children who are asked to think about the processes of thinking, how it could improve their lives, and how the failure to think could ruin their futures. Children receiving Conductive Education can see around them, every minute of the day, other children who are succeeding in becoming independent, and this is translated into an enormously strong, conscious desire for their own independence. The emphasis on conscious motivation and knowledge of what they are doing is considered of extreme importance both by Feuerstein and in Conductive Education, and both systems are antithetical to the mechanistic theories of behaviourism.

A further interesting parallel is the attitude towards the intellectual potential of the motor-disordered child at the Budapest Institute. Retarded functioning is seen largely as a result of the disorder blocking the acquisition of learning skills. It is in many cases, therefore, eminently remediable. The results of intelligence tests on entry are seen as having little value and it is the response to general education after a period of Conductive Education, which is considered more important.

The distinction between children whose intellectual functioning is retarded due to 'peripheral' rather than central causes is very similar to Feuerstein's distinction between those who are culturally deprived for social or physical reasons, and those who are mentally handicapped through hereditary disease or brain damage. The attitudes to treatment of both categories are also very similar. In Hungary all but the very severely mentally handicapped are taken in at the Institute. But it is understood from the start that progress will be much slower and less certain. As with Feuerstein, the Hungarians see mental handicaps as extra barriers that are much more difficult and time-consuming to surmount but should always be confidently attempted.

COGNITIVE EDUCATION PAST AND PRESENT

The idea that intelligence needs to be actively modified and trained is an ancient one. Latin has long been used as discipline for thinking and, before that, subjects recommended for this purpose were arithmetic and geometry. This is rather interesting, given Feuerstein's extensive use of numerical systems and geometric shapes in the instruments. Plato, for example, emphasised the importance of the processes of thinking and learning over the mere content of what is learnt:

> The great philosopher declaimed: 'Have you observed that those who have a natural talent for calculation are generally quick at every kind of knowledge and even the dull, if they had an arithmetical training, although they may derive no other advantage from it, always become much quicker than they would otherwise have been.
>
> 'Arithmetic stirs up him who is by nature sleepy and dull and makes him quick to learn, retentive and shrewd. He makes progress quite beyond his powers.'*

Francis Bacon, in the late 1500s, recommended the study of mathematics to remedy thinking problems such as the lack of attention. John Locke also proclaimed the need for mental discipline:

> All pleasant methods of teaching children necessary knowledge are false and ridiculous. It is not a question of learning or geography or geometry: it is a question of learning to work; of learning the weariness of concentrating one's attention on the matter in hand.

The British public school system has long adopted an

*Quoted from: *On the Trail of Process: A historical perspective on cognitive processes and their training*, by L. Mann. New York: Grunne and Stratton, 1979.

approach of active modification and cognitive training in the education of the sons and daughters of Britain's wealthier classes. And one must say that it has continued to produce the goods: high-level critical thinkers who know how to operate at a high level in society.

The schools can assure parents that they will transform their children into competent academic performers, with higher education opportunities almost guaranteed. Many less well-off parents who see their children failing at state school, transfer them to public schools to great effect.

Better facilities and pupil/teacher ratios, and social advantages to begin with, explain a large part of the success story of public schools. But they do not tell the whole story. Two other fairly unique features of the public school system must also be taken into account. First, the system believes it can transform or 'mould' children and this is executed through 'teaching' of a much broader mediational character within a highly-motivated closed environment. One might not like all the values that public schools instil, but they are part of a complete system which can orientate a child, and which is rich in intention, meaning and transcendence.

The second, many would say more important, part of the job of a public school is to teach children to think well, act well and speak well (research shows that many state schools actively discourage children from talking in class). When it comes to thinking well, Latin has always been consciously taught in public schools as a form of 'mental discipline' or cognitive training; in other words, it has a transcendental objective. Latin is the most obvious example, but teaching in all good public schools traditionally involves more discussion and debate, during which children receive much greater practice in the manipulation of principles, perspectives and analyses than they do in state education. It is a great irony that the state system should have a much more conservative attitude towards intelligence and the modifying potential of teaching than the formally conservative public school system.

The United States

Across the Atlantic the training colleges for the elite also recognised the importance of process over content. Mann quotes a statement, published by Yale University in 1829, describing the essential purpose of college education.

> The two great points to be gained in intellectual culture are the discipline and furniture of the mind; expanding its powers and storing it with knowledge. The former of these is perhaps, the most important of the two.

The Americans have recently sought to revive this tradition of cognitive training as a way of coming to grips with what is now recognised as a serious decline in general educational standards. The original impetus, however, came from those interested in remedial work for children from low socio-economic groups and minorities, and in programmes for the gifted child, particularly the 'gifted under-achiever'.

A significant number of cognitive skills programmes have been developed and are being rigorously tested in the United States with a commitment and thoroughness that, in my opinion, puts the British evaluation of Feuerstein's work to shame. Feuerstein's Instrumental Enrichment is just one of the programmes under trial, but it is the market leader, in terms of scale of its implementation and evaluation, and in general academic reviews.

The three other most common programmes are *Philosophy for Children*, by Lipman, Sharp and Oscanyon, *The Short Course in Comprehension and Problem Solving*, by Whimbey and Lockhead and *The Chicago Mastery Learning Reading Programme*, by Beau Fly Jones.

Philosophy For Children[1] is not designed to teach children philosophical theories, but to train them in thinking philosophically. The authors completely reject the assumption that learning comprises only the transmission of the contents of human knowledge from one generation to another—instead it entails the generation of thinking activities. Learning historical facts is not learning to think historically; learning scientific facts is not learning to think scientifically: there is a similar difference between thinking philosophically and learning philosophical facts.

The authors believe that children are naturally concerned in the same issues as philosophers—in understanding reasons for things, exploring alternatives, questioning assumptions and searching for meanings to experience. But they claim this philosophical process of inquiry is stultified by passive-accepting adults.

Teachers and parents can, and should, keep up this ability to 'wonder' in children: the act of philosophical inquiry will develop children's thinking skills. The goals of their programme include improvements in children's abilities to construct relationships, draw distinctions, to define and clarify, to evaluate information, to distinguish between what is true and what is logically possible, to use analogies, to grasp part-whole relationships, to formulate problems and to draw syllogistic inferences.

The main vehicle for teaching such skills is dialogue which, the authors insist, does not follow reflective thought, as is often assumed, but precedes it. Models for such dialogues are provided in short novels in the programme, which provide 'leading' ideas. The books are based on the principle of the Socratic dialogues: it is no use telling someone how to proceed in a rigorous intellectual inquiry; it is necessary to show how it is done. Alongside the novels are teaching manuals and exercises which stimulate the desired thinking processes.

One story involves a child who had failed to pay attention to a lesson about Halley's Comet. Asked what object with a tail circles the sun every 77 years, he answers 'planet'. He had heard previously that all planets circle the sun, therefore he reasons that the answer must be a planet. The teacher informs him that just because all planets revolve round the sun that does not mean that all objects that revolve round the sun are planets. The ensuing discussion includes the need to look at the assumptions behind one's answers, the non-reversibility of logical 'all' statements and the reversibility of logical 'no' statements, and how such principles can be applied to real life. Some 30 cognitive skills are taught in this way.

Talking through or 'verbalising', as the Americans would say, the steps of a mental operation, forms an important part of *The Short Course in Comprehension and Problem Solving*. It promotes more reflective and systematic styles in children's thinking and renders the elements in a mental operation explicit and, therefore, more open to 'corrective feedback'.

Its authors stress that thinking is a learnable skill analogous to physical skills rather than some mysterious ability that one is born with, or not. The programme is designed to correct 'imprecise' or 'sloppy' thinking which leads to problem-solving failure.

It is possible to see many similarities between this and the Instrumental Enrichment programme, although the 'Short Course' analysis of children's problems in thinking is at a much lower level of theoretical exposition. Breaking problems into their constituent elements, fixing the relations between elements carefully in sentences, and the use of analogical thinking to solve problems, are stressed by the authors in their bid to combat sloppy thinking. For children in high school and colleges who take the course, it is judged to help them become more rigorous in solving certain types of problem, but less so in becoming genuinely critical and creative thinkers able to evaluate and accommodate new information readily. A key feature in effective learning stressed in Feuerstein's Instrumental Enrichment is knowing when there is a need to get more data to clarify given information or relationships, and this skill is not thought to be catered for in the Whimbey and Lockhead programme. Insight-creation is missing.

The Chicago Mastery Learning Reading Programme is different from Instrumental Enrichment, *Philosophy for Children* and *The Short Course in Comprehension and Problem-Solving* because it emphasises learning and studying skills rather than thinking skills. It is based on the view that almost all students can acquire the high-level learning skills that only 'the best' students currently attain.

The programme is designed for children in the fifth to eighth grades (that is 10 to 14 years). Each grade has a separate book within which there are two units, a comprehension unit and a study skills unit. The book for the seventh grade, for example, has within the comprehension unit sections on using sentence context, 'mood' in writing, understanding complex information, comprehending comparisons, analysing characters, and distinguishing facts from opinions. The study skills unit contains sections on how books are organised, understanding and using graphs and charts, how to study text-book chapters, and distinguishing between major and minor ideas.

As with Instrumental Enrichment, the Chicago programme

does try to teach cognitive skills directly, although it is via the teaching of the learning skills that children actually need in their academic careers. The skills taught are, therefore, much limited, falling basically in the domain of reading and verbal comprehension and 'procedural' study strategies and practices. The importance of the latter group of skills should not be minimised: for some unknown reason schools assume that children will develop study skills automatically, in the same way as critical insight is supposed to 'occur' as a function of being bombarded with information. Of course, the vast majority of children never do reach these intellectual levels.

Chicago, the *Short Course* and *Philosophy for Children* all have one important advantage over Instrumental Enrichment: they can be easily slotted into school curricula, into reading or English studies, without a conscious decision by the school to set aside special cognitive training periods required by Instrumental Enrichment. And none of them requires the theoretical knowledge and training to implement that Instrumental Enrichment does.

On the other hand, unlike Instrumental Enrichment, none of the programmes has the depth or the potential to transform teaching. Although the *Short Course* and *Philosophy for Children* are based on psychological theories of thinking, they do not integrate a theory of cognition with one of child development. They cannot, therefore, be employed to diagnose and remediate children whose development has gone badly astray. All three methods described here, apart from Instrumental Enrichment, rely on already developed intellectual faculties—such as the ability to read complex texts, to decode messages and to cope with considerable content. They then sharpen up children's cognitive operations rather than instil basic cognitive functions. A child with very little abstract thought, who lacks vocabulary, has blurred and sweeping perception, and who has a profound impulsiveness, would, in all likelihood, be a non-starter in all three programmes.

[1] Some of the information in this section is gleaned from an article, 'How Can We Teach Intelligence?', by Professor Robert J. Sternberg, Professor of Psychology at Yale University, which appeared in the American journal, *Educational Leadership*, September, 1984.

CONCLUSION

Because of its theoretical basis Instrumental Enrichment offers teachers a great deal more than just a curriculum supplement. If, and it is a big if, they are properly trained they can become expert at diagnosing early signs of cognitive impairment and take steps to counteract problems.

Mediated Learning Theory also offers teachers a practice of teaching which is linked to a theory of child development and cognitive psychology, and opens up the prospect of a scientific practice of teaching. At the moment teaching pretends to be a profession of 'assessed' method and skill; in practice it is largely a profession of dubious custom and practice with the mystique of vocation. Both facets have helped to devalue it in relation to other professions.

Teaching the processes involved in thinking by using Instrumental Enrichment to stimulate discussions, to draw out underlying principles and to formulate strategies, and by using children's own experience to bridge Instrumental Enrichment skills to other areas of existence, is an extremely high-level skill. But it is a taught skill and not a vocation mysteriously given by nature. It is measurable and is linked to a coherent knowledge base. This, and the diagnostic powers which Instrumental Enrichment and the Learning Potential Assessment Device confer, could transform teacher-training and teachers' claims to be serious professionals.

Feuerstein had always maintained that Instrumental Enrichment is a way of 'smuggling in' a theory of child development and under-development. And because it is based on theory, the instruments can be adapted and developed both generally and for specific groups of children, using the theories as guidelines. Neither Instrumental Enrichment, nor the theory of Mediated Learning Experience, form a take-it-or-leave-it package.

The caveat in all this, however, is that if the instruments are to be adapted they must be changed for a valid purpose, in a way that is consistent with their theoretical basis and with the kind of testing and analysis that will show whether the changes are really improvements. The type of 'adaptation' of Instrumental Enrichment being undertaken in the Oxfordshire 'Cognitive Skills Programme' which, in the words of its own personnel, seeks to reduce Feuerstein's materials both to the level of inadequately trained teachers and to the assumed level of backward and inattentive children, is opposed to everything Feuerstein stands for.

The tragedy of Britain's approach to cognitive education in the state system is that perhaps no other country in the Western world probably needs it more. A constant refrain emanating from British universities and industries is that our education system is not producing the 'thinkers' needed to become creative science and technology students and workers, who can keep abreast of rapidly-changing technology and make some of the changes themselves. Yet high technology is Britain's only hope, when the oil runs out, of remaining in the front rank of industrial nations.

At the other end of the scale, the schools in our inner cities and council estates are turning out children who are unemployable. Two complementary forces are responsible for this: it is not that teaching now is necessarily any worse than it was after the War, but that the unskilled working-class jobs that used to absorb our school failures no longer exist. And both a consequence and a determining force here is the cultural fragmentation resulting from unemployment and changing social values.

Our inner cities and council estates now have large numbers of families living on public assistance on or below the breadline. The reality of work, and wages and independence, which used to smooth the transition from adolescence to adulthood and cement the bonds between generations, no longer applies for the 50 per cent of school leavers, or the 80 per cent in especially depressed areas, who have no hope of finding fulfilling work—and who were despairing years before they left school.

Parents who are unemployed, or who have been forced to take early retirement, may have few cultural values that they can feel confident in passing on to their children. There is often no real possibility for many harassed and isolated single parents to give their children the type of experience which they need to partake actively in such a rapidly changing society.

In this situation, teachers in schools must become the conscious agents of cultural reproduction, forcing the pace of child development and the acquisition of thinking skills and culture above the level that can be provided by the immediate environment. In one sense, this is a restatement of an old-fashioned ideology of teaching. But it desperately needs restating against those on the left and the right who discover countless reasons why black and working-class children can never succeed in schools because of 'underlying conditions'.

It is precisely this need to acculturate children who are functioning below the levels imposed by rapid social development that has led North America and Third World countries to latch so fiercely on to cognitive education, and Instrumental Enrichment in particular. Integrating culturally-different and culturally-deprived children into a technological economy—at a time when the pace of technological change makes curricula out of date before they are fully disseminated to schools—requires the training of children in abstract powers of thinking which can be flexibly applied to different subjects.

In Venezuela a government department was at one point established to promote cognitive education programmes within the education system. Instrumental Enrichment was one of the main programmes used. In Africa some governments are asking organisations like ORT, the Organisation for Rehabilitation and Training, (which specialises in technical edcuation) to prepare cognitive education programmes, including Instrumental Enrichment, so that students can adapt to the changing demands of technology. In South Africa some liberal-minded firms, panic-stricken at the thought of a black revolt, have turned to Feuerstein and his Instrumental Enrichment programme to help them train up blacks for management posts in double-quick time.

In America and Canada Instrumental Enrichment is being used as a remedial programme for penitentiary inmates and juvenile delinquents. Cognitive education, and Instrumental Enrichment especially, is increasingly being seen as the 'emerging alternative in special education', as part of the rediscovery of a traditional intellectual training for ordinary high school and college children, and as an important strand in curriculum development for the gifted. In Britain there is a great deal of rhetoric about the need for cognitive skills, along with, in my view, a complete lack of an appropriate intellectual or financial commitment.

There is now widespread recognition that the conventional theories of fixed hereditary intelligence were misguided and led us into a harmful cul-de-sac. To quote the words of Robert Sternberg, Professor of Psychology at Yale University: 'Both the preoccupation with testing and the assumption that intelligence is a fixed entity have led to the neglect of a more productive question: Can intelligence be trained? My research suggests that it can.'

The reason put forward by Sternberg as to why we ventured up this particular cul-de-sac is exactly the same as Feuerstein's.

After all, if intelligence is constantly changing or even potentially changeable, what good could tests be? With scores constantly changing, the usefulness of the tests as measures to rank individuals in a stable way over time would be seriously challenged.

At this point it becomes impossible for psychology to rank individuals in an almost classical fixed hierarchy of IQ scores, related in the last instance to the rankings of class and race. Nearly 30 years after he first challenged conventional psychology, Feuerstein's ideas are being echoed by some sectors of the academic establishment. But his ideas (far more than their echoes) have yet to realise their potential. They continue to have the power to upset the intellectual assumptions which underpin British education and social services and, for that reason, I do not think they will be easily accepted.

BIBLIOGRAPHY OF REUVEN FEUERSTEIN

FEUERSTEIN, R., JEANNET, M. and RICHELLE, M. *Quelques Aspects de Développement Intellectuel chez les Jeunes Juifs Nord-Africains.* October, 1953.

REY, A. avec FEUERSTEIN, R., JEANNET, M. and RICHELLE, M. *Rapport Concernant Quelques Problèmes Pedagogiques.* December, 1953.

FEUERSTEIN, R., and JEANNET, M. *Quelques Aspects de la Representation de l'Espace chez les Enfants Nord-Africains.* Juillet, 1954.

FEUERSTEIN, R., RICHELLE, M. and JEANNET, M. *Quelques Aspects des Structures Effectives chez les Enfants Nord-Africains d'Après le Test de Rorschach.* Juillet, 1954.

REY, A., FEUERSTEIN, R., JEANNET, M. and RICHELLE, M. *Rapport de Voyage au Maroc.* Août, 1954.

REY, A., FEUERSTEIN, R., JEANNET, M. and RICHELLE, M. *Quelques Aspects de l'Etat Psychologique des Enfants Juifs Marocains.* Genève, 1955.

RICHELLE, M. and FEUERSTEIN, R. *Enfants Juifs Nord-Africains.* Youth Aliyah, 1957.

FEUERSTEIN, R. and RICHELLE, M., with collaboration of REY, A. *Children of the Mellah. Socio-cultural Deprivation and its Educational Significance. The North African Jewish Child.* Jerusalem: The Szold Foundation for Child and Youth Welfare, 1963.

FEUERSTEIN, R. and HAMBURGER, M. *A Proposal to Study the Process of Redevelopment in Several Groups of Deprived Early Adolescents in both Residential and Non-residential Settings.* Jerusalem: Report for the Research Unit of the Hadassah-Wizo Canada Child Guidance Clinic, the Youth Aliyah Department of the Jewish Agency, 1965.

FEUERSTEIN, R. and KRASILOWSKY, D. 'The Treatment Group Technique.' *Israel Annals of Psychiatry and Related Disciplines.* Vol. 5, No. 1. Spring, 1967. pp. 61–90.

FEUERSTEIN, R. and SHALOM, H. 'Methods of Assessing the Educational Level of Socially and Culturally Disadvantaged Children'. *Megamot*, No. 2–3, August, 1967. pp. 177–187.

FEUERSTEIN, R. and SHALOM, H. *Problems of Assessment and Evaluation of the Mentally Retarded and Culturally Deprived Child and Adolescent: The Learning Potential Assessment Device.* Paper presented at the First Congress of the International Association for the Scientific Study of Mental Deficiency. Montpellier, September, 1967.

FEUERSTEIN, R. *The Role of Social Institutions and Subsystems in the Causation, Prevention, and Alleviation of Retarded Performance. A Contribution to the Dynamic Approach.* Paper delivered at the Peabody-NIMH Conference, Nashville, Tennessee, 1968.

FEUERSTEIN, R. and SHALOM, H. 'The Learning Potential Assessment Device'. In B. W. RICHARDS (ed.), *Proceedings of the First Congress of International Association for the Scientific Study of Mental Deficiency.* England: Michael Jackson, 1968.

FEUERSTEIN, R. *The Meaning of Group Care within the Residential Setting for the Redevelopment of the Socio-culturally Disadvantaged Adolescent.* Paper presented at the Hadassah Youth Aliyah Specialists Seminar, Jerusalem, June, 1969.

FEUERSTEIN, R. *The Instrumental Enrichment Method: An Outline of Theory and Technique.* Jerusalem: HWCRI, 1969.

FEUERSTEIN, R. *Les Problèmes Psycho-éducatifs Spécifiques du Développement de l'Enfant dans le Milieu Semi-urbain.* Paper presented at Congrès Mondial de l'Enfance, Stockholm, September, 1969, Jerusalem: HWCRI, 1969.

FEUERSTEIN, R., TANNENBAUM, A. J. and KRASILOWSKY, D. *Selected Statistical Data on the Follow-up Study of Youth Aliyah Graduates of North African Origin.* Paper presented to the Hadassah Youth Aliyah Specialists Seminar, Jerusalem, June, 1969.

FEUERSTEIN, R. 'A Dynamic Approach to the Causation, Prevention, and Alleviation of Retarded Performance'. In H. C. HAYWOOD (ed.), *Social-Cultural Aspects of Mental Retardation.* New York: Appleton, Century, Crofts, 1970.

FEUERSTEIN, R. *Interventional Strategies for the Significant*

Modification of the Cognitive Functioning of the Disadvantaged Adolescent. Theoretical Considerations and Techniques. Paper presented at the Seventh Congress of the International Association for Child Psychiatry and Allied Professions, Israel, 1970.

FEUERSTEIN, R. *The Cognitive Redevelopment of the Deprived Low-Functioning Adolescent. Cross-cultural Studies and Interventional Strategies.* Lecture presented at the First International Conference of the Society of Founding Fellows of the Center for Human Development, Hebrew University, Jerusalem, 1970.

FEUERSTEIN, R., HANEGBI, R. and KRASILOWSKY, D. 'The Corrective Object Relations: Theory and Treatment Group Technique'. *Psychological Process*, Vol. 1, No. 2. 1970.

FEUERSTEIN, R. *Les Différences de Fonctionnement Cognitif dans des Groupes Socio-ethniques Différents.* Thèse de doctorat presentée à l'Université de Paris (Sorbonne), Paris, Juin, 1970.

FEUERSTEIN, R. and KRASILOWSKY, D. 'The Treatment Group Technique'. *Yesodot*, Summer, 1971.

FEUERSTEIN, R. *Problems of the Cognitive Assessment of the Socio-culturally Deprived Child and Adolescent. The Learning Potential Assessment Device: An Outline for a Solution.* Paper presented at the NATO Conference on Cultural Factors in Mental Test Development, Application and Interpretation, Istanbul, July, 1971.

FEUERSTEIN, R. 'Low Functioning Children in Residential and Day Settings for the Deprived'. In M. WOLINS and M. GOTTESMAN (eds.), *Group Care: An Israeli Approach.* New York and London: Gordon and Breach, 1971.

FEUERSTEIN, R. 'The Redevelopment of the Socio-culturally Disadvantaged Adolescent in Group Care'. In M. WOLINS and M. GOTTESMAN (eds.), *Group Care: An Israeli Approach.* New York and London: Gordon and Breach, 1971.

FEUERSTEIN, R. *Cognitive Assessment of the Socio-culturally Deprived Child and Adolescent: Mental Tests and Cultural Adaptation.* Jerusalem: HWCRI, 1971.

FEUERSTEIN, R. *Studies in Cognitive Modifiability. Proposal for Extension of the Learning Potential Model for Applied Individual and Group Assessment.* Jerusalem: HWCRI, 1971.

FEUERSTEIN, R. 'Alleviation of Retarded Performance'. In Henry P. DAVID (ed.), *Child Mental Health in International Perspective.* New York: Harper and Row, 1972.

FEUERSTEIN, R. et al. *Studies in Cognitive Modifiability, Vols. I and II.* Jerusalem: Ford Foundation Trustees, 1972.

FEUERSTEIN, R. *Learning Potential Assessment Device: A New Method for Assessing Modifiability of Cognitive Functioning in Socio-culturally Disadvantaged Adolescents.* Paper presented to Israel Foundation Trustees, Tel Aviv, 1972.

FEUERSTEIN, R. *Studies in Cognitive Modifiability: A Proposal to Study the Effects of IE on the Cognitive Functions of Retarded Early Adolescents.* Jerusalem: HWCRI, 1972.

FEUERSTEIN, R. et al. *The Effects of Group Care on the Psychosocial Habilitation of Immigrant Adolescents in Israel with Special Reference to High-Risk Children.* Jerusalem: HWCRI, 1973.

FEUERSTEIN, R. *The Role of Cultural Transmission in the Development of Intelligence.* 1973 Allan Bronfman Lecture, Quebec, Canada, September, 1973.

FEUERSTEIN, R., KRASILOWSKY, D. and RAND, Y. 'The Evolvement of Innovative Educational Strategies for the Integration of High-Risk Adolescents in Israel'. *Phi Delta Kappan.* April, 1974. pp. 556–559.

HOFFMAN, M., FEUERSTEIN, R. and RAND, Y. *Fostering Higher Cognitive Processes in Retarded Performers: Theory, Instruments, and Procedures.* Paper presented at the Second International Congress of Special Education, Madrid, 1974. Published in proceedings of the Congress.

RAND, Y. and FEUERSTEIN, R. *LPAD Group Measurements as an Instrument for Class Composition Decisions.* Jerusalem: HWCRI, 1974.

FEUERSTEIN, R. and RAND, Y. *Mediated Learning Experience: An Outline of the Proximal Etiology for Differential Development of Cognitive Function.* Jerusalem: HWCRI, 1974.

FEUERSTEIN, R. *Family Continuity and Cultural Development.* Paper presented to Seminar of International Association for Child Psychiatry and Allied Professions, Philadelphia, 1974.

FEUERSTEIN, R. and RAND, Y. 'Mediated Learning Experiences: An Outline of the Proximal Etiology for Differential

Development of Cognitive Functions'. *Journal of International Council of Psychology*, (9/10). 1974. pp. 7–37.

FEUERSTEIN, R., KRASILOWSKY, D. and RAND, Y. 'Neue Wege fur Integration von Besonders Schwer Benachteiligten Jugendlichen'. *Israel Freunde der Schweizer Kinderdorfs.* Zurich, 1975.

RAND, Y., FEUERSTEIN, R. and HOFFMAN, M. *Interventional Strategies to Improve the Cognitive Efficiency of Culturally Disadvantaged Adolescents.* Paper presented to the Congress of the Israeli Society for Scientific Research in Education, University of Tel Aviv, 1975.

FEUERSTEIN, R. et al. 'The Effects of Group Care on the Psychological Habilitation of Immigrant Adolescents in Israel, with Special Reference to High-Risk Children'. *International Review of Applied Psychology* (25). 1976. pp. 189–201.

HOFFMAN, M. and FEUERSTEIN, R. *Strategy of Cognitive Redevelopment Through Instrumental Enrichment: Didactics and Materials.* Paper presented at the International Forum on Adolescence, Jerusalem, 1976.

FEUERSTEIN, R. *Mediated Learning Experience: A Theoretical Basis for Cognitive Human Modifiability during Adolescence.* Paper presented at the Fourth International Congress of the International Association for the Scientific Study of Mental Deficiency, Washington, D.C., August, 1976.

FEUERSTEIN, R. 'Dynamic Assessment of Cognitive Modifiability in Retarded Performers. The Learning Potential Assessment Device'. In B. B. Wolman (ed.), *International Encyclopedia of Neurology, Psychiatry, Psychoanalysis and Psychology.* Section XII. New York, 1976.

FEUERSTEIN, R. 'Mediated Learning Experience: A Theoretical Basis for Cognitive Human Modifiability during Adolescence'. In P. MITTLER (ed.), *Research to Practice in Mental Retardation.* Vol. II. Baltimore: University Park Press, 1977.

FEUERSTEIN, R. *Need to Shift Self-Perception of the Retarded Performer from Passive Recipient to Active Generator.* Paper presented at Kennedy Center for Research on Education and Human Development, Nashville, Tennessee, February, 1977.

FEUERSTEIN, R., RAND, Y. et al. *Studies in Cognitive Modifi-*

ability. Instrumental Enrichment: Redevelopment of Cognitive Functions of Retarded Early Adolescents. Jerusalem: HWCRI, 1977.

FEUERSTEIN, R., KRASILOWSKY, D. and RAND, Y. 'Modifiability during Adolescence'. In Dr. James ANTHONY (ed.), *Yearbook of the International Association for Child Psychiatry and Allied Professions.* London, 1977.

FEUERSTEIN, R. *Ontogeny of Learning.* Paper presented at International Brain Research Organisation Symposium on Brain Mechanisms in Memory and Learning, Royal Society, London, July, 1977.

FEUERSTEIN, R. *L'attitude Active Modifiante envers des Difficultés d'Apprentissage par l'Intégration et l'Innovation.* The Dr. M. Sam Rabinovitch Memorial Lecture. Keynote address at the Third Annual Conference of the Quebec Association for Children with Learning Disabilities, Montreal, Canada, March, 1978. Published in proceedings of Conference.

FEUERSTEIN, R. 'Ontogeny of Learning'. In Mary T. BRAZIER (ed.), *Brain Mechanisms in Memory and Learning.* New York: Raven Press, 1979.

RAND, Y., FEUERSTEIN, R. et al. 'Strategies for Improving the Cognitive Level of Low Functioning Adolescents: Theoretical Basis and Empirical Evaluation'. *American Journal for Mental Deficiency.* 1979.

FEUERSTEIN, R., RAND, Y. and HOFFMAN, M. *Learning Potential Assessment Device.* Baltimore: University Park Press, 1979.

FEUERSTEIN, R. et al. 'Cognitive Modifiability in Retarded Adolescents: Effects of Instrumental Enrichment'. *American Journal of Mental Deficiency.* 1979, Vol. 83, No. 6, pp. 539–550.

RAND, Y., TANNENBAUM, A. J. and FEUERSTEIN, R. 'Effects of Instrumental Enrichment on the Psychoeducational Development of Low-Functioning Adolescents'. *Journal of Educational Psychology.* 1979, Vol. 71, No. 6, pp. 751–763.

FEUERSTEIN, R. *Cultural Difference and Cultural Deprivation in New Immigrants: A Diagnostic and Interventional Perspective.* Paper presented at Fifth International Congress for the Scientific Study of Mental Deficiency, Jerusalem, August, 1979.

FEUERSTEIN, R. with RAND, Y., HOFFMAN, M. and MILLER, R. *Instrumental Enrichment.* Baltimore: Univeristy Park Press, 1980.

FEUERSTEIN, R. and JENSEN, M. R. 'Instrumental Enrichment: Theoretical Basis, Goals, and Instruments'. *The Educational Forum.* May, 1980, pp. 401–423.

FEUERSTEIN, R. et al. 'Cognitive Modifiability in Adolescence: Cognitive Structure and the Effects of Intervention'. *Journal of Special Education.* Symposium Edition, 1980.

FEUERSTEIN, R. *Dynamic Assessment (LPAD) in School Psychology.* Paper presented at the Fourth International Colloquium in School Psychology, Jerusalem, July, 1980.

FEUERSTEIN, R. *Modifying the Cognitive Structure of Retarded Performing Adolescents.* Paper presented at the Fourth International Colloquium in School Psychology, Jerusalem, July, 1980.

FEUERSTEIN, R., MILLER, R. and JENSEN, M. R. *Can Evolving Techniques Better Measure Cognitive Change?* Outlooks, (in press).

FEUERSTEIN, R. *Instrumental Enrichment.* Paper presented at NIE-LRDC Conference on Thinking and Learning Skills, Pittsburgh, October, 1980. To be published in proceedings of Conference.

FEUERSTEIN, R. 'Mediated Learning Experience in the Acquisition of Kinesics'. In R. St. CLAIR and B. HOFFER (eds.), *Developmental Kinesics.* Baltimore: University Park Press, 1981.

FEUERSTEIN, R. *Rescuing Youth: New Approaches to Assessment and Educational Enrichment.* Paper presented at a Special Seminar in Memory of Henrietta Szold sponsored by the U.S. Committee for UNICEF, the National Organisations Advisory Council for Children and Hadassah, Fordham University, February, 1981.

FEUERSTEIN, R. *The LPAD and IE: A Unique Approach to the Diagnosis and Assessment of Learning Problems.* Paper presented at the Second Annual Marianne Frostig Symposium on Learning Disabilities in co-operation with Mount St. Mary's College, Los Angeles and San Francisco, February, 1981.

FEUERSTEIN, R. and HOFFMAN, M. B. 'Intergenerational

Conflict of Rights: Cultural Imposition and Self Realisation'. Reprinted from: *Viewpoints in Teaching and Learning, Journal of the School of Education.* Indiana University, Vol. 58, No. 1/Winter, 1982.

FEUERSTEIN, R., RAND, Y., JENSEN, M., CANIEL, S. and TZURIEL, D. 'Learning Potential Assessment'. Accepted for publication in the *Journal for Special Services in the Schools.* 1985.

DOUGLAS, Jo and SUTTON, A. 'The Development of Speech and Mental Processes in a Pair of Twins'. In: *Journal of Child Psychology and Psychiatry.* Vol. 19, pp. 49–56, 1978.

STERNBERG, Robert J. 'How Can We Teach Intelligence?'. In: *Education Leadership* (USA). Based on research for The Organisation Research for Better Schools, Inc. September, 1984.

BERKELEY, R. 'Basic New World of Intelligence Testing'. In: *Psychology Today.* September, 1979.

BÜCHEL, F. P. 'Etiologie des Difficultés d'Apprentissage et Intervention d'après Feuerstein'. In: *Revue Suisse de Psychologie Pure et Appliquée.*

FILSON, A. E. *Cognitive Modifiability: An Interpretative Study of Feuerstein's Instrumental Enrichment Programme.* (MEd Thesis) University of Manchester, 1983.

GORDON, E. W., TERRELL, M. D. 'The Changed Social Context of Testing'. In: *American Psychologist.* Vol. 36, No. 10. 1981.

HEYWOOD, C. *Instrumental Enrichment: Replication and Extension.* 1977.

JENSEN, M. R., FEUERSTEIN, R., RAND, Y., CANIEL, S. 'Cultural Difference and Cultural Deprivation: A Theoretical Framework for Differential Intervention'. In: R. M. GUPTA and P. COXHEAD (eds.) *Cultural Diversity and Learning Efficiency.* London: The Macmillan Press, 1986.

KENNEY, M. V. *Effects of Feuerstein's Instrumental Enrichment on the Reasoning, Non-verbal Intelligence, and Locus of Control of 12- to 15-year-old Educable Mentally Handicapped and Learning Disabled Students'.* (PhD Dissertation) University of Missouri. Vol. 45 (8–9), p. 2452. February, 1985.

MAKIN, J. *Performance of Inner City and Middle Class Children on Feuerstein's Learning Potential Assessment Device.* (MA Thesis) University of Toronto, 1973.

MESSERER, J., HUNT, E., MEYERS, G., LERNER, J. 'Feuerstein's

Instrumental Enrichment: A New Approach for Activating Intellectual Potential in Learning Disabled Youth'. In: *Journal of Learning Disabilities*. Vol. 17, No. 6, pp. 321–384. 1984.

QUILDON, K. *Later Effects of Early Childhood Intervention on the Learning Performance of Low-income Children.* (PhD Thesis).

BOLIVAR, Ruiz, DE MARTINEZ, P. *La Modificabilidad Cognoscitiva en Estudiantes Pre-universitarios.* Universidad Nacional Experimental de Guayana, Centro de Investigaciones Psico-Educatoras. No. 3. November, 1984.

STERNBERG, R. J. *Instrumental and Componential Approaches to the Nature and Training of Intelligence.* Yale University.

STERNBERG, R. J. 'Stalking the IQ Quark'. In: *Psychology Today.* September, 1979.

TZURIEL, D., FEUERSTEIN, R. *Dynamic Group Assessment for Prescriptive Teaching: Differential Effects of Treatments.* Proceedings of the 23rd International Congress of Psychology. Acapulco, Mexico, 1984.

WAKESMAN, M. *Assessment of the Effects of Instrumental Enrichment Cognitive Training on the Intellectual Performance of a Group of Gifted Students at a Local Public School.* University of Toronto, 1980.

FEUERSTEIN, R., RAND, Y., JENSEN, M. R., CANIEL, S., TZURIEL, D. 'The Dynamic Assessment of Structural Cognitive Modifiability'. In: Carol Ltdz (ed.) *Dynamic Assessment: Foundations and Fundamentals.* 1986.

INDEX